THE ROAD TO MOUNT BUGGERY

A JOURNEY
Through the
CURIOUSLY
Named Places of
AUSTRALIA

MARK WHITTAKER
and AMY WILLESEE

MACMILLAN
Pan Macmillan Australia

For Oliver

First published 2001 in Macmillan by Pan Macmillan Australia Pty Limited
St Martins Tower, 31 Market Street, Sydney

Reprinted 2002

Copyright © Mark Whittaker and Amy Willesee

National Library of Australia
Cataloguing-in-Publication Data:

Whittaker, Mark.
The road to Mount Buggery.

ISBN 0 7329 1111 7.

1. Names, Geographical – Australia. 2. Australia –
Description and travel – 1990–. I. Willesee, Amy. II.
Title.

910.014

Typeset in 12/14.5 pt Bembo by Midland Typesetters
Printed in Australia by McPherson's Printing Group
Cover and text design by Big Cat Design
Map by Colin Wynter Seton

Mark Whittaker fled his job as a staff writer for *The Australian Magazine* in *The Weekend Australian* newspaper to write this book. He has since returned to that newspaper as part of the 'Dossier' investigative team. He has previously co-authored two non-fiction books: *Sins of the Brother — The Definitive Story of Ivan Milat and the Backpacker Murders* (published by Macmillan) and *Granny Killer — The Story of John Wayne Glover.*

Amy Willesee has written for Sydney newspaper *The Daily Telegraph*, including a stint as its gossip columnist (writing as Amy Ewen). Before leaving to write this book, she was working as a researcher on acclaimed television documentaries *The Last Warriors* and *Who Killed Sallie-Anne Huckstepp?* She is now working as a journalist in Sydney.

CONTENTS

DARWIN

Escape River
Restoration Island

Skeleton Point
Disaster Bay
Escape Point Point Torment

Mt Misery
Mt Regret

Bungle Bungles

Cape Keerweer

Cape Flattery
Hope Islands

NORTHERN TERRITORY

Massacre Inlet
Hell's Gate
Plains of Promise

Battle Camp
Cape Tribulation

Ophthalmia Range

Lake Disappointment

Mt Treachery

QUEENSLAND

ALICE SPRINGS

WESTERN AUSTRALIA

Useless Loop

Mt Destruction
Mt Unapproachable

Escape Glen

Desperate Bay
Thirsty Point

Mt Carnage

Deadman's Dugout

Paradise

Lake Massacre

Houtman Abrolhos

Hangover Bay

SOUTH AUSTRALIA

Mt Hopeless

Death Rock

Starvation Lake

BRISBANE

PERTH

World's End

New Era

NEW SOUTH WALES

Cactus Beach
Denial Bay

Anxious Bay

Avoid Bay
Cape Catastrophe

ADELAIDE

SYDNEY

Mt Terrible

VICTORIA

Mt Buggery
CANBERRA

MELBOURNE

Cape Grim

Hell's Gate

TASMANIA
HOBART

Isle of the Dead

CHAPTER 1

HIT *the* DOG
FENCE *and*
TURN RIGHT

Broken Hill, New South Wales

MARK ▶ The morning blows pale grey and we're pleased as hell to have the tent packed on the roof-rack. The overgrown paddock, with heavy trucks rumbling down the Silver City Highway just out of sight, is notable only because it is the first in a year of campsites – and because there were no other campers around to see us reading the instructions for our tent.

Relieved to have got this far without incident, we are keen to hit the road, and are just checking under the bonnet like we learnt at four-wheel-drive school when we hear a voice.

'Have you got any dogs?'

It's a man with a rifle under his arm and a fat blue heeler at his heels, which, upon our negative reply, he releases. My thoughts are wavering between, ah, a chance to converse with a friendly local, and, shallow grave, here we come.

'You camping, are you?' he asks.

'Yeah. Is that cool?'

'Sure. Nice spot. Where you headed?'

'Mootwingee', I say, picking a national park up the road.

'*Moot* wingee?' he smirks. '*Mutt* Wingee – that's how the coons say it. Got to be the Queen to say *Moot* wingee.'

He asks where we are from.

'Sydney.' First mistake.

And what we do.

'Journalists.' Second mistake.

'You're part of that New World Order.'

Our morning is now to be a lesson from this armed man in a nylon parka, with his greasy hair combed forward. We go quickly through the disarming of the nation and the back-door republic, to other United Nations inspired travesties. All the while, both his hands are firmly on the .22 Mauser. It is not an invitation to open debate.

I note that there is a thread on the end of his barrel and see an opportunity to get him onto more mundane, blokey issues, like silencers. Third mistake. He says he's been made a criminal for possessing one, and has to hide it along with all the other bundles of gunmetal hidden round about. Out of the grasping hands of the New World Order.

Then he surprises us. He pulls a silencer from his pocket. And having twirled it on, puts a round in to demonstrate its silent killing capacity on some birds cackling away above us.

At this point, I later learn, Amy is seriously braced into fight-or-flight mode. Leaning heavily towards flight. I'm thinking that if he were going to shoot us he would have done so already. I'm looking for the tell-tale changing of mental gears – from normal person to blank, staring automaton – that people who escape from serial killers consistently report. But there is none. Just this amiable, articulate but not especially worldly man who feeds his dog too much and who is angry with the world.

He's with us an hour and a bit. We learn of his not very voluntary redundancy, his dad's pathetic compo payout awarded by a 'government appointed' judge for a ruinous workplace injury.

During one of our attempts to get going, I ask his name.

'Martin. Not Bryant,' he says, alluding to the madman who committed the Port Arthur massacre.

Amy tells him her name, and he answers dreamily, 'Amy, that's a nice name. I've got a niece called Louise.'

It sounds like mental gears crunching. Time to hit the road. Quick.

We'd actually told Martin a small fib. Mootwingee isn't our destination. Our destination goes by the far more alluring and easier to pronounce name of Starvation Lake. But that had seemed too hard to explain.

AMY ▶ In early 1998, Mark was sitting at his desk at *The Australian Magazine* in Sydney, looking to wangle a road trip with photographer Paul Blackmore. He needed another story idea to convince the boss they should go. He pulled out the map of Australia and stared at it for inspiration. There, in the middle of Western Australia, he noticed Lake Disappointment, a substantial blue splodge even on his small map. He wondered what was behind such an almighty letdown. Then he started turning up more misery on the map: Mount Treachery, Point Torment, Cape Catastrophe, Mount Hopeless. Where did they come from and what was out there now? There was his story.

Mark and Paul drove off across the country, but they never made it to Lake Disappointment. Their four-wheel drive went up in flames behind a remote Western Australian beach. They replaced it with a rental Toyota Camry but bogged that trying to reach Point Torment. It was Hard Brown Land: 2, Visitors: 0.

Mark and I met soon after he returned from that trip, and in the way of dreamy new romances indulged in anything-is-possible fantasies. Above all, we dreamt of taking a year out to travel around Australia.

'You know,' Mark said in those early days, 'Paul and I always thought that placenames story would make a good book.'

The idea stuck with us, enticed us. There is something thrilling about discovering a bizarre new name and tracing its dry co-ordinates to a point in the atlas. Wondering if we could get there. The potential of the unknown. It was the start of our journey, our obsession.

Over the next 18 months we found ourselves spending weekends in Sydney's Mitchell Library, tracking down the stories behind the names. And there were plenty of names to choose from. Forty-five Mount Miserys at last count, another nine Misery Hills, Rocks and Bluffs. Behind each name was a story. We found some of them in the library, but many remained a mystery.

We imagined what these places might actually be like. Who lived there now? Why was Australia – the lucky country – such a hotbed of anguish? No-one knows who named a lot of them anymore, but one thing's for sure: they weren't working for real estate developers.

Explorers and surveyors took possession of the land by marking it on a map and naming it. They may not have had the vocabulary to deal with the waterless channels that were put down as rivers, the salt pans they called lakes and the rocky outcrops that became mountains, but they knew the words for how the country made them feel. In an era of stoicism, brave men wore their hearts on their maps.

Early on in our visits to the library, we came across Henry Lawson's directions to find the mythical never-never:

'Where lone Mount Desolation lies,
Mounts Dreadful and Despair –
'Tis lost beneath the rainless skies
In hopeless deserts there;
It spreads nor'-west by No-Man's-Land –
Where clouds are seldom seen –
To where the cattle stations lie
Three hundred miles between.'

That was where we wanted to go. At the very least, chasing these names would force us off the highways, off the tourist trails, and into obscure, tough patches of country; places that would tell a very Australian story.

As the planning rumbled along, a map of Australia rolled out on the dining room table accumulated a rainbow of little dots. Our Map of Misery. Somehow, we hoped to randomly join the dots and draw a picture of Australia.

Two weeks before our departure date, however, we had a lot of dots and not much else. No four-wheel drive, no camping gear, no bush skills and absolutely no knowledge of what lay beneath the bonnet of a car.

How dare we presume we were capable of doing this.

Those final two weeks were chaos. In between packing up the apartment, putting our city lives into boxes, choosing a tent, buying a Landcruiser troop carrier (which we named Frank, in honour of the man who named Lake Disappointment, Frank Hann), and bottling away our self doubt, we began to wonder if the year ahead could be worth all this madness. And could our relationship make it through a year in a tent?

Suddenly, miraculously, we were off, headed first of all for McDonald's at Lithgow to rendezvous for a weekend at four-wheel-drive school, to learn about a vehicle we had owned for less than a week.

We were imposters, sitting up there in our shiny, five-year-old troopie, straight from the city. Embarrassed to admit to our fellow students and teacher how hopelessly underprepared we were, we watched for signs of derision and bemusement as they took in our car and our polished boots – and the news that we were about to head into the killer outback. We certainly weren't going to tell them that just days earlier, when we'd brought Frank home after having a long-range fuel tank fitted, along with all the other accessories we'd read about, we couldn't get him started and were forced to call the NRMA. Ah! That's what points are. Mmmm, you just clean them like that, eh.

So, knowing that there'd be no mechanic on a motorbike making house calls in the Gibson Desert, there we were at four-wheel-drive school, my romantic dreams well and truly in my throat, choking me, as we embarked on our first task: driving along the side of a slope that seemed way too steep. I wasn't even driving, but it was all I could do to stop myself from hyperventilating, bursting into tears and fleeing home.

By Sunday afternoon, however, we had not rolled Frank even once. We had changed a tyre, crawled under the engine, snatched him out of a bog and felt vaguely better equipped for the journey. Frank looked a bit more credible all splattered with mud, and we did too. We had a year and a whole country in front of us. We were ready to go.

Then it rained for three days. Not brave enough to try out our 'thirty-second' tent, we cowered in on-site vans along the Great Western Highway. And, ignoring the first few dots on the Map of Misery, we crawled towards the Centre.

At our first camp off the bitumen we encountered Martin and his fat blue heeler. There was no choice but to go deeper into the tough country. We would forge our way to Starvation Lake.

Starvation Lake, New South Wales/South Australia

MARK▶ We've been driving most of the day over bumpy dirt roads and cattle station tracks that don't do what the map says they do. Are we even allowed to be out here? We're searching for Starvation Lake, which right now is no more than a blue blob on the map straddling the New South Wales–South Australian border. We know nothing about it. Phone calls to nearby stations went unanswered. Searches in the library came up blank. But it's the first name we're actually tackling and we're determined to get there, especially since I'd already tried once before, when Paul and I had been scared off by rain.

This time Amy and I have a whole year to play with, so we can afford to tough it out.

Late in the afternoon we drop in unannounced at Pine View Station, which, it turns out, includes the New South Wales portion of the lake. At the homestead Albert Lacey can't tell us where the name came from, but he's always presumed it's just that the country is so ordinary out there. His directions are simple: follow one of the station tracks west until you hit the dog fence and turn right; when you come to a flat, dry section, that's the 'lake'.

We follow Albert's instructions. Half an hour along the track, Amy is beginning to doubt my ability to judge where west is. Then, as we come up over a sandhill, we suddenly see the dog fence – allegedly the world's longest fence, built to keep marauding rabbits out of the north and west. Having failed at that, it's now meant to keep marauding dingoes away from the sheep in the south-east.

It is a curiously elating experience to bump into the back of New South Wales like this. With all the scrubby dunes it had felt like we were approaching the sea, and now we've hit the beach.

'WA-HOOOOO!' Amy whoops, as we turn right and head north. Pairs of majestic wedge-tailed eagles are perched along the boundary at regular intervals. There's a huge mob of roos and emus in our path. Some attempt to outrun us – and run themselves into exhaustion – while we urge them to please go east. (Australian marsupials sacrificed big calorie-hungry brains for the sake of energy conservation long before the motor car arrived and we wonder if they might now regret it.)

It is a guilty pleasure to watch them. Amy is ecstatic. She eggs them on, laughing, until they decide to go west and slam headlong into the fence, their necks kind of crumpling on impact. It is maybe five minutes before the track is finally clear.

Sailing over the red swells of the dunes, surrounded by 360 degrees of horizon, it's like being on a rolling sea. Then we drop into a flat, dry section. The road and the dog fence continue straight out across it. Starvation Lake.

Despite floods which have recently ripped through surrounding stations, the lake hasn't got a puddle in it. Albert told us it has never filled in white man times. It takes rain like the 1974 floods to put any water in it at all; that water stays for years.

7

Other times, it's just shifting sand and claypan, good for nothing but starving.

At least the floods have turned the scruffy vegetation green – and brought flies worse than an old-fashioned Aerogard commercial, maddeningly thick in our mouths and ears and noses. Around our ankles, swarms of tiny grasshoppers surge in thudding waves. It's a bit of a worry that the flies and locusts are this bad in our first week. Is this what we're facing for the whole trip?

Amy drags out a fly net, inherited from Frank's previous owners – two Swiss backpackers – and struggles with the mechanics of smoking a cigarette through the net hanging from her wide-brim hat. I doubt she'll cop this for a year.

Okay, we're here. Now what do we do?

We set up the tent a bit down the track and ponder what the hell this is all about. More immediately, we are having issues with our equipment. There's a red light flashing on our new nine-hundred dollar fridge, illuminating the word 'ERROR' with each pulse. We only used it for the first time this morning – and what kind of error could we have made plugging it into the cigarette lighter and flicking the ON switch?

'How about we run it off the generator,' I say. It'll give us something to do.

We've never used the generator, either.

I tug and tug at the little rope trying to start it, thinking fondly of all those lawns I haven't mowed since moving out of Mum and Dad's some 13 years ago.

'Have you switched it to ON?' asks Amy, who's been cheating, reading the instructions.

The generator kicks in like a Victa, first time. But it doesn't run the fridge. And it doesn't recharge the sixty dollar light with the allegedly rechargeable battery. Oh, for the refinement of the Nyngan caravan park.

That night, being more used to nocturnal serenades of sirens and screaming, we're confounded by the thudding noises outside the tent. Like someone stomping on something hollow. We're sure we're being stalked by some new madman. The morning, however, reveals the relentless noise to be more roos making their way along the fence.

The journey out of Starvation Lake is less enchanting than the one in. We keep getting diverted around swollen lakes. The maze of wet weather tracks spiralling out in all directions soon gets us what Amy calls lost and I call confused. And then we get what we both call bogged.

It's a scorching day, there's no shade, and we haven't seen another vehicle for more than 24 hours. I love it. I grab the 'entrenching tool' and dive into the thick, red mud, testosterone-charged. I drove us into this mess and I'm going to dig us out.

Within minutes, however, we hear an engine in the distance and Amy, for some reason, isn't at all disappointed.

'Someone didn't know where they were going,' says an old bloke with muscular brown arms as he gets out of the ute. He's referring to a little wet weather diversion we'd missed off to the left. He's not impressed. He drives off to get a more powerful vehicle so he can get us out.

When he returns half an hour later, we look on with eyebrows raised as he prepares to pull us out using techniques we were specifically warned against at four-wheel-drive school. He just pops the snatch strap over the ball of his tow bar, and into our tow bar – which is missing its pin – he jams an old bolt to secure the strap. I can hear our four-wheel-drive instructor telling us someone is about to lose an eye.

'Do you think we should . . .' I butt in like the class captain.

'Nah, she'll be right.'

Still, when he turns his back I throw a towel over the strap like we'd been taught and feel thoroughly wussy for doing so. Amy hides behind a tree.

Frank is wrenched out of the quagmire with everyone's eyes still intact and we make our apologies.

For all his gruffness, the old bloke is clearly delighted that his Nissan ute is rescuing our much larger troopie, and we leave him railing against radio announcer John Laws for talking up Toyotas to city slickers.

We eventually make it to Tibooburra, a remote fleck in the north-west corner of New South Wales where a friend of ours is living. We are exhausted but satisfied at having completed our first mission. For some reason the flies aren't so bad in town and it's amazing how relaxing that can be.

While we're enjoying the conviviality and cold beer out the front of the Tibooburra Family Hotel, we pull out the Map of Misery and again contemplate what the hell we're doing. There's got to be more out here than flies, stinking heat and thirsty red mud. We want a good story.

So we decide to head to Lake Massacre, 300 kilometres to the north-west, in Burke and Wills country. When I first read about the mystery surrounding the slaughter that happened there, I knew we had to go and do some digging.

With our friend waving madly from the hotel car park, we take the road north out of town and head for Innamincka.

CHAPTER 2

A GRAVE RUDELY FORMED

October, 1861. The far inland was alive with the hoof-beats of four parties searching for the heroically boofheaded Burke and Wills expedition. One of them was led by a tall, shy Scotsman, 'Big' John McKinlay. He'd come to Australia at seventeen and now at forty-two was an accomplished bushman. His ten-man, horse and camel expedition had come up quickly from Adelaide to the top right corner of South Australia.

Without much trouble he picked up from his Aboriginal guides a story that the locals had murdered some white men and there was a grave on a lake they called Kadhi-baeri. He made his way over wicked sandhills in the ever-growing heat to a lake where he found 'a grave rudely formed by the natives, evidently not one of themselves, sufficient pains not having been taken'.

His party removed the earth carefully and 'close to the top of the ground found the body of a European enveloped in a flannel shirt with short sleeves'. There was no flesh on the bone and there was little hair. The skull was 'marked with slight sabre cuts, apparently two in number'. McKinlay measured the bones and reburied them.

They found old camel and horse dung, and then another grave which looked like it had been dug with a shovel. As far as

McKinlay was concerned it was the Burke and Wills expedition, for no other white men had ever come this way. 'I fancy they must all have been murdered here,' he wrote. They dug out the grave with the only tool they had, a stick, 'but found no remains of bodies save one little bone. The black accounted for this in this manner, he says they had eaten them.'

The expedition found a few more blackened bones in an adjoining old fireplace. There was also a piece of light blue tweed, fragments of paper, small pieces of a nautical almanac and an 'exploded Eley's Cartridge'.

The next morning they captured one of the locals, and the guide requested McKinlay at once shoot the savage, 'as he knew him to be one of the murderers of the man or party; but we declined, thinking we might be able to glean something of the others from him,' wrote McKinlay. Indeed, the man took them to an old camp and dug up some saddle stuffing, telling the interpreter that the rest of the saddlery was burned, the ironwork kept, and the other bodies eaten.

As testimony to the fighting, he showed them his own body. In front and back, according to McKinlay, were 'the marks of ball and shot wounds now quite healed'. He told them there was a pistol north-east of them, at a creek, and McKinlay ordered him to go and get it. The man said he'd be back the next day.

True to his word, he returned about 4 am, at the front of forty men armed with torches, shields and assorted weapons, 'shouting and kicking up a great noise, and evidently endeavouring to surround us,' wrote McKinlay, who told the guide to order them back. They ignored the warning and advanced to within a few paces.

'Seeing nothing else left but to be butchered ourselves, I gave the word "Fire". A few of those closest retired a few paces, and were being encouraged on to the attack, when we repeated our fire; and until several rounds were fired into them (and no doubt many felt the effects) they did not wholly retire.'

McKinlay doesn't mention how many, if any, Aborigines were killed.

As far as he was concerned he had uncovered the fate of Burke and Wills. He immediately dispatched his journal back to Adelaide with the message that all Burke's party had been killed and eaten. He was sure this site would live in infamy by the name he bestowed upon it: Lake Massacre.

McKinlay was stuck at the lake for seven days until his foreman, Mr Hodgkinson, returned from delivering the journal to civilisation. He brought with him some newspapers. In them was the news that another rescue expedition led by Alfred Howitt had rescued one of Burke's party, the young soldier King, and had in fact found the real graves of Burke and Wills on Cooper Creek.

McKinlay presumed, therefore, he had found the grave of the fourth expedition member, Charles Gray, but that didn't account for discrepencies like the Aboriginal stories of a massacre and the gunshot wounds on the Aboriginal man. So whose graves had McKinlay found?

Cooper Creek, Queensland

AMY ▶ It is pitch black when we arrive to set up camp on Cooper Creek. With our rechargeable light still refusing to recharge, we turn to Frank's headlights for illumination. Only this sets off a blood-sucking frenzy as swarms of sandflies descend so thick we can't contemplate cooking a meal without it being two-thirds unwelcome protein. So we turn the lights off and attempt to do everything by feel.

'This is why we don't set up camp in the dark,' Mark tersely instructs me. I had urged him to push on past dusk so we could camp here by the Dig Tree, a living testament to the follies of the Burke and Wills expedition. It seemed a good place to begin our journey to Lake Massacre.

Right now, though, we are driven to seek refuge in the tent, where a dinner of processed cheese and salami sandwiches – no butter – is eaten in silence.

Morning, however, reveals the vibrant oasis of the Dig Tree camp. The sandflies are gone and the coolibahs shading the banks are screeching with corellas. It's hard to imagine you could die here.

This is Camp 65 where William Brahe whiled away his time waiting for his fiery boss, Robert O'Hara Burke, and the serious, young surveyor William John Wills to return from their mad dash to the Gulf of Carpentaria. Selected to join them was a young soldier, John King, and Charles Gray, a beefy, tattooed sailor with valuable navigation and bush skills. The foursome had set off in the scorching heart of summer, 1860/61, and instructed Brahe to wait three months while they pioneered a south–north route across the continent. Brahe was to build a stockade while he waited for more supplies to arrive from the south. But three months went by, no supplies came and the party didn't return. Brahe waited on another month before he gave up. He buried some food and a note, and famously carved instructions on a coolibah tree for the men to dig. As he saddled up and rode away from the Dig Tree that April 21, 1861, Burke's party was just eight hours away.

Burke and Wills had made it to the Gulf – or at least as far as some mudflats, mangroves and salty water – and were limping back to the Cooper. They had been held up by the thunderous wet season and supplies were running low. Charles Gray had been caught stealing food, for which Burke had given him a walloping. So times were tense when the muscular Gray started complaining he was too weak to walk. Burke didn't believe him. Eventually, though, Gray was so ill he had to be lashed to a camel. He died on April 17. His three companions spent a day burying him. That day of digging cost them the chance to catch Brahe.

Returning to Camp 65, the three survivors dug up the supplies and rested for two days. Burke, thinking it would be too hard to follow Brahe south to their depot at Menindee, decided instead to head west along the Cooper to a police outpost at the top of the Flinders Ranges. It was another bad move in a journey riddled with them. They didn't get anywhere near the Flinders Ranges and turned back to the Cooper, where the search party later rescued King and found the bodies of Burke and Wills.

We head west as they did along the Cooper, driving the forty-odd kilometres to Innamincka, towards the graves McKinlay found at Lake Massacre.

Innamincka, South Australia

MARK It's 38 degrees in the shade and there's a hot wind disrupting the dust. Like the willy-willy that just swept by us, Innamincka rises beguiling and unexpected from the plains of stone they call gibber. It doesn't seem to make sense that a town should exist here. Five hundred metres away, Cooper Creek drives an extraordinary oasis through this otherwise barren north-eastern corner of South Australia. It carries water down from monsoonal Queensland, and therein lies the answer to why we're up here on this infernal plain and not down by the creek in the shade of the coolibah.

In town, the only relief from the heat is in the pub and there it feels strangely invigorating to hear how it rained heavily in western Queensland two months ago and so Innamincka is expecting a flood next week. The town's seventeen residents will soon be living on an island. Cooper Creek is rising by the day.

'They reckon they could be the biggest floods since 1990,' the groovy young barman tells us while a girl at the youngish end of teenaged sketches him and his dreadlocks. 'Everyone's waiting to see how the new bridge goes. If the water gets up to eleven metres it could wash it away.'

Our plan is to ask around town about the state of the roads from here to Lake Massacre, so we can track down the intriguing grave that history has maintained belongs to Charles Gray.

So we head across the wide stretch of dirt that passes for a street to the Desert Parks office, a large verandah-surrounded house which was once the Inland Mission hospital where lonely nurses lost the battle to save the disease-riddled and malnourished indigenous population. Ranger Christine Crafter tells us Lake Massacre is a restricted area.

'You need my clearance to get out there. But you can't go, anyway. The roads have been cut off for months with all the flooding.'

That's a different flood from the one that's coming down. You'd think all it ever does is rain out here.

According to Crafter the name Lake Massacre probably would have reverted to the Aboriginal name, only there was another massacre there in the early 1900s and so the name remained out of respect.

'Anyway, it's not even Gray's grave,' she says by the by. 'It was probably one of Leichhardt's party.'

What?

'Yeah, some bloke came up from Melbourne to write a book about it or something. Gray died further west.' She says the researcher also found factors in McKinlay's account that made it seem unlikely to be Gray. Crafter isn't too sure of the details, but going back over McKinlay's journal we presume that the cuts to the skull and the amount of decomposition are enough to create doubt that it was Gray's body. Not to mention the Aboriginal man's gunshot wounds.

Certainly, Crafter seems to believe that the lake is where the intrepid German explorer Ludwig Leichhardt met his end. His disappearance in 1848, while attempting to be the first to cross the continent from east to west, has remained one of this country's most enduring mysteries.

Crafter tells us to read *Drought or Deluge*, which has a good account of the subsequent history of the Lake Massacre area. We buy a copy at the little store, along with a fly net for me, and set up camp on the banks of the Cooper.

Within twenty years of Burke and Wills passing through, the country around the Cooper was full of cattle and sheep. White men were crawling all over the place; poor men looking for work, ill-prepared for life on the track. They died deaths equally as harsh as the explorers, but with none of the glory. Best they could hope for was something as simple as a name like Deadman Sandhill, where four unemployed men died while attempting to walk from Birdsville to Innamincka searching for work.

Lake Massacre was taken up as part of a station called Land of Promise or Promised Land, whose owner J.W. Wylie, folklore insists, killed many Aborigines. The station's name was later changed to Coongie and its stone shearing shed is now a tourist attraction.

Having given up on reaching Lake Massacre, we spend a very pleasant few days watching the Cooper rise past little sticks inserted in the bank, feeling more at home in our tent. Flies in our tea are beginning to matter a lot less. We feel like we could stay forever in the shade of the river red gums, but we're forced to clear out before the Cooper overflows into Strzelecki Creek and blocks our way south.

Mount Hopeless is the next dot on the Map of Misery.

After John King was rescued by Howitt, King revealed that Burke's intention had been to reach the Mount Hopeless police outpost – which was their undoing.

We're interested in the 'mountain' not only because it was Burke's last hope, but because the story of how its name came to be is synonymous with the hardships of the South Australian outback and its explorers.

To get there we follow the Strzelecki Track, which once had the reputation of being the toughest of all the stock routes and was seldom used. Now, it's one of the trails that draws us city four-wheel drivers to the Centre, and is so well maintained because of all the Moomba Gas Field trucks using it, you could do it in one of those 14,990-dollar Korean hatchbacks.

But if we needed a reminder about taking the country lightly, it's to be found in *Drought or Deluge* where we read of the pregnant wife of a local stockman who decided to take her four kids to Moomba for a swim one summer's day in 1970. Her four-wheel drive broke down ten kilometres from town so she began to walk the eleven kilometres back to their camp. It was

57 degrees Celsius. Six kilometres down the track her seven-year-old daughter got too tired and took shelter under a tree. Two more of her children became ill and she carried them to an abandoned rabbit chiller less than two kilometres from home.

She got the oldest child to the camp and left him there. By the time she got back with water, the two youngest children at the rabbit chiller were dead. The daughter she left under the tree was alive, but died as she carried her back to camp.

'Three children had died within a few kilometres of ice-cream, air-conditioning and a swimming pool, because the car broke down on a summer day.'

CHAPTER 3

THE VIEW *from* MOUNT HOPELESS

Mount Hopeless, South Australia

AMY ▶ A rusted drum marked with the letters 'MH' and several empty beer bottles tossed onto the gibber alert us to the entrance of Mount Hopeless Station, 330 kilometres south of Innamincka. Locusts thud against our windscreen as we turn off the Strzelecki Track, unsure what we will find through the gate with its dirty great padlock hanging uselessly. Bumping over three kilometres of driveway, we pass plump cattle in the dry Mount Hopeless Creek and arrive at the homestead. It is abandoned. There are vague remnants of a once-loved garden now overgrown with weeds, and more empty beer bottles. The windmills are turning though, and the solar panels look shiny and new.

Continuing down the track the only other cow we see has its white ribs poking through its rotten carcass. We're not entirely sure where this track will take us – hopefully to Mount Hopeless, the sad lament of one of South Australia's most heroic explorers, Edward John Eyre.

Apart from the glorious dusty pink and blue Flinders Ranges in the distant south, however, the biggest bulge we can see is more nipple than mountain, and the track we're on is not heading towards it. According to the global positioning system (GPS), which we're using for the first time to pinpoint the spot, that's got to be it. We return to the homestead looking for a different route west, and find one back off the Strzelecki Track.

We startle a mob of cattle watering at a bore, and they race off down the track in front of us – the track softer underfoot than the huge red rocks of the plain. A few peel off to the side when we cross a dry creek bed, but a group of old girls with swollen, swaying bellies, calves in tow, opt for a galloping convoy towards Mount Hopeless. We stop and wait, we accelerate, we slow down, we beep, but these fat, well-groomed women in their ill-fitting heels only step it up a gear, and suddenly they are sprinting along the track and we are horrified that we may be driving them kilometres from water and killing them with the stress.

Then suddenly they display a stunning sense for the dramatic and veer off into the shadow of the hill, as if, ta da! to present Mount Hopeless. We round the base of the stony breast. A beautiful pale grey donkey bolts away with lightning little steps – the urgency of an animal who knows what it is to be hunted.

Having chosen a campsite in a field of stones, we wonder how effective our thin air mattresses will be. The light and the fridge are still lost causes. At least we've got the hang of the tent.

The first thing I notice when I get out of the car, however, is a crusty old snake skin, the sight of which will haunt me throughout the night. I'm never going to get the hang of snakes.

But before the sun disappears we take out our photocopies of Eyre's journal, made in the wood-panelled library that now seems so far away, and we head for the top of Mount Hopeless to take in the view.

Edward Eyre was a Yorkshire vicar's son only too aware that he was descended from gentry. He wrote: 'The consciousness of belonging to a time honoured race is in itself an incentive to exertion of no slight kind. There is generally the hope of repairing fallen fortunes. There is always the power of preserving the respect which attaches to the name . . .'

The vicar scraped together the money to set up his tall, thin, sixteen-year-old son in the colonies. Eyre had led an outdoor life, but his features were delicate. A portrait of the young man shows big eyes, a narrow face and foppish hair more suited to his father's footsteps than a pioneering life.

With 400 pounds to his name, Eyre set himself up as a farmer and grazier, but his sheep and wheat were hit by disease. He was forced to sell his farm and he took to the dangerous and specu-lative world of overlanding livestock, literally following in the wheel ruts of the explorer Thomas Mitchell to the new settlement at Port Phillip. Then from Sydney to the newly created colony of South Australia.

Eyre was only the second person to overland to Adelaide, arriving in July, 1838. The colony was just twenty months old. The place was a shambles teetering on the edge of bankruptcy and certainly a long way yet from the images of parks, piety and sicko murders that would portray it in the future. Indeed, its harbour was called Port Misery, a name first given it by shipping interests who had wanted the new colony based at Port Lincoln.

When Eyre arrived in Adelaide, he couldn't get a good price for his cattle so he started building a butcher's shop. He'd get his money back if he had to do it one steak at a time. When the locals saw he was serious, their offering price rose and he sold the herd for a personal profit of 650 pounds. He brought another mob of sheep and cattle from Sydney and made 2000 pounds on that trip, so he had money and time to spare. He was twenty-three and had been in the colony just six years. He would go exploring.

In later life, he described the forces that drove him to this turning point as 'an innate feeling of ambition and a desire to distinguish myself in a more honourable and disinterested way than by the mere acquisition of wealth. I was wrong no doubt – as many are who take a similar course – though I think it is a noble fault to fall into . . . You may win the distinction or honours but it by no means follows that wealth is ever again within your reach.'

In 1839, people still thought South Australia had boundless acres of fertile soil. Hopes were high. Eyre first went west in search of those boundless acres, to what is now known as Eyre Peninsula, as far as Denial Bay and present-day Ceduna, and decided the country was far worse than it later proved to be. The following year, in an expedition that he largely paid for himself, he was the first man to set out for the centre of the continent. At a farewell lunch at Government House, Governor Gawler handed over a silk Union Jack 'worked' by the good ladies of Adelaide to be planted in the Centre where it could 'wave for another 1000 years over the peace and prosperity of the mighty population which immigration is pouring upon us'.

The expedition set out at a canter, but as it left the gates of the Governor's residence, the cheering and the waving of hats stirred the 'gallant steeds' into a gallop, barely under control. Men on horses and women in wagons followed them for a few miles before the eight men slowed to a walk and began the lonely business of exploration.

They were three weeks north of Adelaide when they crossed Mount Eyre, the previous extremity of Eyre's northward journeys, and gazed towards the giant Lake Torrens, shimmering white in the distance, ambiguous as to whether it held water or salt. When he got to it, he found there to be a crust of salt over a muddy bog. Even then, he thought there was water in it, a few miles off, but was unable to trust his eyes with all the haze and refraction. 'I stood gazing on the dismal prospect before me with feelings of chagrin and gloom.'

Eyre pushed on north where, near present-day Marree, he saw and named Termination Hill. Not because he stopped there, but because the country looked so bad and waterless he reasoned he wasn't going to get much further on this track to the north–north–west. He pushed on nevertheless and saw an infernal salt lake ahead of him and imagined that it was Lake Torrens looping around, hemming him in. He was unaware that it was in fact Australia's largest salt lake, which would later bear his name.

Heading back south, 'melancholy' and thirsty, he pondered the way he would be received. 'The traveller who discovers a rich and well watered district, encounters but few of the hardships, and still fewer of the anxieties, that fall to the lot of the explorer in desert regions, yet is the former lauded with praise, whilst the latter is condemned to obloquy.' Eyre had already decided that his only hope of continuing north was via the Flinders Ranges, further to the east. He needed the water in the pools of the rugged gullies, for there was none on the flat. He crossed boggy plains to a hill he named Mount Distance, because it was much further away than he thought it was going to be, and then he gazed towards 'a distant low haycock-like peak'.

This little hill was the northernmost point of the range, so he knew his journey was over. He would go there to take one last look into the centre of the continent because he felt he owed it to his backers. He named it even before he had climbed it and saw what lay beyond. Mount Hopeless.

Heading towards it, he found salt water springing up from the land, 'presenting the most miserable and melancholy aspect imaginable'.

But he pushed on and climbed the hill. 'Cheerless and hopeless indeed was the prospect before us. As I had anticipated, the view was both extensive and decisive.' He saw salt lakes to the east, north and west, and was certain, beyond all doubt, that Lake Torrens encircled him like a giant horseshoe. 'This closed all my dreams as to the expedition, and put an end to an undertaking from which so much was anticipated. I had now a view before me that would have damped the ardour of the most enthusiastic, or dissipated the doubts of the most sceptical.'

Mount Hopeless, South Australia

MARK▶ The view is indeed desolate, made soft and warm in the red light of late afternoon, but it is also exhilarating. We go on a photographic frenzy around the cairn at the top.

Unlike Eyre, we can see no lake through our binoculars and wonder if he wasn't imagining things; if indeed he had had enough of his trip to the north. He also recorded that he looked around the eastern side of the Flinders Ranges, but they stretch further east than we can see around. Given this lonely view from Mount Hopeless, though, we certainly can't blame him for turning back and facing that damned obloquy.

Eyre was always disappointed. Given his melancholy opinions – not to mention his pessimistic nomenclature – nobody bothered following his tracks into northern South Australia until gold fever sent out a new wave. The next bloke to get there, sixteen years later, was B.H. Babbage, who found no gold but did find a fine canal-like body of permanent water, Blanchewater, just ten kilometres from Mount Hopeless. Heading south of Mount Hopeless he expressed his opinion of the country in the naming of a hill thirty-two kilometres away. He called it Mount Hopeful (later renamed Mount Babbage). Land applications came flooding in and as an editorial in the *Adelaide Register* noted: 'Many districts are now covered with flocks which years ago were denounced as hopelessly sterile.'

The reason this dry, salty land Eyre thought to be so worthless could support grazing was a plant called saltbush. The light green bush is ubiquitous in much of interior Australia. Eyre didn't know that it was succulent, full of nutrients, and that cattle would get fat on it. Cattle and sheep rushed into the north, overgrazed the country and when the inevitable droughts came, as they do every decade or so, Eyre's name for Mount Hopeless became entirely appropriate once more.

A cattle station and a police station were established at Blanchewater, but people still referred to the district as Mount Hopeless, and that's how Burke and Wills had come to see it as their last hope. But in the days when you needed more than a Hyundai for the trip, their hopeless attempt cost them their lives.

Lyndhurst, South Australia

AMY ▸ We are keen to find anyone who may have lived in the shadow of Mount Hopeless. Someone lovingly tended that garden now given over to beer bottles. So in the morning we head the two hundred kilometres south-west into the nearest town, Lyndhurst – best remembered as the end of the bitumen for north-bound travellers into the outback and for the name of its pub, the Elsewhere Hotel. As in, the barman elucidates, 'Where are you going tonight?'

Happy to be elsewhere, we order a couple of steak sandwiches and learn from the publican that the guy who had planned to do up the old Mount Hopeless homestead a few years back went broke when he got into foreign currency loans.

The Brown sisters are in town, though. The Browns were the last family to live out there. 'You would have passed Ronnie a couple of hundred kilometres back, driving the grader along the Strzelecki Track,' he says.

'Yeah, we saw her a long way back. Two days ago.'

'That's her, but her sister Junie Wilson should be home – the first house on the left coming into town.'

'You're too late,' June Wilson apologises as we step over a couple of teenagers working on a motorbike on the front step, and into the busy, narrow Wilson home. Too late by seven years to talk to her father, who worked at Mount Hopeless for two long spells, and too late by twenty-five minutes to catch her brother Dean who did a bit of growing up there. We sit at the small kitchen table and June makes tea. Her husband Frank joins us. His dark features are 'Afghan', his voice pure outback. June's features are those of her Aboriginal mother and white father.

There's a black and white picture of her dad, John Brown, in the kitchen. It shows a young man on a horse, his hat, shirt and attitude every bit James Dean in a poster from *Giant*. He could have told us stories about it and all the other places around about with names like Quicksand and Skeleton and Donkey Corner. 'Yeah, Dad worked at Mount Hopeless before he married my mum. Mustering in the camps, that sort of thing. Anything with horses. He loved horses.'

'Was it an outstation then?'

'Yeah, of Mumpie. That's what we call Murnpeowie Station.'

Her dad moved around a lot, working at various stations. By the time he did his second stint at Mount Hopeless, from 1980 until 1987, he and June's mum Margaret had ten kids. Only the youngest two were still living at home.

'I'd moved to Calcutta with Frank – that's an outstation of Mount Lyndhurst Station,' June says.

'So what happened to Mount Hopeless?'

'The beginning of the end for Dad, and for Mount Hopeless too, I suppose, came when he had his accident. He was riding a motorbike out there. He was a horseman. He was never much of a bike rider. Hated bikes. They were mustering and he hit a sandy bump on a clay pan. You know those bumps,' she says, as though we'd all naturally know the hazards of clay pans.

The bike flung over and the exhaust pipe broke his ankle. He crawled three or four kilometres towards the gas pipeline that comes down from Moomba.

'He reckoned there'd be gas workers along, come and get him. His leg was giving him that much trouble as he dragged himself, he took off his belt and used it to tie his bad ankle up under his bum. That didn't really work so he crawled back to the bike and tried to ride it again. He fell off and this time he broke the leg really bad. The young fellas in the camp finally decided to come looking for him the next day.'

They found him about 2 pm, alive but pretty crook.

'I remember it 'cos I was six months' pregnant with my daughter Erica at the time. I had to get on the motorbike and ride from Calcutta to Mount Hopeless so I could take Mum to be with Dad.'

But June got a flat and do you think those road trains would stop for a pregnant woman in the middle of nowhere? The second bloke pulled up, but only reluctantly, she thought.

'I asked him if he could give me a lift to the Mount Hopeless turn-off. I was really hoping he'd take me in the last three kilometres to the house.'

But the truckie looked at her funny and, sure enough, she found herself walking that last stretch over the rocky red plain.

'Mum and Dean [her younger brother] were at home and heard the little dog barking. They looked out to see what was up and they seen me wobbling down the track, my big belly out front.' It didn't seem so funny at the time.

Johnny Brown was never the same. Physically, nor maybe mentally. 'He was spooked.'

'Yeah, you're twenty years too late,' June says. 'You want all the old-timers. They're all gone now.'

Even into the early 1980s when June and Frank were working for Mount Lyndhurst, every station employed about ten men. But during the savage drought early in that decade men were laid off everywhere.

'Fair enough, it was tough times, but they were never put back on,' Frank says. There hasn't been anyone permanently at Mount Hopeless since John Brown left in 1987.

Upon leaving, we learn that June's sister Ronnie is back in from driving the grader up the Strzelecki. She has gone 'elsewhere', however, and doesn't want to chat.

Lyndhurst, South Australia

MARK ▶ Our plan is to push north up to Marree and the Oodnadatta Track. But perusing the Map of Misery, there are a number of dots that we want to have a quick look at first.

To the east, near Arkaroola, there is Humanity Seat, which sounds like some organisation based in Geneva, but is allegedly a lump of rock that the shitkicker miners who were scraping low grade copper out of the Flinders Ranges named because it reminded them of an arse. When we get to the privately owned nature reserve of Arkaroola we learn that the only way to see it is on a sixty-dollar tour. Although I think the woman has said six dollars, which makes it a whole lot easier to say yes.

We had been a bit shy about showing too much interest in Humanity Seat, so we hadn't asked too many questions. Then, after enduring two hours of driving up and down rough hills in first gear we see it and we can't make out anything remotely resembling a derrière in the rough, orange rocks.

'Yeah, never could see it myself,' says the guide, Richard. 'I hear you can see it from the air.'

Heading south to do some shopping in Port Augusta, I'm infuriating Amy by insisting on the indigenous pronunciation 'Port Agutta'. In the pressure-cooker car we trainspot our names. We have a squiz at Mount Desire, so named by surveyor Samuel Parry because of his desire to go home. Stoically, he pushed on.

Death Rock is an interesting lump by a waterhole. The Aboriginal name for it, Kanyaka, means just a piece of rock, but the early white settlers noticed that the sick and dying Aborigines all wanted to go there to drop off this mortal coil. Hence the name.

Devils Peak, at the top of the Pichi Richi Pass between Quorn and Port Augusta, is one of those sharply jutting rocks that early settlers seemed to connect to his satanic majesty. Quite pretty, actually.

After getting our Sunday night dose of *Popstars* in the rec room of a caravan park, we turn around and charge back up to Lyndhurst and on to Marree, where the road north splits into the Birdsville Track to Queensland and the Oodnadatta Track to Alice Springs in the Northern Territory.

We drive up the Birdsville Track for twenty kilometres to Illusion Plains, where the heat shimmer off the gibber had the surveyor Samuel Parry all aflutter: 'At times a vast sea appeared to surround us and saltbush was magnified to huge trees, hillocks to mountains and but a little distance could be penetrated by the eye.'

Alas, it just isn't hot enough for any acid trip illusions out there this day, so we head back to Marree.

I'd been up this way once before, on a story with Tim Flannery, the prolific author and then curator of the Australian Museum. I asked him if he knew of any interesting placenames we might seek out. He couldn't think of any in particular but he had a good laugh: 'You know, almost all the towns around Australia with variations of the word "coon" in their names actually mean shit. It's an amazing thing that across all the Aboriginal languages and dialects, the word for shit is remarkably common. It looks like in a lot of cases when the explorers came through, their guides had a bit of a joke at their expense telling them that this or that place was called shit water or mountain or whatever.'

According to *Manning's Place Names of South Australia*, Oodnadatta may well have the same derivation. It might come from one such 'coon' variation, Cudnadatta, meaning 'excreta water', there having been an artesian bore sunk just west of the town that bubbled soda and foul-smelling minerals. But then again, it could mean 'yellow blossom of the mulga'.

We've got to get to the bottom of this.

CHAPTER 4

MUSTERING UP PARADISE

Coward Springs, South Australia

AMY 'It's not pretty out there,' Mark warns me. 'Sorry, babe, but your bikini top suffered.'

I step out of the tent into a mud-wrestling arena. Where the mud stops, a wide brown puddle begins. We don't have to be told we are trapped. All night an almighty storm has thudded rain onto the tent loud as a tin roof and flashed green light through the canvas.

It is still now, but our patch of paradise at Coward Springs on the Oodnadatta Track isn't quite the same.

For some reason, the spectacular lightning display we'd admired before going to bed hadn't inclined us to move anything under cover. We were in the desert, after all.

Like my bikini, all of our stuff is spattered brown, but looking around at the other campers with their sleeping bags hanging out to dry, we've done okay. The only thing for it is to have a spa in the warm artesian pool, made, like most things new up this way, out of sleepers from the old Ghan railway line. Coward Springs was a rail siding until the switch to diesel in the 1950s meant the trains didn't need to stop here anymore. It's now an extremely pleasant, privately owned campground where you pay at the gate in an honour system.

There was no big milksop who inspired the name Coward Springs. It was an honour bestowed on Tom Coward, a police corporal who accompanied the explorer Colonel Peter Egerton Warburton through here in 1858.

Everything's drier by mid–afternoon, when a barefoot woman turns up at our tent to let us know that, provided there is no more rain, the road out should be open by morning. Oh, and by the way, do we smoke? Their supplies have been cut off and she is hanging for a ciggie. Her name's Vivien and it turns out she's a friend of the owner, Greg Emmett. So I donate a couple of cigarettes and we invite ourselves round for a cup of tea.

We find Greg, Vivien and her partner Steve at the kitchen table in one of the rundown old railway cottages. Swallows dart in and out, and the little room is full of people who turn out to be an ABC TV crew doing an *Australian Story* on Lake Eyre. The only place left to sit is on the floor.

Greg tells us he took up the lease at Coward Springs in 1990. The buildings were run down, there were no roofs. 'It was a wreck, basically. The only decent thing about the place was the tamarisks and date palms,' he says. Some of them were planted a hundred years ago by the Afghan cameleers. Greg and Steve are camel men, lured into the profession by one of Australia's modern cameleering pioneers, Rex Ellis, back on Kangaroo Island. 'He gathered together all the layabouts on the island and we all started working for him,' says Greg, who now spends half the year down on Kangaroo Island and the other half up here restoring the ruins.

Scruffy and lean, Greg and Steve are hitting their forties now, but have a young feel about them. They talk eruditely about the explorers and about obscure bush creeks and birds and animals. Right now, though, they've got boxes to unpack. The TV crew brought Greg's supplies with them and they are clearly keen to open them up and get to their food and cigarettes. So we leave them to it, and Greg loads us up with tubs of gooey dates from the historic trees – some for us and some for a mate of his up at William Creek.

It's not far up the Oodnadatta Track to William Creek, the last town on the way to Oodnadatta. We have to deliver the dates and we also want to visit Lake Eyre before we push on. The trade-off for enduring the sodden obstacle course of creek crossings, wheel ruts and cows is a magnificent scene: the glistening wet red gibber and a blue sky wallpapered with cartoon clouds.

William Creek, population about ten, is South Australia's smallest town. Light aircraft contend for parking spots outside the pub, and the extended family that runs the hotel airs its dirty laundry in the bar to we strangers amid the clutter of bras and knickers, photos and dirty poems.

We've just taken a perch when in walks a stout young jackaroo with sunken eyes looking out from under a white ten-gallon hat. While buying a takeaway slab for the boys, we overhear him say he's been mustering up Paradise.

Paradise, eh? We don't have that on our Map, but it sounds like somewhere we'd like to go.

First we have to drop the dates off to Phil Gee, another of the mad cameleers, who's just over the road. We figure we can ask him about it.

We lob at his door and he asks us in for tea, apologising that he only has powdered milk. He has a fabulous long explorer's beard and a cheeky grin. His double swag is rolled out on the floor of the sparsely furnished house, his laptop open on a desk. He's preparing for a weekend camel trip, although it looks like his tourists may not make it because of all the rain.

'Paradise? It's just a paddock,' Phil laughs. 'It was originally the area between town and the next sandhill. The name's a bit facetious, that's all. Nothing overly exotic.'

So William Creek, it turns out, is the gateway to Paradise. Well, it probably is for Phil. He's been fascinated with the area since he first got here and started retracing explorers' journeys

with his string of camels. He's turned up a few curious placenames in his travels, and some that never made it on to any
maps.

'The Dead Woman Dreaming, for example, which is a major
history through this country, is all about a fella dragging this
dead woman all over the country, and a lot of placenames are
named after the way she was looking as he was dragging her,
depending on how you were looking at her. Quite obscene –
they're not sort of like European placenames. There's one that
means her legs are wide open and looking very ugly, that sort of
thing. Sensitive stuff. Certainly there's a lot of them – men's tes-
ticles, penises, everything sort of features really prominently,
women's tits . . . He was dragging this woman along naked, and
they were all shouting abuse at her and calling her everything
under the sun.'

'Where did you get that story?'

'Oh, I couldn't say, 'cos all this stuff's sort of really sensitive.
In many ways I'm being entrusted with it now because no-one
in the country knows the Aboriginal history and Aboriginal
people themselves are not telling anybody, so there's quite a bit
of political manoeuvring going on. Some of them don't want
whitefellas to know their history so they can't use it as a commercial commodity, and I don't.'

Phil's happy enough to buy into the Oodnadatta debate.

So does it mean blossom of the mulga, or shit water?

'How can it mean blossom of the mulga when there were
never any mulga trees for miles around the area? It's all just a
bloody joke. The locals introduced that name, oh, probably a
hundred years ago, you know. Oodnadatta is from Cudnadatta
(shit water). It's documented way back from the 1800s. It's well
known, it's just not well known in the popular press. Don't fall
for the blossom of the mulga bullshit.

'The funniest thing is that they promote what they call an
Oodna Burger up at . . .' Phil cracks up and then checks himself.
Should he really be telling us that the burgers at the famous Pink
Roadhouse are shit burgers?

'But the thing is they're good mates of mine up there. Never mentioned it to 'em. That's the last thing they'd want me to tell the press.'

You get the feeling Phil enjoys a stir. When a bloke got busted for drink-driving a camel up there a while back, Phil, as editor of the *Australian Camel News*, fronted to the court case in Coober Pedy, foot-long beard and all, with a 'press' card stuck in his ten-gallon hat.

'So how'd you get into the camel business?'

'How'd I get into it? I bought ten wild camels on Master-Card. The bloody stupidest thing I've ever done. That was '84. I just went up to Alice Springs and bought them off one of the camel men up there. I went up to buy two tame ones and he talked me into ten wild ones . . . It was a bit of a romantic sort of thing.

'Three years later I left on my first trek, which was an absolute bloody horror 'cos I didn't know what I was doing. The camels were bloody scared shitless. I was scared shitless. That was from Adelaide to William Creek.'

From William Creek, Phil began retracing the journeys of early explorers, doing it the hard way.

'We're very hard core actually. Sort of go pretty hard.' Like the time he followed John McDouall Stuart's ghost across Dismal Plain, named during one of Stuart's surveying expeditions before he made his momentous journey across the centre of Australia. Dismal Plain was a great, flat, stony stretch of nothing.

'It's treeless and it's barren and it's hard walking for camels and horses, and it goes for about thirty, forty kilometres, big sharp stony gibber all over, great big cracks like this. Stages when I really bloody thought I had to watch my camels, they didn't fall down, you know. And it takes a couple of days to cross it. It'd take (Stuart) bloody one day. It took me a couple of days . . . I did that trip with three girls. Best trip I ever did. My wife thought it was the worst . . . But places like that are dismal, no joy.

'We were actually trying to work out where Stuart crossed

the Stuart Highway . . . and it was really hard to pick up his routes. It was 1858 – bloody hell, he only had a compass and a crappy map, and no-one worried about it too much after he did the trip because he never found anything of any significance. He didn't find an inland sea, he just found crappy country, and in that same year they discovered all the mound springs a bit further north of where he was. But he did actually cross the Stuart Highway – as it turned out he went right though Coober Pedy. It's quite amazing. He walked right through the biggest opal floater field in the world.'

Since we left Sydney, talk of all the water flowing into Lake Eyre has been getting us excited. In the past week we've heard everything from it being three-quarters full, to the cynicism of the publican at Marree who reckoned we might not see a drop. 'We had a bloke come in and say, "Well, now I can die happy. I've seen Lake Eyre full." But there wasn't any water in it. Still, if he thought he'd seen it, who was I to tell him otherwise? He was happy.'

With Mark behind the wheel, we leave William Creek late to drive the rough seventy-kilometre track to the lake. The guy at the little William Creek shop told us a convoy of four cars had returned from the lake earlier today after having been trapped out there for days by the rain. One of them got bogged, but they made it through, so at least we know it's passable. Still, I'm not entirely comfortable with the idea of going out there just the two of us.

About thirty kilometres along the track we see a simple wooden cross: 'Dec 11 1998 Caroline Grossmueller Perished'. We get out, and even in April it's hot. The flies are bad, and the saltbush and rocky plains stretch on forever.

There's a cattle trough maybe 200 metres further on, overflowing with water pumped from underground. The dark, deflated hide of a long-dead beast sags metres from it. We can't help but imagine how divine such a pool would appear in thirsty, fifty-degree heat. Caroline Grossmueller, in her delirium, must never have seen it. When she was found dead here, the five-litre water bottle in her pack was full and a two-litre bottle lay beside her, three-quarters full.

That's a funny thing about the outback and the north: just about the only people to come here in summer are German-speakers. We bought our troopie off a Swiss couple who had just done the trip. All the English-language guide books simply tell you not to come between November and March, but the German books, catering to some sort of sauna madness, have the Germanics keeping little places like William Creek alive during the long, fiery summer.

And so it was that the two Austrians – Grossmueller and her boyfriend of eleven years, Dr Karl Goeschka – drove out to Lake Eyre in the brilliant solitude of December. They signed a register at the William Creek Hotel on the seventh, saying to expect them back by lunch the next day. According to Goeschka, the publican's son told them: 'If you're not back at this time then you're in trouble and we have to get you out.'

They were driving a rental Landcruiser converted to a campervan. In the last few hundred metres before the lake, they got bogged in sand. They weren't overly concerned; they'd registered in the book, after all.

They waited out the next day expecting a rescue party, growing angry at the people back at the pub as time passed and no help came. Grossmueller wrote in her diary that they were in hell. They decided to walk out the next day, even though they had food and there was about 200 litres of drinking water in a tank out there for just that purpose.

We're imagining Grossmueller's vision of hell as we drive in and top a crest. Suddenly everything is black. Mounds and mounds of bizarre, ebony gibber. I imagine it is what hell will look like when the fires go out – an awesome, horrifying vista in which barely any vegetation survives. What must Grossmueller have experienced walking through it?

As the couple walked, they apparently had a fight and Goeschka turned back to the vehicle while his girlfriend pushed on. She made about forty kilometres over three days. Her body was found four days later by a couple of German tourists. Goeschka was found alive and well back at the vehicle. The car was driven out of the sand simply by deflating the tyres and locking the front wheels. Apparently the companies that rent out these four-wheel drives forbid customers taking them off road, and so don't demonstrate the tricks of four-wheel driving.

We hit the sandy entrance to the lake and I get nervous, barely breathing as Mark pushes Frank through. This is where Grossmueller and Goeschka got stuck. But we're lucky – sand after rain is nothing compared to the scorched, slippery stuff of midsummer.

The beachy stench of rotten fish and salt air hits our nostrils. Seagulls screech overhead. We read in our guide book that Lake Eyre hasn't been continuously filled for over 20,000 years. It has only filled four times in the past hundred-odd years. For the last couple of months, though, its name has been splashed across newspapers around Australia because of all the water that's been gushing down from Queensland.

It's a bit hard to tell where the water actually starts, but we can tell the Marree publican was way off the mark. We had imagined ourselves swimming, but trudging through all the thick black goo to get to the water proper is hard work, so in the end we settle for getting little more than our ankles wet.

We stay at Lake Eyre a couple of days and for the most part are alone. It is a thrill to stand in the shallows of this big lonely thing at sunset; the expanse of still, pink water, the dance of lightning in the soft pink distance.

It's 9 am on a Saturday and the beer is flowing freely through the gates of Paradise. William Creek's main street has sprung into a tent city, the population swollen to twenty times its usual size with zealous jackaroos, jillaroos and cockies. The annual William Creek gymkhana and race weekend is due to kick off, but when Mark and I arrive back in town from Lake Eyre there is a curious pall hanging over the pub. It turns out that with the roads blocked by the rains, the booze and boobs fest is in limbo. The horses aren't here and the barmaid is grim: the VB van from Coober Pedy hasn't made it. At this rate, supplies won't last the day.

The morning hours pass in the vain hope the problems will somehow disappear. They don't. And so the William Creek gymkhana is metamorphosed into a games day, with such party favourites as the Dummy Spit, Toss the Can, and an auction that sees a jar of crab sell for over three hundred dollars.

Sydney journalist Kendall Hill, here to do a story on the floods filling Lake Eyre, decides to stir his paper's 'basket weavers' by volunteering the broadsheet as sponsor of the wet T-shirt competition. Others come to the party all wanting this corporate glory and a fierce bidding war ensues. Kendall drops out around the 250-dollar mark but leaves the money – his own – in the Flying Doctor kitty. Soon 1500 dollars has been raised by Kendall's little stir.

The crowd is under strict instruction to respect the local beauties who climb on the back of two utes to show their wares. Even when the water is splashed on and the brand new T-shirts prove water-resistant, the red-blooded mass is well mannered. Only two contestants are prepared to flash the real thing, one of whom has apparently been flashing them all afternoon anyway. She does, however, do it well, and takes the crown.

The VB is long gone but these guys are flexible. They make do with West End. We clearly don't have their stamina and retire early, just as a crinkly old guy who specialises in silly hats and has been going hard all day sinks to the ground. Yet, before we've even finished our goodnights, he's back up, beer in hand, kicking on. What a trouper.

It's with more than a little trepidation that I pick my way through the debris to the loos the next morning. The first man I pass lets rip with an astonishing belch as his Bonds singlet strains to hold in his beer belly. Another stops me: 'I've lost the keys to my plane.' A wheelbarrow full of empty beer cans is parked up against the toilet block, evidence that at least someone in town is on top of things this morning.

One by one the planes taxi down the dirt airstrip and the swags are tossed on to the back of utes. Only the stragglers remain. The road to Coober Pedy has been opened, but the sign on the pub door urges extreme caution. The road to Oodnadatta – the one we want – is still closed, so we decide to check out Paradise.

Paradise is to be found on Anna Creek Station, which at 24,000 square kilometres bills itself as the largest cattle property in the world. We phone the station and Tracy, the manager's wife, tells us that as well as Paradise, Anna Creek has Whatchemacallit, Starvation, Poverty and Skeleton Dams.

'But I wouldn't send you out to any of them. They're all way out across pretty tough country.'

We are, however, welcome to visit Paradise.

We find the handwritten sign marking the turn-off directly beneath the one pointing to the rubbish dump. 'Paradise 22km.' The road's a bit boggy but doesn't look too bad, until we hit a patch of virgin mud at sixty kilometres an hour and nearly take ourselves out. Coming to a slow motion stop off the road, neither of us knows quite what to say, so Mark gets out and grabs the Butternut Snap biscuits.

Gingerly, we drive the car back onto the road and immediately there's that sinking feeling. We're bogged. Great. These people have been generous enough to let us come on to their land and here we are carving ugly scars into their road and they're probably going to have to come out and rescue us. Mark is more positive. He grabs the shovel with admirable zeal and, with a little rocking and the creation of a makeshift bridge, gets us out. He's happy.

Paradise itself is hard to distinguish from the rest of the country. There's a dead cow and a wooden cattle yard and a coolibah-lined dry creek bed. Paradise is okay, we suppose, but we wouldn't want to live there.

Back at William Creek, the Oodnadatta Track is still closed. We ponder our dilemma over a pie in the pub, but when the barmaid takes up where she left off with her all too personal conversation about the in-laws, it looks like we're going to Coober Pedy to see a dead man on the outskirts of town.

Right on the edge of the opal moonscape that is Coober Pedy is Deadman's Dugout. Local lore would have it that a lonely old miner died in his underground home and his hungry pet dogs gnawed away at the corpse until it was found. Phil Gee had told us about it and given us the name of a local historian, Anne Johnson, who he said knew something of the story. So from the Coober Pedy caravan park, Mark calls her up.

Johnson says when she stumbled on the 1946 police records of the death of Jack Stanley she was somewhat disappointed to find there was no such reference to pet food, just that he was found in his doorway and he'd been there a long time. Old Jack was meant to have been a gruff old chap, didn't get along well with others, which is why he lived way out there on the edge of town. They took him over the track and buried him in his own workings.

We find old Jack's rough wooden cross on the road from William Creek, just north-east of the intersection with the Stuart Highway. It is penned in by a little stick fence and flanked by some very old car bodies. Just over the road is his dugout, still in use today. There are two dugouts there, actually, both neat, almost landscaped. Jack's neighbour has an old Mercedes in the drive, near a '60s caravan and a metre-high Grecian statue. No-one is home.

We retire to the caravan park where we read in the local paper that there are twenty-five tourists trapped in Oodnadatta. We wonder if they have eaten all the burgers because helicopters have had to drop supplies for them. We are still keen to find out more about the contentious name so we ring the Pink Road-house. Evidently Adam Plate, on the other end of the phone, has no misconceptions about the 'shit burgers' they serve up.

'Basically, Oodnadatta is a town of public servants and transient Aboriginals and no-one could give a rat's arse what it means. The public servants just made it up, basically. It's supposed to be a misquoted conversation where the Aborigines told the whitefellas to keep away from the bog that's in front of you, but the public servants have said that it's got something to do with the blossom of the mulgas. That's crap.'

So that's that then.

As it turns out, it is more than a week before the road opens up into Oodnadatta, and by then we're flooded in at Alice Springs.

CHAPTER 5

JUSTIFIABLE ARREST

Alice Springs, Northern Territory

MARK The rain starts soon after we cross the Northern Territory border, swirling down in a great sweep from one of the tropical cyclones whose names of late have blurred one into the other, giving the north one of its best soakings in years.

So wouldn't you know it, when we tune into ABC local radio one of the first items we hear is about bushfires. Bushfires. But they don't talk of tinderboxes. Up in the Territory it's 'firebombs'.

'The fires that will come from these grasses will beggar the imagination,' declares the talent. 'They will incinerate trees, massively changing ecosystems.'

Hard to believe right now. Everything is a lovely soft green, except the spinifex, which is deep British-racing-car green.

It rains all the way to Alice Springs, where it has been raining for three days. The normally dry Todd River, home of the Henley-on-Todd regatta and innumerable local drunks, is a raging brown torrent. Already this year the Alice has had twenty-four inches of rain, three times the annual average, causing the biggest floods in twelve years. We book ourselves into the last on-site caravan in town.

Next day, the roads north and south have been closed, blocked by the Palmer and Finke Rivers respectively. We book back into the van and stare wistfully at the Map.

We want to get to Mount Treachery near Yuendumu on the Tanami Track, but the roads up there look like being closed for some time. I'd been there two years earlier for the magazine article; Paul Blackmore and I pulled up at Yuendumu for petrol, and I asked an Aboriginal man passing the pump about Mount Treachery, sixty kilometres north-east of town. He said the name came from the Coniston massacre: 'Rounded 'em up doing their ceremonies, minding their own business. Just shot 'em. Cut their head off. Drove 'em all the way up to the Granites (220 kilometres up the Tanami Track). Killed many relatives. Nobody talk about it much. Very sad.'

Asked when it happened, he said without hesitation: '1928. Before this place was built.'

The people at the Walpiri media centre around the corner weren't so sure of its connection to Coniston. The white media people put a map over the bonnet of an old Kingswood with a Hawthorn scarf across the dash, and invited passing elders to try to figure out which hill it was. But no-one knew where Mount Treachery was nor what story it told.

In August 1928, Fred Brookes was a sixty-seven-year-old white station hand at Coniston. The station had been in drought for four years and couldn't afford to keep him on, so he bought some camels and took two Aboriginal boys out bush to hunt dingoes for their ten-shilling bounty. There had previously been tension between the whites and the 'wild blacks' who had been pushed off soaks so cattle could water, but when Brookes's little party came to a soak not far from the Coniston homestead, they were pretty much ignored by the thirty or so Walpiri camped there.

An Aborigine with the white name of Bullfrog came over to trade tobacco and sugar, but Brookes had little of either and didn't want to part with any. Two days later, Bullfrog turned up again with his wife, Marungali.

'Let that woman go washin' clothes for me,' said Brookes, according to an account in *The Killing Times*, by John Cribbin.

'Let her go after washin' clothes, I'll give you tucker.'

Marungali washed Brookes's shirts and stayed the night, while Bullfrog fretted. 'Under Walpiri law there was nothing greatly amiss with a man sanctioning his wife in service to a white man, but what was essential was that there should be payment rendered in return . . . All night, Bullfrog waited, expressing growing anger to his uncle Padirrka . . . When dawn broke, Bullfrog was to see his wife getting out of Brookes's bed. In a fury he rushed the camp, closely followed by Padirrka.'

Bullfrog was armed with a boomerang and stone knife. Brookes was half naked. The first blow with the boomerang severed an artery in his neck. Lurching with a strangled scream, he was grabbed from behind by Marungali, who pinned his arms as Bullfrog and Padirrka hacked away. They put the body in a hessian sack and jammed it into a rabbit hole, one leg protruding.

Padirrka and Bullfrog fled the camp, but the others in the tribe made no attempt to flee, since they understood that white man law only punished the perpetrators.

Brookes's two Aboriginal companions alerted the authorities to the murder. So began a far more orchestrated and outrageous treachery. A hero of the Gallipoli campaign, Mounted Constable George Murray, came whooping through the black camps at the head of a posse of police and civilians. Among the many Aborigines killed over the next fortnight was Marungali, but not Bullfrog nor Padirrka, who got away.

The matter would have rested but for the trial in Darwin of two other Aboriginal men for the murder of Brookes. The charges were laughed out of court but a diligent missionary had drummed up media interest from the eastern states. The outcry caused by Murray's frank admission to killing seventeen Aborigines prompted Prime Minister Stanley Melbourne Bruce to call an inquiry.

The Chief Government Resident in Alice Springs, Mr J.C. Cawood – who was a player in the drama, having sent out the posse – was a member of a three-man commission of inquiry, along with a Queensland policeman and a police magistrate.

They cleared the police involved, notably Mounted Constable Murray, on the basis that if he had intended to go out and massacre the Aboriginal population he had ample opportunity to kill many more than he did.

The finding was that the thirty-one who were officially noted as dead – as opposed to Murray's figure of seventeen – had been killed while 'resisting justifiable arrest', and that every single one of them was implicated in the murder of Brookes. The inquiry found that, among the many causes for Brookes's murder and the general surliness of the blacks, missionaries preaching equality with whites and 'a woman missionary living amongst naked blacks' had 'lowered their respect for whites'.

It's a white man thing. We won the war, we name the battle-fields. Mount Treachery first appeared on the official register, near Brookes Soak, in 1930, apparently in reference to Brookes's murder and not the subsequent massacre.

Murray continued to be regarded by the white population as a good man who did what needed doing. Subsequent oral histories revealed that up to seventy people may actually have been murdered by his party.

MARK▶ This morning, I look for instructions on the Spam tin. There aren't any, but I manage to figure out how to scoop it out all by myself. I'm making a surprise breakfast for Amy and don't want to ask for help. I consider this to be personal growth.

The menu is toast grilled with cheese, tomato, Spam and John West garlic. Served with instant coffee. Nescafé Blend 43, in fact.

We used to be card-carrying citizens of Latte Land; owned two plungers and a stainless steel espresso thingy. But Amy vetoed bringing them with us due to space considerations. We decided to become tea drinkers for the duration, but something just drew us back to the stronger caffeine hit in the morning.

And get this: the cheese is Kraft Processed Cheddar. The sort you haven't eaten since school, and if you have, you haven't mentioned it in polite society.

You might be thinking that when someone as refined and

sophisticated as Amy is served up a breakfast such as this, she would instinctively turn up her nose, get on her trendy little chrome scooter and make for the nearest café. Not only does she stay, she loves the Spam.

'Tastes a bit like devon,' she declares. 'I love devon.'

She hasn't had devon since fourth class, but we are reshaping our lives. Going back to basics. If it was good enough to last the morning in her Barbie lunch box without turning the bread gooey, it's perfectly appropriate for long road journeys without a working fridge.

We got onto Spam after trying a tin of corned beef back at Lake Eyre. We liked that and decided to graduate to the harder stuff. We had already accepted Kraft Processed Cheddar into our lives and we aren't afraid who knows it. It is like renouncing all worldly possessions.

Deb instant mashed potato, cask wine, Vesta curry prawns and rice, socks with sandals and dirty hair – we have embraced them all.

Amy turns from the sink: 'You know at home how we have all the stuff: the plates, the cooking utensils, the chopping boards, the dishwasher, well . . . it's so easy here when we haven't got anything.'

That is a lesson the wise masters have been trying to teach the human race for several millennia. And we've discovered it here in a caravan park on the outskirts of Alice Springs.

AMY ▶ It's a week before things are nearly back to normal in Alice Springs. The sandbags are still out. There are road closures and debris everywhere, but the local Aborigines have finally returned to their drying riverbed. The slanting afternoon light silhouettes their black figures against the pale sand and river gums.

Since the road to Mount Treachery is still shut, we decide to see how justice looks these days in the wet heart, and wander one morning into the Alice Springs court building, a square, white, modern pile in the middle of town.

In the magistrate's courtroom there is a juvenile case where no details are given, just an Aboriginal boy sitting forlornly next to his grandmother, proud in a purple scarf. He gets bail on condition he reside with her at Old Timers, a camp on the outskirts of town. His face is blank as his lawyer explains that, yes, he can go, but no drinking, okay? As he is led out we see his bare feet and skinny legs.

Then there is a man, whose age is given as thirty or thirty-one, who was caught carrying twenty casks of wine into a dry community. He had a flat tyre and when questioned by police drove off on the rims. He made it four kilometres before the car would go no further.

He says, through his lawyer, that he was involved in the crime but was not the instigator. When asked to plead to being in control of liquor, his guilty plea is more implied by his lawyer than spoken. The lawyer, a thin woman in a pinstripe suit, has a sharp young face, yet silver-grey hair. She tells the court he actually wants to do time; he doesn't trust himself to stay off the grog: 'He's not very happy at the moment.'

He sits there quietly. The large fluoro lights overhead, the wood panelling and amplified silence all adding to the unreality of the scene.

Another young man is brought in, and unlike those before him he slouches into the chair with defiance, staring down the world. The prosecutor alleges that he, with another guy, had been drinking before they entered a property on the southern outskirts of town, about 500 metres from our caravan park. They found an axe and an iron bar in the yard, and tried to push a Landcruiser down the driveway.

Meanwhile, inside, the owner heard the noise, went to investigate and tried to call the cops. But one of the accused followed him inside. The owner lashed at him with an ornamental spear, nicking his neck.

The defendant then smashed the owner's head with the iron bar, fracturing his skull. The two men struggled, while the co-accused broke his way into the house with the axe and began weighing into the householder.

They got fifty dollars and the Landcruiser, which had had the keys in it the whole time. They drove to a vacant lot where they bogged the car and abandoned it, taking the axe and the iron bar with them to a house at Old Timers.

It's only upon hearing this that we realise it is the same address the shy kid who was up earlier was remanded to. He is apparently the co-accused.

The prosecutor says the owner of the house was operated on last night and is in intensive care. He has, though, spoken to police and made a positive ID of these two.

The older defendant has no record of such attacks, but has five car theft convictions, the latest in 1995. His lack of recent form seems to owe more to the fact he hasn't turned up to court since 1997 than his good behaviour. He's got a string of out-standing warrants.

The weary magistrate says he's not going to give this guy bail again. He's facing life imprisonment. Yesterday may prove to be his last day out in the world. He is nineteen and married with a child.

Once again, the defence lawyer has to explain the magistrate's ruling to her client: 'No, you didn't get bail, you have to stay here, okay?'

The session ends and we wander back out to the hallway. We decide to drop into the next courtroom, where the Supreme Court is in session. It is full-on wigs and gown territory. And the regalia of the British legal system couldn't seem more odd than when compared to the small man wearing the orange tracksuit top hunched in the dock.

We see virtually nothing more than his curly brown mop of hair, though we later learn that his name is Clifford Ebatarinja. His defence barrister, Kim Kilvington, grabs our attention from the start with one word: 'payback'.

We don't know what Ebatarinja has done yet but this is just a bail application and payback is usually only taken into account by judges when *sentencing* traditional Aboriginal people. If they know they are going to cop a tribal spearing when they return to their community, then the judge can lighten the whitefella sentence by some degree.

In this case, however, Kilvington argues that if Ebatarinja doesn't get bail and return to his community to face payback, the elders will 'sing' a snake to come and get him. The equivalent of pointing the bone. He explains that the snake is a traditional method of tracking down a guilty person.

'My client has a psychiatric report which notes a number of people dying of these beliefs, and my client may die in prison if he has not faced payback, and if he believes the snake has been sent to him.'

Kilvington reads from the psychiatric report, which says people have died by 'complex presumed psychological mechanisms' after they have been 'sung'. The psychiatric report continues, 'Mr Ebatarinja has a fixed and unshakeable belief that if he is sung he will inevitably die. I have no doubt this could occur in this man.'

Kilvington says that 'even if there has not been a decision to send the snake, but the applicant fixates that the snake has been sent, it will have the same effect.'

A barefoot woman comes in and sits beside us in the gallery, waiting for the next case. She is breastfeeding a newborn baby wrapped in a white blanket.

The judge, Justice Dean Mildren, says he is likely to grant Ebatarinja bail, but adjourns the matter until next week. Kilvington explains to his client what has happened in slow, careful words, but, as he later tells us, he's never sure if he is understood. The client just nods.

We wait outside the courtroom for Kilvington. He sits down on a bench, revealing a pair of red, green and yellow socks beneath his sombre barrister's robes, and juggles a pile of recalcitrant folders. He says we got lucky today. Payback cases come up every week, but the magic involved in this one is different.

Ebatarinja was originally up for murder, but that was dropped to 'dangerous act causing death', which means that there was no intention to kill or seriously injure, and that death wasn't foreseeable. Ebatarinja allegedly hit a woman in the head with a tin while he was drinking, bruising and cutting her. What wasn't immediately obvious was the tiny lesion it caused on her brain, which slowly bled. She died three or four days later. 'It was essentially an assault that unfortunately, and in many ways accidentally, lead to the death of his wife.'

'Oh, it was his wife.' I say, taken aback.

'Oh, who knows? I had one client give me instructions, much to the infuriation of the magistrate, that he was eighteen, when he was probably closer to sixty-five, because the boss at the station told him once he was eighteen, and he told me that the boss doesn't lie. So having once been told he was eighteen, that's how he travelled through life.'

He says Ebatarinja is probably in his late thirties. The frail, hunched-over man we saw in court had seemed so much older.

'You've got to remember the life expectancy out here for (Aboriginal) men is only about fifty-two, so it's fair to describe some men as being old men after they're about forty, really.'

Kilvington is a talking whirlwind. Sentences stream out of him, long and complicated, and bright and fascinating. He tells us about a 'doozey' he's got coming up in a couple of weeks where the client, who has been charged with murder, is profoundly deaf and mute. Can't communicate in any way other than enough sign language to establish 'hungry', 'thirsty', 'father', 'sick', and a clenched fist to show anger.

'How old is he?' Mark asks.

'Oh, he's in his twenties, but he comes from probably the most dysfunctional family in Australia, all of whom are totally alcoholic, all of whom have long criminal records. His brother's in jail charged with attempted murder of a fourteen-year-old girl.'

'Where are they from?'

'Larapinta Valley Camp, in town, which is the most dysfunctional, alcoholic camp in town, which has probably the highest killing rate in the world, if not, definitely, in Australia. The rate of killings – he would have personally witnessed probably half a dozen killings, so as he evaluates life entirely by visual perception, he has probably accepted (that) it's like a standardised form of behaviour.

'Our killing rate here [Alice Springs] is . . . it depends – some years only about eight, and some years a dozen or more killings . . . in this town which notionally only has 26 to 27,000 people. So, on an average year, one in every 2,200 people in town will be violently killed, usually by knife, so it's actually got quite a high homicide rate.'

This, plus the marriage of traditional law with the British system, makes for an interesting legal practice.

'How strong are traditional beliefs in the drinking camps around town?' asks Mark.

'A lot of the time when they're sitting down drinking they are in fact reinforcing the traditional beliefs and customs, that's what they talk about. They sit down. You say, "What do you do?", like you might say "What have you done in the last twenty years?", and it's quite frequent for the client to say "I've sat down". And sometimes I used to get annoyed: "But you can't have sat down for the whole twenty years. Have you worked?" "No, I sit down". And that quite literally is what they do as a lifestyle. They sit down and they talk, and they sing, and they sing the traditional songs which relate to a particular area, or episode or the ancestors, and they participate in a lot of ceremonial business, always moving around, going around to ceremonies.'

As an example of the strength of traditional beliefs, Kilvington cites the case of another of his clients who is in jail for murder. Never to be released. 'The community were never satisfied that he'd killed the person, so they organised people from hundreds, if not thousands of kilometres, all the senior men, to go to this very powerful snake dreaming ceremony, where they could sing the real killer . . . And they had a belief that it might have been a fella – I won't mention his name. And everyone knew that it was going to happen, and the psychiatric nurse here at the prison was keeping a close watch on my client because he knew it was going to happen, and if he was the killer he would have died, because the information we have about that ceremony is that the person starts frothing at the mouth, then vomits, and then dies.

'So they conducted the ceremony, and sure enough the person who'd been nominated as the probable offender started frothing, started vomiting and duly died.

'But of course we don't have an autopsy report to prove cause of death, for the purposes of getting this client, who someone else acted for once upon a time, out of jail.'

In order to make a case, Kilvington would have to prove the existence of the custom, prove that the deceased belonged to that belief system, and prove that he was aware of the ceremony taking place. More importantly he would have to show that the deceased's beliefs were so deeply held that they could cause him to react with the symptoms expected from the guilty person – that is, to die. He would also need medical evidence of the condition of the deceased's health prior to his death to eliminate other possible causes.

'And then we'd have to ask the court to construe all of that as being an admission of guilt by the person who died. It's never been done before, the logistics are frightening, and I can't use it to get our client out of jail, although now that this business has been done all those people in that wide geographical area firmly believe, without any question, that the wrong person's in jail, and that the person who killed the woman died. And they all feel aggrieved with our justice system because they perceive that an innocent member of their extended family is in jail. And I can't do anything about it.'

Kilvington's got so many things on the go, including a few constitutional cases he hopes will see 'draconian' slabs of Territory legislation overturned, and he sure can talk.

Until, suddenly, 'I've got to go,' he interrupts himself. 'It was a good one.'

We later learn Justice Mildren did grant bail to Ebatarinja, recognising his beliefs as a reason.

The Tanami Track is still closed, blocking our intended route north-west into the Kimberley. We are forced into a reappraisal back at the Map of Misery over a glass of cardboard shiraz and a piece of processed cheese. We dwell on a trail left by the explorer Ernest Giles south-west of here, around Ayers Rock – Uluru – and beyond.

He left some lovely names on the map – Fairies' Glen, Titania Spring, Mount Oberon, Ruined Rampart and Ediths Marble Bath. He left some horrors, too – Mount Destruction and Ophthalmia Range.

In the quiet of the Mitchell Library in Sydney, Giles's journal had taken us to these places he'd tackled with optimism and humour, while the Romantic in him indulged in the joy of beauty and torment. Desperately thirsty, hungry, crazed by flies and heat, Giles would comment whimsically on the 'ivory moonlight' or the 'charmed surroundings'. Maybe he was off with the fairies.

We'd applied for permits to visit some of Giles's placenames, which are on Aboriginal land, when we first arrived in Alice. Now we have to wait for the wheels of the Central Land Council's bureaucracy to turn.

CHAPTER 6

UNAPPROACHABLE

Uluru, Northern Territory

MARK ▶ We head to Uluru (formerly Ayers Rock) and the caravan park at Yulara to await a permit from the Central Land Council so we can have a go at approaching Giles's Mount Unapproachable, 150 kilometres west–north–west of the Rock.

The caravan park is all nice and green. The resort apparently holds 5000 people and a good portion of them are camped here on Lawn 1, a twenty by thirty-metre patch of grass as far away from the toilets as it's possible to get and still be in the same postcode.

The couple next to us has matching shiny tracksuits, and a sticker on their Nissan Patrol: 'Celebrate Jesus' Love'. We never once hear a single noise from them. We hear every move, however, of the family behind us, and we know that little Brigid needs to go to the toilet every morning about 4 am otherwise there are accidents. Other than that, they are perfect.

There are two peak hours at the camping ground. One before dawn as cars roar off to catch sunrise at the Rock. Needless to say, we skip that one, and little Brigid would have preferred to as well, if the amount of shouting it took to rouse her is any indication.

And when I rashly yell, 'Shut up!', it sets the tone for a tense few days of camping next door.

We feel like Boo Radley. We love those kids. They are so cute. Yet they won't come near us. A rough-looking workman turns up to paint a fence and they're all over him, but they never say a word to Amy or me.

Standing at the base of the Rock, we contemplate the climb up. A busload of Japanese tourists brings to mind the pilgrimage up Mount Fuji. But suddenly they are gone, and we are surrounded by large people with German-sounding accents; the women in shiny impractical shoes climbing the first few metres. They gradually disperse and some Americans arrive.

'Harry, did you take a photo of this lady with a snake around her neck last night?'

'No, it wasn't me, sugar.'

We stretch, fill the day pack with muesli bars, and begin the ascent. It is steep. The chain doesn't start until about forty metres up – obviously a technique for weeding out the old and sick and high-heeled.

A woman is sitting in a large cleft of rock about ten metres below the chain. Chicken Rock, it's called.

She says she's been there for two hours. She got this high and froze. 'My husband went up, but I couldn't. I can see him now, coming down.'

Meanwhile, Amy is freezing too. It is steeper and scarier than either of us had imagined. Amy's not going any further, but at least she can claim cultural sensitivity. She had been feeling uncomfortable; the traditional owners prefer tourists not to climb the Rock. I tried to tell her that they don't have any strict taboo against it. Mainly they get saddened by the people dying up there. Anyway, she's not going to be one of those . . . if only she could get down the little way she's gone up.

We decide to walk around the base, leaving the culturally insensitive act to me, tomorrow. I like the idea that in this era of the Nanny State I'm still free to climb it and die as I please.

The 9.6-kilometre walk is beautiful, following the folds and patterns and watery gullies. The Rock's huge surface like the upturned rusty hull of a supertanker.

After a week here, it is time to leave. I did a load of washing in the communal laundry yesterday. When I brought it back Amy pointed out a sanitary pad mixed in with it.

'It's not mine,' I said.

'Well, it's not mine either!' she screamed.

'At least it's clean.'

'Yuuuuuuuuck.'

It really is time to go. We're still waiting on the permit from the Land Council for Mount Unapproachable. The whole bottom left-hand corner of our map of the Northern Territory is shaded brown, indicating Aboriginal land. Permits to drive across it are simple to obtain, but we want to leave the main track and write about it, so it's a whole new bureaucratic ball game. We, perhaps naively, thought we could play it in the two weeks we had in the area.

We try calling but the permits person, Nerida, is off sick. When we do get through to somebody who knows something, we're told it can't be arranged in our time frame. We could do it in maybe six months' time and then we'd have to pay for elders to escort us. We'd practically begged Nerida to tell us as much when we put our application in two weeks ago, but then it was all, 'Oh, no, should take about a week'.

And so Mount Unapproachable lives up to its name.

Instead, we organise the easier to obtain permits that allow us to follow Giles's footsteps into Western Australia and across the Gunbarrel Highway.

 Ernest Giles should have been a poet. A dreamer with a dandy's black moustache, he devoured literature and recited verse. Enchanted by stories of Robinson Crusoe, Cook and Leichhardt – 'the pleasure and delight of visiting new and totally unknown places' – his dreaming could take him in only one direction.

It was August 1872. Giles had just turned thirty-seven, and the Overland Telegraph Line from Adelaide to Port Darwin was finally completed, dividing the continent in two: the explored and the unexplored.

For years Giles had fancied himself the person to penetrate the unknown western half, 'where, for a thousand miles in a straight line, no white man's foot had ever wandered, or, if it had, its owner had never brought it back, nor told the tale'.

So Giles scraped some money and horses together with the help of a few well-connected friends, and with a small party, started up along the telegraph line. His plan was to head west from the Charlotte Waters telegraph station south of Alice Springs and across to the Swan River, today's Perth, in Western Australia.

He wrote in the preface to his narrative *Australia Twice Traversed*: 'There was room for snowy mountains, an inland sea, ancient river, and palmy plain, for races of new kinds of men inhabiting a new and odorous land, for fields of gold and Golcondas of gems, for a new flora and a new fauna, and, above all the rest combined, there was room for me!'

For all his floral fancies, Giles was actually an accomplished bushman. Following a classical education in London, he joined his family in Australia and worked at various stations along the upper Darling River, surveying new land for station owners.

Historian Geoffrey Dutton, in his biography of Giles, paints a lovely image of the explorer on the track, 'modestly, humorously conscious of being a small bony man with a high, domed forehead and a straggly moustache, wearing an overcoat of flies, fighting his way thousands of miles to discover little but desert'.

Unfortunately for Giles, this was the story of his travels. On this first expedition, his small party made it just 500 kilometres from their starting point. Certainly Giles didn't want to turn back, but by November his band was falling apart. They had wasted much energy on never making it through the salt bogs to what he called Mount Unapproachable. The newly christened Glen Thirsty paid tribute to a desperate lack of water.

Finally two of the men, Alec Robinson and Samuel Carmichael, deaf to their leader's pleas, threw in the towel and Giles followed. They returned in icy silence, retracing their steps up Petermann Creek in the Levi Range.

CHAPTER 7

CHICKEN TRACKS

Warakurna, Western Australia

AMY ▶ We're at the Warakurna Roadhouse, just inside the Western Australian border, trying to pay for a tub of butter and it's chaos. There's a woman hanging out the front door screaming for someone's attention, two boys are laying into each other behind us – one of them in tears – and the woman behind the counter has a thin hold on her frustration as she struggles to deal with the large convoy passing through.

Outside, the bowsers are locked behind cages, and there's an amazing array of old cars scattered around. Ships of the desert with soft tyres, crunched bonnets and odd doors. A couple of naked kids and amorous dogs run around, ignored by the young men in assorted Aussie Rules regalia putting oil into a clapped-out 1980s Ford Falcon.

It turns out we've been caught up in the exodus from the inter-community footy.

'It's always disorganised, but it's good for business,' the woman behind the counter says, managing a laugh.

Warakurna consists of the roadhouse, the nearby Aboriginal community – off limits to us outsiders – and the Giles weather station. Set up in the late 1950s at the top end of the Woomera rocket range, the station's primary function was to tell the boffins which way the wind was blowing so they could estimate where

THE ROAD TO MOUNT BUGGERY

their toys might land. The weather bureau took over when the rocketeers finished and now its primary function is to launch two weather balloons a day, simultaneous with forty-five other launches around the country which feed information about temperature, wind speed and barometric pressure into a central computer.

When Giles came this way, he saw a mountain and headed for it, thinking there would be water. But he lost four horses in an horrendous retreat from the barren hill. He wrote: 'The very sight of the country, in all its hideous terrors clad, is sufficient to daunt a man and kill a horse. I called this vile mountain which had caused me this disaster, Mount Destruction, for a visit to it had destroyed alike my horses and my hopes.'

We'd hoped to visit that mountain, too, but our permit strictly forbids us leaving the main road.

Instead we visited the Giles weather station last night. As we drove in, there was an old yellow grader in a cage on the right. At first it looked like the grader had been given the same treatment as the petrol bowsers back at the roadhouse, but on closer inspection we realised it was on display. 'Gunbarrel Construction Crew' was written on the side in copperplate. Nearby, a great section of a fallen rocket, shiny gold like it came from a cheap sci-fi set, played second fiddle to the grand monument to road construction.

A plaque on the grader indicated it had belonged to Len Beadell. We quickly learn that Len's a legend out this way for having built all the roads for the rocket range, now collectively known as the bomb roads. (The rocket range, Woomera, later lead to the A-bomb tests at Emu and Maralinga.) The Gunbarrel Highway, though, built between 1955 and 1958, was Beadell's crowning glory, and the reason his grader is given pride of place. It was the first road to join Central and Western Australia.

Embarking on our journey along the Gunbarrel Highway, we soon appreciate the value of a grader; a rare and treasured piece of equipment out here. The corrugations on the Gunbarrel are high and widely spaced. In places we have to slow to about 10 kilometres an hour or listen to Frank make excruciating noises. Mark is contemplating walking, and I'm wishing I'd worn a bra. Suddenly the journey looks like taking three times longer than we'd expected.

'They should have called it the Rattlesnake Highway,' says Mark. 'All we do is rattle and snake.'

Beadell's aim had been to make the track as straight as possible, but the naming of the highway was by someone with a sense of irony at the Surveyor General's department. Indeed, we'd even laugh at the word 'highway' if the shaking would stop long enough.

For long sections people have found it easier to forge new tracks through the spinifex than face the bumps, and we can't help but follow these 'chicken tracks'. We're not sure whether they're named for their resemblance to small bird tracks or because chickens like us take them.

Still, there is a certain pleasure in crossing the Centre at walking pace. We're on the edge of the Gibson Desert, unusually green at the moment and with all its wild flowers in bloom. Alone in one of the most remote areas of the country but for the occasional camel.

Having travelled only about 180 kilometres in ten hours of hard driving, we pull over and set up camp by Mount Beadell, which glows red as the sun sets. It is a glorious spot and the distant strangled howl of dingoes only adds to the mood as we snuggle up in our tent.

Bumping onwards the next day, we start to get some great gunbarrel action: dead straight road as far as the horizon, with the spinifex and scrub forming high walls on either side. We gun it up to sixty, seventy kilometres an hour, and cheer the memory of Len Beadell, and just as we do, we hit some new washout or corrugated section and we curse him. And we understand why they've got his old grader in a cage.

Surveying this desolate section in the atlas, we are interested to see one of Beadell's bomb roads is named Sandy Blight Road. Curiously, we are now approaching a similarly unenticing Giles placename, also inspired by a nasty eye infection.

The failure of Giles's first attempt to reach the West Australian coast from central Australia had only whetted the dreamer's appetite. He was also no doubt encouraged when, upon his return from that trip in 1873, he learned that two other expeditions were leaving for the west coast. They had all the camels and money and hoopla they could want but he had a psychological claim on this virgin turf.

On his second expedition, he covered over 1000 kilometres of unknown territory but didn't make the coast. He quite literally lost fellow expeditioner Alfred Gibson in what he called the Gibson Desert. The rest of them suffered 'misfortune and starvation'. Crazed with hunger and thirst, Giles describes the relish with which he pounced on a baby marsupial, rejected from the pouch of its mother, and tore into it while still alive.

He escaped the Gibson Desert to learn he had been beaten by two separate expeditions. 'Still I have been told by a few partial friends that it was really a splendid failure.'

Admirably, if not a little obsessively, Giles pursued his goal again and again, until, on his fifth expedition, in 1875, he saw the Indian Ocean. It was a bittersweet victory. Giles subsequently wrote to Sir Thomas Elder: 'I travelled during the expedition 2500 miles [about 4000 kilometres], and unfortunately no areas of country available for settlement were found. The explorer does not make the country, he must take it as he finds it . . . Still, the successful penetration of such a region has its value, both in a commercial and scientific sense, as it points out to the future emigrant or settler those portions of our continent which he should most religiously shun.'

An anticlimax, but he had conquered his demons. After huge celebrations in Perth, he saddled his camels, turned around, and walked home. Only on the return journey, he travelled about 640 kilometres north of his east-west track, through the dreaded desert, and was blinded from repeated attacks of ophthalmia – sandy blight.

'My eyes had been so bad all day, I was in agony; I had no lotion to apply to them. At length I couldn't see at all, and Alec Ross had to lead the camels, with mine tied behind them. I not only couldn't see, I couldn't open my eyes, and had no idea where I was going.' So when they came across a range of rounded hills, Giles had to take his co-explorer Ross's word for it.

'I called this range, whose almost western end Alec ascended, Ophthalmia Range, in consequence of my suffering so much from that frightful malady. I could not take any observations, and I cannot be very certain where this range lies.'

Newman, Western Australia

MARK Had Giles been able to see the Ophthalmia Range, he still might not recognise it if he came back today. The rusty red mountains have huge gouges taken out of them, and at their base is the town of Newman, neatly set out around a shopping mall.

Unsure what ophthalmia and sandy blight are, we drop in on the eye doctor in the mall, a bubbly blonde called Sandy Mackenzie.

When Sandy was an optometry student, she had a long-distance love affair with her future husband. He was in the mining business and she made the mistake of telling him, 'When I finish uni, I'll follow you anywhere in Australia except Port Hedland.' Eighteen months later the Sydney girl was living in Hedland. She said she'd give it five years. No more.

Seven years later they moved 500 kilometres down the road from Hedland to Newman where she's been for seven more.

'So that's how come we've got an optometrist called Sandy, actually I'm Alexandra, living on the edge of the Great Sandy Desert looking at sandy blight patients . . . Most Aborigines who come in here have had it at some stage in their lives, several times.'

Sandy blight and ophthalmia are the same thing. 'The official term is trachoma. The Aboriginals still get it. It's still quite a concern and is still pretty much endemic in isolated low socio-economic areas,' Sandy says in her girlish voice.

'It's a type of conjunctivitis. Usually one of the contributing factors is poor hygiene . . . It's spread quite easily. Somebody touches their eye, shakes your hand, and you touch yours. Or a fly travelling from eye to eye. It affects the conjunctiva, the skin covering the eyelids, and they get sort of follicles, bumpy things that feel like sand when you're blinking. You have blood vessels growing on the eye,' she pulls out a picture of an eye with a light pink cloud over it. 'And in some people it's so bad this starts to happen to the eyeball, and they go blind.'

Modern treatments mean blindness is no longer an issue and, interestingly, they're finding that the incidence is much lower in the communities with swimming pools because they add so little water to the chlorine, it kills everything.

The bulk of Sandy's business, though, is testing the eyes of the truck drivers from the local iron ore mine. She tends to send them down to Perth for treatment a line earlier on the eye chart than is usual practice, and this used to raise eyebrows down there. Then some of the Perth people came to town and Sandy took them on the tourist run through the mine. When they saw the giant four-wheeled beasts these truckies were driving, there were no more questions asked.

Newman doesn't need a giant banana or pineapple: one of its iron ore trucks parked outside the tourist information centre is an irresistible photo opportunity. However, it's when we're sitting in a minibus on the side of what's left of Mount Whale-back and one of these babies comes towards us that we get a true appreciation of them. They are the size of an outer suburban mansion. And mansions have atrocious cornering. So when the one thundering towards us turns sharply away and roars up the hill, we are awed and thankful.

In 1957, prospector Stan Hilditch was here in the Ophthalmia

Range in the Pilbara looking for manganese. With his wife Ella sweltering in their 1951 Ford Thames doing her needlework, he'd go and climb a high peak, get his bearings on all the watercourses and then go pottering around with his hammer in the rusty rocks. Ella's loyalty was to pay off.

As Stan climbed a nameless hill, some 805 metres above sea level, he could see he was onto something. It had been known since the previous century that the Pilbara was full of iron, but it was so far from the coast as to be useless. Iron is high volume, low value. But Stan could see from the way a creek cut into the side of the hill he named Mount Whaleback (he thought it looked like a beached fish) that this iron ore deposit ran deep. He knew it was high quality.

That night he told Ella, 'Now, listen. This deposit's going to be enormous. We probably won't have a chance to do anything in our lifetime, but we may.'

The ore tested sixty-eight per cent pure. High quality, but you needed a big imagination to think you could mine iron more than 400 kilometres from the coast. Stan's partners told him to forget about it.

Twelve years later, after major haggling and dealmaking between some of the biggest companies in Australia and Japan, a railway had been built in record time – with record amounts of beer drunk. The town of Newman had popped up as a tough-living tent city and Port Hedland had been converted from a swampy village into a major sea port doing the most tonnage of any in Australia. It's a big story. Everything's big in Newman. It's the only adjective you need. If it ain't big it ain't worth describing.

The tour guide, Sue, has already dazzled us with the stats. 'Fully loaded, the ore trucks are seventy tonnes heavier than a fully loaded jumbo.'

You want to buy one it'll set you back 2.5 million dollars and if you can scrape that up, don't get a flat because tyres go for 25,000 dollars. The price of iron ore is twenty-six dollars a tonne. Doing our sums quickly and inexpertly, we fail to come up with

an answer to how many loads a truck has to carry to pay for itself
– considering that it goes through better than a set of tyres a year.

Our tiny bus climbs to a lookout on top of Mount Whaleback and I ask whether you can still make out the whale in the
mountain.

'You're sort of in its belly now,' says Sue. 'It used to go nine
levels higher.'

We look across a large valley where we can see the ore trucks
pottering around on the terraces, small against the huge, dark ore
mountain. 'That valley used to be the mountain.'

Where we are standing, the new peak is 135 metres lower
than the old mountain and the little trucks down below are
some 390 metres into the carcass. To keep going down into the
ore, however, they have to move all the dirt and rock in what's
left of the whale a kilometre away. So in fifty years we'll have a
new Mount Whaleback. And they'll stop pumping out all the
underground water that seeps into the hole. Each week, eighty-
two million litres pour into the valley.

'When they turn off the pumps we'll have Lake Whaleback.'

Sue tries to impress us with talk of all the 'rehabilitation' of
the vegetation that mining companies go on about these days.
That's great, but what's really dazzling is her claim that 'the total
area of land used for mining in Australia takes up one-third of
the space of all the hotel car parks in Australia.'

Amy still thinks it's sad to see a mountain go, but I want to
know who goes around counting the acreage of hotel car parks.

Our plan has been to head east out of Newman to Jigalong and
on to Lake Disappointment, the name that inspired this whole
journey, way out on the Canning Stock Route. But dropping in
at the shire office, we learn that the Talawana Track is still closed
due to the effects of last month's Tropical Cyclone Rosita.

So we're stuck in Newman, where Chicken Treat appears to
be the hub of the city, and the pub is curiously empty at seven
o'clock on a Saturday night.

After hanging out in town almost a week, Shane, the helpful

guy at the Shire, tells us that while the road isn't strictly closed, we've got Buckley's of getting to the lake.

'We were getting ready to send two graders out there to work on the road – if one got into trouble the other could pull him out – but we phoned the local community and they said, "forget it. There's water everywhere".'

We are disappointed.

Still, we entertain the thought of maybe just giving it a go. Particularly if it is going to cost a fortune to fly out, although for the life of us we can't get a quote from Nigel at By Air Pilbara.

Then we meet Joe Furulyas of Pilbara Iron Country Tours, who cruises the caravan park spruiking for business. From April to September he takes tours, but in the off-season he pays the bills by going out and picking up tourists who've got themselves in trouble.

He motions towards Lake Disappointment and the Canning. 'I'm the only bugger who'll go out and get 'em so they don't mind paying. It's fifty-five dollars an hour, plus mileage, plus expenses.'

He tells us about a French couple. Had all the gear on a troopie like ours. 'They zigged instead of zagging. Got stuck. They had their wills written out and everything when someone came across them.' Our second thoughts firm up in our chicken livers. We are getting flogged in our battle with the Hard Brown Land. The score isn't looking good as Lake Disappointment lives up to its name.

Anyway, we've had an invitation to join a mob of traditional owners going 'back to country' in Purnululu National Park, better known as the Bungle Bungles. Wendy Attenborough of the Kimberley Land Council tells us the elders are taking their kids there to maintain their connection to the land while some long-running dispute with the Western Australian Government simmers away. It sounds like an opportunity too good to miss.

So we say goodbye to Newman and begin the 1700 kilometre hop to the east Kimberley.

CHAPTER 8

LIKE RIPPING UP *the* TITLE DEEDS

Purnululu, Western Australia

AMY ▶ Shirley Drill, wearing an improbably bright orange dress, drives off first with her mob piled into a rental ute; three in the front, thirteen in the back. We take up the rear of the convoy heading into Purnululu National Park, bush-bashing our way in search of long forgotten tracks, when the kids on the back of one ute jump up, pointing and yelling, 'Turkey! Turkey!' In a moment, someone has a .22 aimed out the window and is cracking off a couple of shots before the bustards take to their huge wings.

We arrive at the Ord River and the kids run down to the water with fishing reels. A little girl wearing only a nappy, her dark hair gathered up in a palm tree on top of her head, toddles down last with an oversized handline.

Within minutes there's a commotion down by the water and two shots ring out. Shirley's son Ricky Drill has shot a fresh-water crocodile clean through the top of the skull and the kids descend on the body for a piece of the action, bringing it triumphantly up to shore above their heads. They stroke the dead beast, poking curious little fingers into its mouth and the tiny bullet hole.

Then Shirley takes over. At fifty-two she is head of her mob, a big woman, just coming out of a two-year grieving process for her uncle, whose name she cannot speak. Sitting cross-legged on the pebbles, she slits through the leathery skin behind the left shoulder and reaches deep inside to remove the guts and eggs. Delicacies. The heart pulses on the ground. The crocodile will be cooked in a pit for hours.

The different campfires are spread out in family groups. We are at the whitefella fire with our adopted family, anthropologist Ian Kirkby and his partner, schoolteacher Judy Taylor. Ian and Judy have been living with the community for years. They are no-nonsense and candid, and the kids clearly look up to them. Judy won't abide people asking her if she gets lonely in the isolated community. She has plenty of girlfriends. For her, the implication is she has no *white* girlfriends.

Ian, lanky and dark-haired, first came up here for the West Australian Museum but says he quit because his anthropological information was given to mining companies. He stayed on and is now the 'community co-ordinator', and as such acts on behalf of the families, particularly in dealing with bureaucracy when 'high English' and legalese become a barrier. With us, he is also something of a go-between. Perhaps we are being sussed out.

The camps consist of foam mattresses rolled out close together on tarps, with thick bundles of blankets and doonas. There's no risk of rain now that we're in the dry, so we do away with the tent, too. It is liberating.

Next morning, Shirley invites us to sit down at her camp. She is widely recognised as the traditional owner of this country. She tells us stories from when she was a little girl and travelled through here with her mother getting bush tucker, and of the ceremonies her grandparents would use to protect the country. Notably missing from her story are placenames and Dreaming stories. We later learn that in these days of Native Title, you don't give them away. And it's a land dispute, it turns out, that Shirley wants to tell us about. What's really on her mind is the woman she refers to as 'this silly idiot down the river'.

6 9

When equal pay for Aboriginal stockmen was introduced to the Kimberley in 1972 it caused a mass migration from the land to the shanties on the edge of small towns and missions. The fragile grip the elders had managed to keep on their people for the eighty-five-odd years of white settlement was broken.

Shirley's uncle, Raymond Wallaby, could see his people being crushed by despair and grog, living in humpies or under car bodies in the new ghetto of Turkey Creek. The only way forward was to get 'back to country'.

Bungle Bungle outstation was then an abandoned cattle camp in clapped-out country the State Government had resumed in 1967 for fear its exposed soils would silt up the Ord River Dam. Wallaby grew up there. His mother was buried there. No tourist had ever heard of it.

When Brian Burke's Labor Government assumed power in 1983, promising Aboriginal land rights, the old man bundled his family into his Toyota with confidence. They were going to squat at the outstation and give it its proper name, Kawarre.

About the same time, a television series, *The Wonders of Western Australia*, highlighted the incredible beehive formations suddenly billed as the 'lost world of the Bungle Bungles'. A tourist boom was ignited.

The State Government moved to create a national park jointly managed with the traditional owners, so the Purnululu Aboriginal Corporation (PAC) was formed in 1986 to represent the traditional owners. Wallaby was chairperson and twelve other families were represented. A woman called Bonnie Edwards came forward to help him with her superior English skills. Bonnie's half-sister, Tanba Banks, was recognised by Wallaby and the others as being the traditional owner of the land south of the Ord River on the park's fringe. According to the Purnululu mob, though, because Bonnie had a different father to Tanba, Bonnie was never recognised as a traditional owner.

By 1992, as negotiations for joint management of the park bogged down, Bonnie dropped one almighty bombshell. She announced she and her sister Tanba were the real traditional owners of all Purnululu, an area far larger than the land south of the Ord to which Tanba was already entitled, and which encompassed much of the land claimed by the other families. What's more, Bonnie declared, Purnululu was not even the place's proper name. No, it should really be Billingjul National Park. She set herself up as Billingjul Aboriginal Corporation in direct opposition to PAC – Shirley's mob and the eleven other families who have the weighty support of the Kimberley Land Council.

As a result, neither party now has any input into the management of the park as they await the outcomes of their competing Native Title claims.

Shirley, sitting by the fire on the bank of the Ord, has no doubt who is to blame for the stalemate: 'Old people been living in this place no trouble. Now we got trouble. We got trouble CALM (Department of Conservation and Land Management). We got trouble with this silly idiot down the river here.' Shirley is sad and angry, because with Bonnie's opposition – and with CALM recognising the validity of Bonnie's claim – the community wasn't able to secure land tenure within the park. Without land tenure, PAC couldn't attract the necessary funding for infrastructure. Their little community in the park, Kawarre, where Wallaby had first gone to squat, building houses and a school, simply wasn't viable. So in 1993, after ten years there, the decision was made to move to a relative's outstation outside the park. They thought they would be away for a few months, but seven years later are still making do with occasional visits like this one.

The animosity has festered over those years to become a bitter, personal battle. Just days before we met up with the Purnululu mob, the whole thing erupted in a physical confrontation between Shirley and Bonnie over access to Blue Hole, a traditional neutral ground and meeting place for local Aborigines within the park.

Bonnie has set up a camp in the park by the side of the Blue Hole access road, where her half-sister Tanba lives. It is also the base for a cultural tourism operation run by Bonnie.

Bonnie got wind that the Purnululu mob was planning a visit to Blue Hole. As far as she was concerned it was a rude and deliberate attempt to barge through her sister's camp. So when eight carloads of them turned on to the road to the Ord River, they found tacked to the gate a handwritten but unsigned note, later published in the local paper: 'If you mob come down to Blue Hole we'll bash you . . . s up. So . . . off you Turkey Creek mothers.'

Shirley was defiant and led a convoy of Purnululu mob vehicles forward until they came to a large bog. Parked in the middle was Bonnie's four-wheel drive, and there she was – a tall, strong woman, holding an axe and ready for a fight.

The way Bonnie puts it when we later meet her, she just happened to be using the axe to lay branches and stones through the bog on the day before she was due to meet Western Australian Environment Minister Cheryl Edwardes, who was opening the new Bungle Bungles visitor centre. 'And as I walked across the creek I still had that axe in my hand, and they thought I was going to bash them with that, but if they rushed me I would have, probably.' She told them they could not go any further; that they should just go to Kawarre. The group was determined to continue to Blue Hole.

'Right, anyone comes across there I'm going to pelt youse with rocks,' Bonnie yelled.

Shirley was so mad she drove the rental ute straight into the bog.

In telling her version, Bonnie mocks a high-pitched scream. 'She was going on and I just grabbed her round the shoulder and I threw her on the ground, and I thought by throwing her on the ground I'd hold her down and talk to her, "Listen listen listen", I was talking to her like that, and she turned up and she bit me there.' Bonnie pulls her black shiny dress down to reveal a bite mark on her left breast. 'She bit me there while she was on the ground, so I just ended up punching her in the face.'

Spats like this have seen the dispute written off publicly as two groups of blackfellas bickering. On the one hand, it is typical of post-Mabo/Wik feuds tearing at Aboriginal communities around Australia. Roughly half of all Native Title claims have overlapping claims – some amicable, many not. Then there are the groups without the resources or inclination to challenge rival claims in court.

The way Bonnie sees it, she is in a David and Goliath battle, up against the large numbers supporting Purnululu, with all its lawyers, anthropologists and Aboriginal bureaucracy.

To Shirley, it's a blatant land-grab by someone who doesn't belong to country. Back in Shirley's grandparents' day, 'they kill 'em for speaking out for wrong country. They tell 'em not to and if they keep doing it they kill 'em . . . Bonnie shouldn't be doing it. It's not her country. Don't know what she's talking about. She's putting wrong name on these places. She's calling it Wallardi – it's not Wallardi, it's N____. Bonnie been giving that name. Wrong people,' Shirley tells us.

We ask Ian Kirkby, by the by, for the spelling of N____. He says he can't tell us. Knowledge of traditional placenames is a potent weapon in Native Title cases.

'In these cases the only evidence you've got are the names. The names are like title deeds,' Ian says. 'By publishing this information it's just like ripping up the title deeds and handing it over bit by bit to the opposition for them to paste back together.'

Also at stake is the cultural value of placenames, such that PAC's Native Title application lists, amongst other rights, the ability to 'bestow and/or reveal place-names of the land and waters'.

One of the more popular tourist destinations within the park is called Echidna Gorge. This really gets up Ian's nose. 'They never bothered asking what its real name was. They called it that because some ranger has gone down there and seen an echidna.'

There's been a lot of hesitation at the front of the convoy we're travelling in. We're moving on to a new camp within the park, after much discussion between the elders this morning over whether to try another visit to Blue Hole. We thought they had decided to give it a miss. But suddenly Shirley's ute breaks away from the convoy and swings back across a grassy plain towards the Blue Hole track. Shirley rides regally in the tray packed with a dozen of her mob.

Ian and Judy's ute follows and we – 'interview mob' – pull in behind. We cross a heavy bog and see a single-pole tent and a rough shelter of lumber and metal supporting some canvas. This is where Tanba lives now, a slender toehold in the park which she claims as hers alone under Native Title.

We stop about seventy metres from the camp as Shirley charges in, her dress a beacon. To our surprise, we see much handshaking and we are motioned forward. Then Tanba comes towards Ian with an axe in her hand. She raises it. 'I'll kill you if you come in here.' She lowers the axe and laughs. They embrace.

'That Bonnie been causing trouble,' Tanba says of her half-sister. She mentions they're a bit short of tucker and Judy quickly produces four loaves of sliced white bread and Tanba asks how they are for tobacco and, yes, Shirley is a bit short, so Tanba produces two tins for her. Then Judy comes back with a big chunk of frozen meat for Tanba.

'See how well everyone gets on when there's no Bonnie,' says Judy to us.

We quickly explain to Tanba what we're doing and ask her and her son Peter for a photo.

'Who speaks for this country, Tanba?'

'I do,' she says in a high-pitched voice with something of a what-a-stupid-question tone. But then she continues talking about different places in the park and some that she doesn't go to, but we can't understand her heavy Aboriginal English. Ian translates: she says she only visits the areas Uncle (Wallaby) gave her.

We move on to Kawarre, the little community within the park Wallaby set up to save his family, and which they were forced out of seven years ago. This is the first time the group has been back in over two years, since the death of the old man. Their absence was part of the mourning process, and there is still sorry business to do.

We can't go to the main camp because the buildings have not been smoked (the ritual cleansing following a death). Grief is heavy in the air: for the old man, for their home, for the school Judy established here.

Judy has been psyching herself up for this return for weeks. The first thing she notices when we drive in is that the canvas roof of the school, which she tells us once won an architectural award, has blown away.

Ian sits forlornly under a verandah in the dirt. Kids are rummaging through paints and exercise books in a trunk on the floor. A glockenspiel is caught in a tangle of vines. The school is now an award-winning passionfruit trellis set between the deep green pandanus and the spectacular red escarpment.

Someone pulls out a pencil case with the name Alberta on it. 'Alberta — she's the mother of two now,' says Judy. 'We never expected to be away for more than a few months.'

Halls Creek, Western Australia

MARK▶ After leaving the Purnululu mob we know we've got to find Bonnie to get her side of the story, but first slip in a quick morning on the tourism trail through the bizarre domes of the Bungle Bungles. We drive out of the park through a rollercoaster of creek crossings with water up to the bonnet.

The old gold town of Halls Creek is then an hour south down the bitumen. Bonnie Edwards is at the supermarket she runs with her English husband, Malcolm, a local councillor. We talk in the tea room. The Elvis clock rotates through two hours and Bonnie barely pauses as she takes us through her life. How she wasn't stolen generation because her white father married her Aboriginal mother. How she learned all the traditional ways while growing up in what is now the national park while her father worked for the owners, Vesteys.

'Since 1986 to now, every year we've been going out there to the park in April when it opens for the tourists and coming out in November when it closes,' Bonnie says. 'We've been asking tour operators in the park if we could work with them and show them different cultural activities and how to manage the park and what fruits they can eat, what berries they mustn't touch and what sort of plants will stop erosion, fire burning, things like that . . . And CALM has been very happy with us for doing that.

'We haven't sort of sat back and griped about why we haven't got any land, why the government isn't helping us. We haven't got any support at all, whereas Purnululu's got lawyers, anthropologists, Kimberley Land Council, everyone helping them.' She's bitter about ATSIC – Aborigines Talking Shit in Canberra, she calls it.

She claims this dispute is between two language groups, Kija and Jaru, and alleges Ian Kirkby can't admit he got it wrong on his earlier anthropological work when he found that it was Kija country. She alleges that a number of senior Kija men stole what she calls the *daroogu* – bundles placed in rock crevices as a traditional type of title deed. She claims the men were warned that if the *daroogu* wasn't replaced they would all be placed on 'a voodoo type of thing'. The *daroogu* wasn't replaced and three of the men subsequently died, including Wallaby.

'Tanba and I didn't have to do nothing. It's men's business. We not allowed to even look at *daroogus*.'

She says she doesn't know why Ian's holding the stories and names back, but then says she's holding hers back, too: 'If those people know the Dreamtime stories for the area I will accept them as traditional owners of the area, but none of them do. I know that for a fact.'

Now Bonnie is up pacing in and out of the tea room, drawing back on her cigarette, making all sorts of violent threats against Ian who she styles as the meddling white administrator. She is a formidable figure, promising to fight for as long as there's breath in her body. 'They haven't passed any courtroom battles or anything yet to recognise them as traditional people. If they disprove us as traditional people, well, then we'll back down and go away.'

We leave Bonnie battling away at the supermarket. The struggle looks to continue bitter and twisted for a long while yet. We had gone into the supermarket positive that Bonnie's claims were invalid, but she has convinced us she deserves a hearing. Regardless of the outcome, there is no doubt that both sides are passionate about their claims and that the past decade has caused a lot of pain. However, when we later call the anthropologist Bonnie suggested would back her up, he tells us he has nothing to do with it. He'd recently copped a hard time from ABC current affairs show *Four Corners*, which portrayed him as a stooge for mining companies.

Anyway, it turns out it's Reconciliation Day, and we are drawn to the crowds outside the Halls Creek Shire building for the festivities. We sit on the grass and listen as some elders share their stories. Some talk in language. Others are difficult to hear. One middle-aged man tells of the first time he ever encountered white people; riding on their truck and being amazed at how the trees sped by. His voice is just a whisper, but it seems a relative of his was shot in some confrontation. He finishes his story by forgiving the white people who took them away from their country, and forgiving the man with the gun.

The Australian and Aboriginal flags are raised together and a few hundred adults and school kids set off on a march through town.

As for us, the coast is calling. After two months inland, it's time to get onto the trail of a chipper young English gent named John Lort Stokes who left a string of dots on the Map of Misery right across the top of Australia. So we're going to the beach, more than 600 kilometres away, but distances shrink out here with a good road and a cool sea at the other end.

CHAPTER 9

THE HIDEOUS NAKEDNESS

Dampier Peninsula, Western Australia

MARK We watch the couple approach along the white sand. I take off my shirt and give it to Amy. All her clothes are way up the beach. We hadn't expected company.

'What are you doing on our beach?' calls the man.

'Your beach?' I reply. 'I thought it was ours.'

They come nearer to reveal themselves as older than they had looked from a distance, maybe about fifty.

'We've been here a week and you're only the second people we've seen,' he explains. 'We were on our way to Cape Leveque. Everyone says it's lovely but how could it be better than this? So we stayed.'

The deserted strip of beach skirts the coast, north of Broome, before it becomes Aboriginal land further north on the Dampier Peninsula. It's free camping and there's hardly a soul around. The beach drops away sharply to be rocky at low tide and then brilliant white sand for the top half of the awesome ten-metre tides.

The only tracks we see are those of a wild dog and the intriguing hermit crabs.

The solitude is sublime, but after a couple of days writing up

our notes from the Bungle Bungles, it's back to the placenames.
First up: Skeleton Point.

 Her Majesty's Sloop *Beagle* was in the process of being
immortalised. Two years earlier, in 1836, she had off-
loaded the young naturalist Charles Darwin back in
England after a six-year round-the-world trip. He was busy
writing himself and the boat into scientific fame with several
published accounts of the journey, like *The Zoology of the Voyage
of HMS Beagle*.

The publication of *On The Origin of Species By Means of
Natural Selection* and subsequent superstardom, however, was still
more than twenty years away when the *Beagle* was sent back to
Australia in 1837 to chart the last bits of coast still undiscovered
or inadequately mapped.

John Lort Stokes, aged twenty-five, was second in command
at the start of this journey but was to take over after the retirement through ill health of Captain John Wickham. For Stokes,
it was all one big tally-ho adventure.

After carrying the news to Australia of the death of King
William IV and the ascent to the throne of young Queen
Victoria, the *Beagle*'s first task of exploration was to begin at
Disaster Bay in King Sound, north-west of present day Derby.

Disaster Bay marked the end of the explorations of Phillip
Parker King in 1822. The thing is, it's hard to see from reading
King's account what was so disastrous about his visit. He lost his
second last anchor on the rocky bottom, a 'foul' bottom as they
used to say, and so had to give up exploring and return to
Sydney. But it seems that Setback Bay or Blast It Bay might have
been more appropriate.

Anyway, just before Stokes and the *Beagle* reached Disaster
Bay, the crew had to go ashore to look for water. On the second
attempt at digging a well they got lucky at eight feet with a great
abundance of red-tinged water flooding the hole.

Nearby, they found 'the remains of a native, placed in a
semi-recumbent position under a wide spreading gum tree,

enveloped, or more properly, shrouded, in the bark of the papyrus'. The bones were piled up, with the larger on the outside and on top 'the fleshless, eyeless scull (sic) "grinning horribly" over the right side'.

Shortly, the locals arrived, and 'made no offer of remonstrance at the removal of the mortal remains of their dead brother', as Stokes's party gathered up the bones. Stokes wondered if they thought white people were dead relatives taking the bones to be reincarnated: 'to clothe the hideous nakedness of death with the white man's flesh; or whether, deeming us indeed profane violators of that last resting place of suffering humanity . . . they left the office of retribution either to the spirit of the departed, or the more potent "boyl-las" (medicine men) . . . I know not.'

Dampier Peninsula, Western Australia

MARK▶ We slip and slide up a sandy track for 200 kilometres to Cape Leveque at the tip of the Dampier Peninsula. King Sound is to our right, the Indian Ocean to the left. We hope to learn what the Aboriginal people did think of Stokes taking off with one of their dead, and to find where the skeleton ended up.

The Cape Leveque camping ground is owned by the Aboriginal community at nearby One Arm Point, which is close to Skeleton Point, so I ask at reception who speaks for the country in that area.

Eric, an Aboriginal local who seems to be just passing through, is a bit puzzled by the name. He thinks he knows it, but *gardiya* (whitefella) names have not quite stuck in the hearts and minds of the Bardi people. The map on the wall features Aboriginal names exclusively.

I grab our trusty 1960s Reader's Digest atlas from the truck, and Eric is pretty sure he knows which point we want.

'That Vincent,' he says.

We dodge fallen coconuts on the sandy tracks that pass for streets in One Arm Point where we find Vincent Angus. It's not a Tidy

Town, but the brash bougainvillea and decorative buoys dotted about give the place an irresistible tropical flair.

Vincent is on his mum's verandah where a big polished turtle shell hangs from the wall. His knee is bandaged and he is lifting weights with his foot.

'Just had an operation on it in Derby. An old football injury. I've waited twenty-nine years for it.'

'Did it end your career?'

'No, I played till I was forty-four.'

He's forty-eight now, a big man with a barrel chest bulking out an Orlando basketball singlet. An old man with long white hair tumbling from under a baseball cap wanders over and is introduced to us as 'the old man'. He is Vincent's step-dad, Fred.

We ask about Skeleton Point and the graves out there.

'They used to put them up on sticks. Have you seen how the Indians do it? Well, we do it the same. When the body has deteriorated enough, you roll the body in paperbark and find a good cave or a gap between the rocks and put him in there.'

Fred says his grandfather was one of the last to be buried that way.

Vincent's mum comes out onto the verandah. Like Fred, she has white, white hair. She's in her seventies and has the tentative gait of a very old person, but she sits down elegantly, her graceful hands moving to her face or absentmindedly stroking her arm.

'Have there been stories told about these first white men to come?' I ask.

'William Dampier, you know, there in Cygnet Bay. He wrecked his ship there.' They all chorus the name William Dampier.

I read from Stokes's narrative – the part where he wonders why the Aborigines didn't protest at the taking of the skeleton.

'They didn't know in them days,' offers Vincent. 'Didn't know what he was doing. They been frightened of guns.'

'Boosh,' Fred makes the noise of a distant gun. 'In those days they used to shoot 'em. Hide in the bushes.'

Vincent expands, 'There's skeletons everywhere from here to Broome. Crews dying of beri-beri. Our people being shot, poisoned. That bloke at Hunters Creek used strychnine.'

There's a lot more talk, most of which we can't understand and which is made more difficult to hear because Ricki Lake is on high volume inside, being watched by the kids.

The conversation moves on and it turns out that Vincent is the youngest surviving hard-hat pearl diver. He was in the training course in 1970 just before scuba gear was introduced. The crew was all Malay. That's how he became a chilli addict.

'They were happy days. We didn't worry about money. We got seventy dollars a month. Thought it was good money then. Everyone at Lombadina (the local mission) was still getting rations and three dollars pocket money,' says Vincent.

'Did you keep doing it when the scuba gear came in?'

'Nah, there was no fun in it. It was too easy.'

Returning to the subject at hand, Vincent says someone from Derby was buried in the old way, up in a tree, just last year. 'They brung his body back by helicopter from Derby. They made a bed for his body on poles.'

'Do any of you want to be buried in the old way?'

They turn sombre on this one. Mum says she wants to be buried in the ground.

'They put a cemetery at Skeleton Point when Harry O'Grady had his sheep station there. He didn't want them doing what they been doing all their life so he put a cemetery there for them. The people get sick they go to his camp and if they pass away he put them in the cemetery.'

'There was a sheep station out here?' I say, surprised because the country is so sandy.

'Yeah, he was Irish. They have a habit of doing silly things. He shot himself in the end. Gone mad.'

There's much animated conversation between Mum and Fred on this, and Vincent translates.

'No-one would report the suicide because they frightened the police would come and think they did it and start shooting the people for nothing. Everybody cleaned out. After he shot himself they all been leave that place. Moved up to Lombadina. That was the end of sheep up there. You know what Irish people are like.'

They all have a hearty laugh at that.

'You ain't got any Irish in you do you?'

'Well, I do have a little.'

They politely tone down their laughter.

Next morning we take up Vincent's invitation to visit his place at Skeleton Point. We turn up there to find him drinking tea out of a mug the size of a saucepan. He shows us his treasured chilli plants and as we drive him down to the beach he points to some scrub on the left. 'That's where I'm gunna have campground. Campers over there and tours over there.'

Shortly, the soft blue sea appears before us. He grabs his crutches off the roof-rack and hobbles down to the dazzling white sand fringed by mangroves.

Stokes never made any mention of Skeleton Point's tourism potential; the beach and brilliant blue water are divine.

Vincent is constantly pointing out shells to us; what's good eating, what's bait. Then he gets back on to football.

'In 1997 I went to the AFL grand final. St Kilda and Adelaide. Then got on a plane that night and went to Sydney. Stayed at Darling Harbour and next day went to the Rugby League grand final. Manly and Newcastle. Never seen a League game live before but even I was getting into it with the crowd. Two grand finals in two days.' He shakes his head at this astonishing feat. 'I was a lucky man that year. Two grand finals. That was the high-light of my life . . .

'That's the caves up there,' he says, pointing to a small rocky outcrop at the end of the beach where the ancestors' bones used to be put. He slowly makes his way along the shore, pausing to rest his knee twice in 150 metres.

'Go and have a look,' he urges.

'Is that okay?'

'Yeah. It looks like the sand's covered it up.'

He stays on the beach while Amy and I clamber up over a few rocks and branches. There is sand and leaf litter in the crevice he has pointed out. A whopper tide must have come up to it and we can't see anything of interest. We look into another fissure slightly to the left, not expecting to see anything.

'There's a bone here,' I call out.

'That'd be it,' says Vincent. No big deal. 'That's Fred's grand-father. His grandfather's brother,' he corrects himself, adjusting to the white system of kinship. This was Fred's country but he's passed it on to Vincent, who is building Fred and his mother a place to retire.

Amy and I pay our respects to the bone, which looks like a forearm. You don't see many human bones in our world. It's a little unsettling. And we're unsure how to react. This bone just exists in its crevice at the whim of the elements. There must be plenty more below it in the sand.

We make our way back down and Vincent points up the hill to where he thinks Stokes's well would have been.

'That's the only place where there's wells and gum trees. Our people were always covering their wells up so the police couldn't find 'em. They'd walk along the beach at low tide so the water cover their tracks.'

We're sitting here writing this at Middle Lagoon, 'Natures' Hideaway', run by Tracey and Peter Howard.

'No relation,' Tracey informs us, as if everybody's always seeing a resemblance with the Prime Minister. 'We're the black Howards.'

We've just polished off a lovely trevally caught around midday as the tide rushed into a little mangrove-lined creek. Amy hooked one within seconds of casting and as I tried to get it off the hook for her, my rod started to shake. Amy grabbed it but couldn't pull the bugger in, so I left the first fish flapping on the slope and rushed to pull the second in.

The first fish was lunch, just thrown over the fire on a rusty old grill, then eaten with a tomato and onion salsa. The second was wrapped in tin foil with garlic, chilli and red pesto for dinner. Bellissimo.

We've had some time to kill, so we emailed the Royal College of Surgeons in London – where the skeleton Stokes took ended up in 1841. It turns out the skeleton stayed at the college until 1941, when the collection was bombed. It was then moved to what is now the Natural History Museum, where it still resides, hidden away.

Still on the Stokes trail, we drive around the bottom of King Sound to Derby, nervous about what miseries await us at Point Torment.

CHAPTER 10

HALF MAD *with* INSUFFERABLE ANNOYANCE

With the Bardi skeleton safely on board the *Beagle*, Stokes took the yawl and the whale boat to go exploring down what had just been named King Sound. Stokes was filled with the sort of enthusiasm that would surely have got him beaten up at high school.

'Nor can I describe with what delight, all minor annoyances forgotten, I prepared to enter upon the exciting task of exploring waters unfurrowed by any preceding keel; and shores, on which the advancing step of civilisation had not yet thrown the shadows of her advent, nor the voice of that Christianity, which walks by her side through the uttermost parts of the earth.'

He set out east across King Sound and still could not see the other side, but could sense that he was in the mouth of a magnificent river.

In the clear atmosphere of the next morning he looked through a telescope and saw land off to the east. 'I hoped and believed we should hereafter date the first great event of the voyage', but the breeze dropped off and the men were forced to take to the oars with the thermometer at 110 degrees Fahrenheit in the shade. Large trees drifted by, and each cast of the lead showed the channel was getting deeper as they neared land.

In the afternoon, they came to the only sandy beach in the area and pulled the boats up to the high water mark for that first momentous event.

'A name was soon found for our new territory, upon which we with rueful unanimity conferred that of Point Torment, from the incessant and vindictive attacks of swarms of musquitos, by whom it had evidently been resolved to give the new comers a warm welcome.'

Stokes climbed the highest tree he could find, and looked south 'over a wide prospect of nothing but mangroves and mud banks'. He took some observations, 'but alas! The sleep all could have enjoyed so much after our work was rendered impossible by the swarms of musquitos, who at sunset relieved those of their tribe upon whom the day duty had devolved, and commenced a most unsparing attack upon us: all devices to escape them were tried in vain, and some of the men were really half mad with the insufferable annoyance.'

At 8 pm, at their wits' end, they heard a welcome peal of thunder. The lightning flashed and they thought the impending storm would blow away their persecutors. It didn't. 'I was at length compelled to order the people to take to the boats, fairly driven from the shore by our diminutive but invincible assailants.'

Thus the 'advancing step of civilisation' took one step back.

Derby, Western Australia

MARK▶ White men steered well clear of Point Torment for the next hundred years until leprosy hit the Kimberley and they suddenly needed somewhere to hide all the victims. That's what brings us to Derby fifty kilometres south of the point – and to the front door of a nun who devoted much of her life to lepers. Amy's been a bit crook so I leave her sleeping in the truck while I go in to talk to Sister Francis.

The Sister is one of those women who puts people at ease. She seems a bit tired of talking about the leprosarium. So many want to know. But she proceeds to do her duty. She and some other retired nuns have just moved into these new digs. The iconography leans unhung against the wall. The living area has a computer, a large television, and a statue of St John of God in a blue robe carrying someone in his arms.

When Sister Francis was twelve in Victoria in the 1930s, she heard a priest preaching about the injustices to the Aborigines. 'That prompted me to want to do something about it, and at school in religious instruction you'd get talks on the various saints and they'd talk about Father Damien of Molokai and lepers.

'Well, that turned my head, and then there was the Bible story about our Lord curing the man with the withered hand. That's something that got into it too – love and compassion.'

The local priest had also had an operation at the St John of God Hospital at Ballarat, and there was something about that name that got into her head. St John of God.

So there she was, a twelve-year-old who already knew her future lay in lepers, the Aboriginal people and St John of God. She just didn't know how she was going to make it happen. The years went by. She was working in Melbourne for an organisation supporting Irish missionaries in China when she saw a little paragraph in a monthly church magazine: 'Girls wishing to devote their lives to the care of lepers, the care of Aboriginals, apply to the mother superior of St John of God, Broome.' She recites it like it were in today's paper.

'The three things I wanted were there, she says. So I just packed my swag and came up. Of course I had to be accepted first.'

'It seems like it was directed solely at you.'

'Yes. It was.'

She was twenty-three when she left Melbourne in June 1943. The war was on. She had to wait for permission to fly. When it came, she was on a plane with another girl who was going to be a nun and two more girls who were going to Exmouth to be barmaids.

'When we got there, the soldiers saw four girls getting off the plane, and they said, "We'll put on a dance". But we'd had it. We went to bed. I don't know if the others went to the dance.'

After her novitiate and nursing training, Sister Francis didn't get to the leprosarium until 1951. It had been opened by the government fifteen years earlier to combat the rising tide of leprosy among Aborigines in the Kimberley. Looking for a good, isolated spot, they established it at the bottom of the peninsula that forms Point Torment.

At first it was run by just one secular matron, but the number of patients grew too quickly. The health department advertised for nurses. Mother Gertrude of the St John of God Hospital applied to supply all the nurses for the leprosarium. The government didn't particularly want the place staffed by a religious order, but there wasn't a lot of competition for the jobs, so the nuns got it for three months. They stayed fifty years.

Sister Francis explains that it's not clear whether the disease was the same as leprosy you read about in the Bible, but it had all the same agonies and attracted the same fear. While most patients could carry on a normal life, there were two wards of very sick people in terrific pain.

When Sister Francis arrived, the doors had two handles – one for patients, one for everyone else. When strangers were around, patients politely put their hands behind their backs.

'Did you expect to die from it?'

'No, that never entered my head.'

The treatment, though, was just as frightening as the disease. Chaulmoogra Oil was heated over a kero stove and injected hot into the patients' lesions. It was painful and not very successful, but the patients submitted themselves to it because they wanted to be cured.

'There was really nothing you could do for them other than dispense painkillers,' says Sister Francis. 'They could be in bed there for weeks at a time, languishing in pain.'

All patients' feet and hands were examined and bathed every day except on weekends.

'They say that fingers fall off, feet fall off. The trouble is, because there's no feeling, they can have a stone in their shoe or a nail in their boot or they can pick up a hot pot . . . they don't know and then, of course, it gets infected. The infection goes into the bone. It's because of the infection that things fall off. With the nervous effect, the contractures, they get claw hands.

'Nowadays that can be prevented. A lot of ours from the Lep did have the claw hands and the mutilation and deformity because we didn't have the know-how to prevent it.'

It was hard to contain people coming in from the remote regions. Absconders were put in the jail. But Sister Francis gives an overall impression of hope. Inmates planted gardens, making the institution largely self-sufficient. The patients from the mission at Beagle Bay had been trained by the Palatine monks as carpenters, mechanics, cementers. They did all the maintenance. Patients went fishing, hunting and gathering, and when darkness fell the sound of old men singing, didgeridoo and clapping sticks would float up to the nurses' quarters. When there were enough dancers, there would be corroborees.

There was meant to be no mixing of the sexes at the Lep after 5 pm, but babies were born – and taken from their mothers, who were not allowed to even touch them.

Sister Francis left the Lep in 1961 and went to the mission at Balgo, in the Tanami Desert, then to Beagle Bay and Broome. When she returned in 1975, antibiotics had come and changed everything. 'The drug was introduced say in '69 and it was mirac- ulous how they were cured and were discharged in droves. Some who'd been in there for years. There were close on three hundred when I left in '61. I got back in '75 and it was down to eighty and it just went down from there. When we closed in 1986 there was only eight left, and there was only one, really, who should have been there, who really needed the care. One was blind, didn't want to go out to live outside. They were mostly in their sixties. They were transferred into a nursing home in town.'

The Kimberley still gets two leprosy cases a year. Because of the long incubation period, people can have the disease for years without knowing, and pass it on. These days it's a fortnight in hospital and they're free to go.

Sister Francis directs us to the old leprosarium out on the road to Point Torment and tells us to speak to Trevor Mitchell, the caretaker.

Large and long-haired, Trevor's been out here ten years now, since it was decided to use the facilities as a conference centre. He's had to redo the bush wiring and be generous with the paint. He came to the Kimberley twenty-five years ago with the Commonwealth Employment Service. Went to work for some Aboriginal communities until he burned out and the quiet life here beckoned.

Many of the old buildings are gone, but there are still patterns of street lights between the spread-out bungalows and the boxy examples of 1960s government architecture.

He points across the site. 'Men were on this side of the hill, women on that side. All segregated. The nuns were over this side. The animals and the vegie patch were through there.'

In the fifty years it operated, 1250 patients came through; 357 are still in the graveyard. The plain white crosses make it look like a war cemetery in some foreign field. They bear no markings.

We finish our tour and Trevor points us down a narrow track in the direction of the mosquito-infested Point Torment. His only real instruction is to turn left at Blue Hole (a different Blue Hole from the one at Purnululu). We might have to go through a bit of mud. But stick to the track, Trevor tells us, because it's usually pretty firm.

'You'll be right,' he says, nodding in Frank's direction.

The road to Point Torment, Friday 10 am

AMY I'm writing this covered in mud. Hot, drying, pinching mud. We have been trapped here for nineteen hours.

Trevor was wrong.

I was already feeling sick and sorry for myself, getting over a virus I'd had for a couple of days. And Mark and I weren't really talking: he was being unsympathetic, sick of my moaning.

So when we arrived at the muddy surrounds of Blue Hole, I wasn't in the mood.

'Are you really, really sure you want to do this?' I asked. (As I do, admittedly, at every patch of mud.)

Cowboy Mark, as usual, drove straight in.

'Way to go, Frankie boy,' he whooped as we made it through the first patch of sludge, then the next. But for every stretch we made it through, there was another, boggier one to come. Frank started to struggle, grunting in low range, slowing down until he wasn't even grunting anymore. And we were going nowhere.

I started to cry. I felt stupid. I didn't have the energy to deal with this.

Mark got out and cleared a bit of mud away from around the tyres, stuck a few branches in the track. He actually wanted to push on to Point Torment. It soon became apparent, however, that we weren't going anywhere.

'It's worse than I thought,' he said.

Mark attempted a futile, sweaty dig down to the belly of the car. And then we realised we were in the middle of a soak. Our footprints were filling with water.

We got out the 'bullbag' – the thing you inflate using the exhaust pipe and which is meant to lift the car in these hairy situations. I turned the ignition and it inflated quickly, lifting the wheel a couple of centimetres out of the water before the hose blew off the exhaust.

'Well, do you want to set up camp?' he asked.

That was exactly what I wanted.

We were in an open patch of country with mangroves fifty metres away to the right and scrub just to the left. The driest spot we could find was about fifty metres back down the track. We trudged back and forth, carrying what we would need for the night, fighting off the midges that were swarming with their little needle stings in the late afternoon light.

This morning we were up early, refreshed and ready to tackle this bastard. We took stock: we had thirty litres of water and plenty of food, so we had some time up our sleeves.

We drank only one cup of coffee each for breakfast, instead of the usual two, already making small efforts to deal with dehydration and ration water. Washing up was suddenly not a necessity. We could be here a while.

The morning was spent digging with gusto, but it was all for naught. The trench Mark had dug to drain the water away was still flowing strong, replenished with saltwater from underground. We gave the bullbag another go, but either it's crap or we're crap.

It was time for plan B. We'd never used the winch before so Mark checked that it actually worked – it did – before he started digging the biggest hole of his life. With no trees nearby, the mangroves a way off and only a few small dead things around, we need to bury the spare tyre to act as an anchor. So that's what he's doing now, slaving away out there, while I'm sitting in the shade, covered in mud and tormented by itchy bites, writing this.

The road to Point Torment, Friday night

MARK 'If we were going to die, what would you want to do while we waited?' asked Amy just then.

'I don't know. Play cards or something.'

'No. What about make love, have a wedding ceremony, write a will, go fishing?'

'I suppose.'

After more than a day here, our thoughts have turned to that lonely cross on the track to Lake Eyre. Rationally, we feel quite safe, but still our minds wander.

We are being buzzed by huge, loud moths. The full moon is rising bright. But it is still light. The billy is hissing softly on the fire.

'So, are you still having a good time?' she asks.

'Yeah, I am. In fact I would say I am having the best time of my life.'

'I'm finding it hard to believe you.'

'Fair dinkum. I'm sure I've told you about how I read *Day of the Triffids* and *Deliverance* back to back and noticed how similar they were.'

'You have told me that,' she sighs.

'They've both got exactly the same theme: that man is happiest when he's in the wilderness facing life and death situations.'

Our situation may not be quite as acute as vicious trees and depraved hillbillies, but it is our little challenge in the wilds. The main thing is, we're only twenty-four kilometres from the Lep and Amy remembers we were in mobile phone range there, so we probably don't even have to walk that far if things get desperate.

Today, after the bullbag didn't work, it took over two hours to dig the hole for the tyre. Mainly because all the water seeping in meant I had to bail every few minutes.

Meanwhile Amy was getting down and dirty digging the mud away from in front of the springs and front diff. As the sun got hotter through the morning she gave her left arm and thighs a good layer of mud to cool and protect her delicate skin. I was so proud of her. She had on little grey gym shorts and a small pink top and looked extraordinarily sexy.

'I'm going to be embarrassed if we get rescued with you looking like that. Any bloke that sees you will think I'm mad for wanting to be saved from this.'

We got over our irritation with one another – adversity brought us back together.

So I finished the hole and I was very proud of it – perfectly round and about sixty centimetres deep. I had no idea how deep it should be, so I just thought the deeper the better. Never having done an honest day's work in my life, my back was killing me. After a bit of jumping, the tyre went down into it, and I filled the hole in with slop. Oh yes, this was going to be one glorious escape.

We started Frank's motor and after a few nervous glances to each other, I turned the winch on. Click. It tightened one centimetre. I pressed it again. Click, click, click. We checked all systems, but the winch wasn't going anywhere. My back ached a hell of a lot more when I realised I had to dig the bastard tyre out again.

'Let's go and have lunch.'

We sat forlornly in the shade beside the tent for most of the afternoon waiting for the thirty-five-degree heat to pass. Things were looking bad. So sure were we that we would be fine out here, we hadn't rung home to relay our plans, like we have done in the past when we thought the drive could get hairy. The only person who knows we are here is Trevor from the Lep, and we never told him when to expect us back.

We had no plan C. Even if we did, with the winch attached to that tyre we couldn't go anywhere till I dug it up.

About 4 pm, with the heat abating, we got moving. The dried mud ripped at the hairs behind our knees. My left sandal had been ruined by the constant suction on it in the mud. Now we had to get the tyre out – a tyre with forty times the surface area of the sandal. It was a drawn-out feat of engineering, but we got the thing out and laughed stupidly at the small victory. It felt like we had won a grand final. Two grand finals, even.

We washed up in the wheel ruts, cleaned our teeth in their salty water, and are now spending the night picking mud from between each other's toes.

Saturday, same place

We move Frank two metres backwards before the front wheels sink into the holes the back wheels had been in – only deeper now. We dig some more and rest again through the heat of the afternoon. We hear a car in the distance, but it goes away.

Sunday morning

Amy wakes up in tears. The itchy bites are driving her crazy.

I have a melodramatic feeling that this diary of mine may yet be read by the coroner.

'I really hope we get out of here today,' says Amy, scratching her left calf.

We have about twenty-three litres of water left and food for a week. This is our third day here. We really did expect fishermen to come along for the weekend. If nobody comes today there's no reason why they'll come during the week. So we decide we will walk tomorrow at dawn. We know you're not meant to leave the vehicle, but the weather isn't that hot except through the afternoon, and the Lep is only twenty-four kilometres away. We've got the emergency beacon, but pride will stop us using that till we're half dead.

Paul Blackmore and I had actually got closer to Point Torment than this in our rental Camry, although we were hopelessly underprepared. It was much hotter then, and I can now see we may well have died had a vehicle not rescued us within minutes of us getting bogged in sand a kilometre or two further along the track.

Lunchtime

We hear an engine. Louder and louder. The vehicle's a long time coming into sight, but there it is. A troopie with another four-wheel drive behind.

'I suppose a pull's out of the question,' I say, moseying on over to the troopie. It's got Point Torment May River Tagalong Tours written on the side. The tour leader, Ian Ferguson, grabs his new manual winch and Barry, the tagalonger, grabs his axe and chops tea-tree branches while telling us all the things we shoulda done.

'You're not greenies, are you?' he asks while throwing the thick bushes into the wheel ruts.

'No. no. I've done a bit of damage to these bushes myself,'

I say, even though I had only thrown the dead branches into the ruts.

'I got bogged for two weeks once,' says Barry. 'Got out and 200 yards further on I got bogged for a week.'

Can't even give us the glory of three days.

We are heartened to hear Ian bagging other tour operators in their Okas, the huge four-wheel drive buses endemic in the Far North. 'They break through the surface and the road's ratshit. I've never seen this road like this in twenty years.' He decides that this is as far as he'll go today, too.

He starts heaving on the long winch handle and Frank moves a fraction. I get in and we ease Frank along. I see a little crab scurry before the landslide of mud created by the tyre. We are free.

Derby Caravan Park, that evening

Everything we own is still caked with brown mud but we are clean. The caravan park has a rustic charm. There's a man reciting a bush poem. His partner has just finished yodelling a country song. Real yodelling. Now a fellow is talking through a song about 'My Old Dog'.

Word of our rescue has spread throughout the place. We're famous.

Our rescuer, Ian, who happens to own the caravan park, comes over for a chat. He's dark-haired, bearded and has a radio voice. Been in Derby for twenty-five years with a few years off for good behaviour, he says.

He tells us that had we gone a few more kilometres to Point Torment, we would have come to 300 metres of mudflats, then a fringe of mangroves and a beautiful sandy beach. Unless the tide was out, in which case there would have been two to three kilometres of mudflats in front of the beach. There's a Landrover wreck there. About five years ago a guy got trapped. He buried the spare and winched, buried the spare and winched, but the tide beat him. It's almost completely rotted away now.

We talk about the massive tides here in Derby. The water goes by so fast it's hard to believe it's just a tidal movement. So fast, in fact, that they want to harness it for electricity.

Ian tells us how he'd sometimes pick up a little old Aboriginal lady he'd see with a huge mulloway over her shoulders walking the long, straight stretch of road across the desolate mudflats between the wharf and town. She really loved fishing, and a few months ago, she'd hooked a big fish and wrapped the line around her hand. Then there was a bite on her other line. She went forward to tackle that one when the first one gave a tug, caught her off-balance, and over she went into the swirling brown waters way below the Derby wharf – a huge structure built for the ten-metre tides. Some young guys dived straight in – crocodiles be damned – but it was 500 metres before they reached her. She was dead.

Ian's seen dinghies trying to come into the jetty when the tide is going out, full throttle and only just holding their own against the current.

One time, he and another guy were out fishing when the engine died. His mate had forgotten to check the fuel tank. They didn't stand a chance rowing back, so they drifted until they hit a sandbank. Night came. They couldn't see their hands in front of their faces. All around them they could hear crocodiles coughing, but couldn't tell where they were. It was terrifying. Ian huddled in the middle of the little dinghy, listening, just waiting for the tide to come back in.

All this makes us seriously nervous about our next destination.

CHAPTER 11

WE'LL SEND *the* GIRLS OUT FIRST

Derby Caravan Park, Western Australia

AMY ▶ Greg Prouse listens carefully as we explain what we want to do. He had been recommended to us by our rescuer, Ian, who first scared us silly with his talk of tidal horrors around here. If anyone would know how to get to Escape Point, Ian said, it'd be Greg.

Now, sitting under the tent awning, Greg studies the map. He is blond and tanned, his reading glasses incongruous with his rugged face. He has a good think and comes back with a verdict. No, he doesn't think we should try it.

The combination of the tides, the crocs, the sandbars, the mozzies and our lack of experience really gives us no hope of making it alone. Even if we could navigate our way to Escape Point successfully, Greg explains, we probably wouldn't find a camping spot out of the mud and we'd end up spending the night in the dinghy anyway.

Nobody around here really goes out that way. Even Greg doesn't know too much about it. This all slams a healthy wedge of fear into us – particularly me. But, strangely, getting bogged for three days has made us feel more adventurous. We want to give it a go so we ask Greg if he'd be interested in taking us.

He is a bit off-colour today, having just had a tooth pulled, but his face lights up at the prospect of an adventure. Watching him read through passages from Stokes's escapades up this way, we can see we've got him.

'How about tomorrow?' he suggests.

After escaping the mosquitoes at Point Torment, Stokes and his men got into the boats and headed off in search of what was then the holy grail of Australian exploration: a navigable waterway into the centre of the continent. In 1839, they still thought this a real possibility.

The tide hurried them towards this unknown river 'with a rapidity agreeable enough but not quite free from danger . . . I had never known a sensation of greater delight. Doubt, disappointment, difficulty, and danger; all, all were unheeded or forgotten in the one proud thought that for us was reserved an enterprise the ultimate results of which might in some future year affect the interests of a great portion of the world!'

When Stokes stopped his gibbering, he realised there was a dirty great flat across the river in front of him, 'over which the tide was boiling and whirling with great force'. So he made for a mangrove point a mile away and anchored for the night watching the tide run by at five miles an hour.

With Captain Wickham's permission, he later named the river Fitz-Roy after the former captain of the *Beagle*.

That night, Stokes was roused from sleep by 'a loud roaring, which I at once recognised to be the voice of thunder, heralding the advancing tide'. The turning of the tide came on as a wall of water. It brought the anchor away and threw the boat on its side. They were saved because Stokes had anticipated the tide race and lashed the masts to the shore. Stokes named the point where they were anchored Escape Point. But there was worse to come.

Dawn saw his mighty river as a mighty disappointment. There was no regular channel at low water, just an extensive flat drained by little streams. The 'circling flight of the ever wary curlew, and the shrill cry of the plover' only served to heighten the feeling of solitude. Stokes reconnoitred on foot with an officer, Mr Helpman, and a seaman, William Ask. The boat would pick them up from the nearby point.

But the returning tide soon filled in the streams they had to cross to get back to the boat, and only then did they learn that Ask could not swim. As the water rose to their ankles they walked, feeling with sticks for the streams, 'over each of which Mr Helpman and myself had alternatively to swim in order to pass the arms undamaged; and then Ask, making the best jump that he could muster for the occasion, was dragged ashore on the opposite side'.

But soon they reached a stream too big for Ask. The water was now above their knees, still with several hours to rise. The mangroves around them were too slender to climb. Ask found a piece of driftwood for security and Stokes went off to signal the boat. They weren't far from the rendezvous point now, so they weren't too worried – until Stokes saw the boat anchored way upstream, unable to make headway against the incoming torrent.

'Mr Helpman and myself might have reached her by swimming; but even could I have easily reconciled myself to part with our arms and instruments, at any rate to abandon poor Ask in the dilemma into which I had brought him was not to be thought of. By repeated discharges of my gun I at last succeeded in attracting the attention of the boat's crew, who made an immediate and desperate effort to come to our assistance: while their strength lasted they just contrived to hold their own against the tide, then, drifting astern, were again compelled to anchor.' They tried again and failed. A bank stopped the boat creeping along the shore.

The water rose up the three men's torsos at an inch a minute. Stokes prayed and shouted encouragement, and as the water topped their shoulders, the boat skimmed over the bank that had previously blocked it and pushed through the almost submerged mangroves, rescuing the men 'barely in time to confirm upon this locality its former title of Point Escape!'.

Escape Point, Western Australia

AMY ▶ We are fanging through a milk-coffee sea as the last of the tide gushes in, filling this eight-kilometre wide stretch of river. Greg and his partner, Anna Bonython, are in one dinghy, Mark and I in their wake. We have only half an hour of high tide to get to the mouth of Alligator Creek, where shortly after Stokes's rescue, he saw a large crocodile and knew how doubly lucky he had been.

Rounding Escape Point, we see country that is flat and sparse, just a few dark green mangroves lining the muddy bank. We turn left into Alligator Creek. The tide is pouring in, water bubbling and churning over a sandbar. Greg stops to check it out and decides we are all right to cross it. Tentatively, we motor in. Silver flashes of popeye mullet skim the surface. They flock to the shallows to avoid the barramundi, flying out of the water when one gets too close. Then they have to look to the skies with their huge pop-eyes for the birds hovering above.

Greg points to a magnificent bird heaving its enormous white and black wings into flight.

'Jabiru,' he yells over his shoulder.

It's getting late and the tide is dropping. We find a dryish claypan up from the mud and mangroves, and set up camp as the sun sets tangerine over Escape Point.

Greg builds a raging fire, topped with a driftwood tree: 'I like to have one on the fire all night, to keep the crocs away.'

'Does it work?' Mark asks.

'I don't know. The way I see it, each of us has got a one in four chance of being taken by him. And I never win shit, so it's not going to be me.'

'Do they attack people in tents?'

'I had one stalk me once, and it scared the shit out of me. I woke up and its tracks were right there next to my swag.'

With the fire blazing, Greg puts on his glasses and pulls out Stokes's journal, squinting over the details, comparing it with his modern chart.

'Now, what we've got to do is put you up to your neck in water and I'll try and paddle to you,' he says to Mark, his eyes twinkling.

Greg would probably do it, too. At fifty, he is tall and strong, completely assured out here. He came up from Perth about twenty-five years ago. Got himself involved with a bunch who were into bush survival. One of his first big trips, him and a mate took a five-metre dinghy, loaded it up with two forty-four-gallon drums of fuel and headed north.

'We killed a bullock, sun-dried it and basically lived off it for three months. We cut into it with axes. It was brutal. We had a net and we caught a croc and a dugong in it. Cut the net to pieces and it was meant to be our last resort. Made a still with a metal cup to make fresh water. It worked pretty well.'

He has settled down now. Runs a dinghy hire and fishing charter business out of Derby, but he still needs to get the old adrenaline pumping every now and then.

Greg has taken Anna, bright and pretty with soft blonde curls, into some hairy situations since they met. She has recently started her own business, so she's able to join him on a lot more of his trips. They recall the last time they were out this way, a few months ago, just after Tropical Cyclone Steve. The weather was still ferocious, the tides were huge and the Fitzroy River was in flood. They went upstream and launched the tinny to motor back to Derby through huge swells and whitecaps, the rain biting their skin. Anna didn't think they'd make it, and Greg concedes it was a close call, but they weren't going to miss an opportunity like that. They wanted to visit Greg's old mate Helmut.

While Anna cooks us up a delicious pot of beef stroganoff (the real reason Greg likes her to come on the trips, Anna says), Greg tells us about Helmut, with whom he used to live further up the Fitzroy. A former Luftwaffe pilot ('he doesn't talk about that much'), with skin like leather, Helmut lives in a house made of beer cans. Greg would swim out into the river to set their barra nets across the channels at Swordfish Point. That was just a couple of years after crocodile shooting had stopped and there weren't many man-eaters about. Those that were there knew to avoid humans. He wouldn't do it anymore.

The night is so calm, all we can hear is the snapping of barramundi. Or the snapping of something, but we try not to think about the possibilities.

Next morning, we head off for a walk around the point. Within minutes we are up to our thighs in mud, laughing so hard we can barely heave ourselves up out of the troughs. By the time we have squelched around to the point, it is low tide and the channels Greg had been talking about are clearly exposed. What had yesterday been an eight-kilometre wide sheet of water, is now a fast-flowing brown stream about forty metres across.

We watch a small shark and a barramundi torment a school of mullet. The shark and barra both beach themselves to snaffle the fish that cling so desperately to the edge. Such scenes of abundance make these otherwise bleak flats quite wonderful.

The tides aren't as big today as when Stokes was here. And there are less mangroves. We see their stumps scattered along the bank, killed by who knows what. Some are huge.

We get a picture, however, of the streams Stokes crossed, like ditches, mostly about four metres wide and up to ten metres deep, depending on the tide.

With the bed of Alligator Creek now mostly exposed, we walk out onto the firm, rippled sand. Greg wants to check out potential fishing, and he leads us straight into the channel. Mark and I take each other's hands as we wade through the thigh-deep water powering sideways against our legs. This wasn't part of the plan.

'Watch behind you,' Mark whispers to me, his head swivelling from side to side. He's just finished reading the book *Crocodile Attack in Australia*.

'Do they sneak up from behind?' I ask.

'Mmm.'

I can see Greg is also looking over his shoulder. God, you can't see anything in this brown water.

We make it the forty metres to the other side, too relieved to contemplate the return journey.

'If a croc's been watching us it'll be waiting for us to come back,' Greg laughs. 'We'll send the girls out first.'

Ha ha.

'Don't they wait for the last one?' Mark asks.

'Yeah.'

On the way back, Anna takes up the rear.

'Come on darlin',' Greg calls to her.

'It'll be a lot less paperwork if I get taken,' she says.

We make it, but now Greg wants to net the mullet trapped in the backwaters so we can do some barra fishing. They're crafty little creatures and keep escaping his throw net to get back into the main channel. So Mark, Anna and I stagger ourselves across the entrance like a rugby backline. We close in, eyeing off the opposition, splashing and kicking, but the mullet skip through the gaps as we look over our shoulders, waiting to be king-hit by a giant reptile at any moment.

A few stragglers don't make it, though, and they go live on our hooks. Mark and I get good bites from barra, but we both blow them. It looks like packet pasta for dinner again.

We turn our attention to the tide as the last of the outgoing water drains from our creek.

Greg says he can't understand the size of the wave Stokes was describing, it just sounds too big for this part of the river. 'At Swordfish Point way up stream they get that big, but not here. It must have been a really big tide.'

Alas, there is no great wave, but the changing of the tide is a distinct moment as the water comes swirling over the corrugations in the sandbar. We pull our lines in, grab the gear and make a brisk return with the water lapping at our feet all the way. We hear loud splashes against the wall of the opposite sandbank. Sandslides? We turn to watch but, no, it's a feeding frenzy as barra attack mullet trapped in a bend of the river.

The tide is overtaking us and now we have to run. We still have to cross a channel to get back to the bank. The water is already at the top of our thighs and swelling up as it greets the outgoing creek water. We know that crocs drift back into their territories with the incoming tide, but we are all laughing, carried away by the awesome power of water and nature.

In the twenty-five minutes it takes us to fold our tents and pack our gear in the tinnies, the creek rises two metres. We race back out in the dinghies and around Escape Point to Derby.

Derby, Western Australia

MARK A short day's march south of Derby, and just a little inland from Escape Point, is a giant, hollow boab tree. They used to lock up Aboriginal prisoners inside it, chained by the neck, on their way to court in Derby. Now it is neatly fenced and sign-posted – 'Prison Boab' – for us tourists.

Tom Baxter's place is a short drive past it. We'd read about Tom in *The Australian* a few months ago and basically just want to meet the guy. You could say he's harbouring Australia's most famous escapee.

Tom won't actually say that he stole Ned Kelly's skull from public display in the Old Melbourne Gaol – that would be admitting to a felony – but he does admit to possessing it.

Tom has an active manner about him, and a head that seems to sit very erect on his shoulders. He apologises for having such a nice place, explaining that it's the first decent house he's lived in since moving to the Kimberley in the late 1970s. The large architect-designed shutters are normally left up for shade but the ones down the kitchen wall are closed against the easterlies that howl through in May and June.

His road here has been a long one. Back in the 1970s, he explains, he was young and radical, wore army surplus gear, and would catch the old red trains into Melbourne for protest marches. He was living with an Aboriginal woman from Fitzroy Crossing.

He introduces us to his son, Sonny, the product of that relationship. Sonny's mother isn't around anymore, says Tom, offering no further information. Sonny is making a giant pot of bolognaise sauce that smells divine. He makes us good coffee.

The skull went missing in 1978, continues Tom. 'I didn't know much about (Kelly) really. I think I was just more outraged that here's this thing, in the possession of the police, the most amazing trophy, and here it is on public display, and they're actually making money out of it, getting people through the gates.'

Suddenly he had the skull and didn't really know what to do with it. At first the story was all over the radio and papers, but it died within a day or two. He went to author Frank Hardy for advice, and he got a QC mate to contact the Kellys who were still on the family farm at Greta. They didn't want the thing.

So he cleared out in his old Landrover to his girlfriend's country in the Kimberley. Found himself living in the bush with a big mob of about 350 Aborigines who'd walked off Christmas Creek Station. There were some who'd only been in from the desert ten or twenty years, a very tribal situation. He was the only whitefella there, a boy from the city with Ned Kelly's skull in his Landrover.

'Things were pretty wild then, and I just kind of stayed,' Tom says.

He showed the skull to quite a few of his new brothers and was surprised they knew about Ned. Not only did they know Kelly, he had found his way into their Dreamtime creation story. 'The only other white guys that are in there are Moses and Noah and Jesus. The white guys in there are supposedly of high moral courage or whatever. More and more it's an issue of morals and values, when you realise that Jandamarra was treated in the same way.'

Jandamarra was the Bunuba renegade/freedom fighter who lead the authorities of the Kimberley on a merry dance through the 1890s. When they eventually killed him, his head was taken as a trophy and ended up in the private collection of an English arms manufacturer.

At forty-five, Tom is a grandfather already. He has this place and a ten-hectare block on the south side of the Fitzroy where he runs a few camels. He's about to take a bunch of troubled kids bush on camels for two weeks. See if he can talk some sense into them before they go right off the rails.

After he went public with the skull in *The Australian*, the phone never stopped ringing. He covered the whole nation on the radio, and had a really sore ear at the end of the day. Among the callers was one of the Kelly family, and Tom's now working with him to organise a funeral for Ned at the spot where Ned's brother Dan and Steve Hart were buried after their charred bodies were taken from the pub at Glenrowan.

The publicity, however, prompted the police to come and search for the stolen skull all over this place and at his other block on the Fitzroy. 'They were pretty reasonable. I just sort of said: "Well, look Sarge, it's okay, you can go away, because this is not about the laws the public of Western Australia expect you guys to administer. This is about a natural law, and it's a spiritual matter and you guys simply aren't trained for that kind of thing." '

The way Tom puts it, the police came down to his shed and said: 'Look, we're under a lot of pressure from the Victorian Police. They're gunna stick a couple of guys in the plane and they're gunna send them up to Derby and they're going to walk into the Clerk of Courts and he only needs to stamp this thing and they'll be taking you back to Melbourne. What are you gunna do with your kids then? You've got two little kids to look after, mate.'

'Well, look Sarge,' said Tom, 'if I've got to do time for Ned Kelly, I would be too fucken proud. You can take me now if you like.'

The police said they'd give the skull to the National Trust if he handed it over. But Tom wasn't buying that.

'This is a Crown possession. Put one piece of paper in front of me, mate, that might vaguely suggest that this belongs to the National Trust and I can take you a bit more seriously.

'I've had legal advice about the whole thing – it belongs to the Queen of England. And if the Queen wants her skull back, I'll get you to pass on me phone number to her, and I'm more than happy to talk with her about it, mate.'

Tom's on a great voyage of discovery. He's kind of proud to be the person who's advocating a burial service for Ned Kelly. It's caused fantastic things to happen to him. It's like a full-time job, but it's worth it.

It has brought him into contact with people like author Tom Keneally, Aboriginal leader Pat Dodson and leading Kelly historian Ian Jones. Writer Peter Carey rang a while ago and wanted to come and talk about how Kelly has crept into Aboriginal mythology. 'He introduced me to the idea that (Kelly) occupies the place in Australia that George Washington and Abraham Lincoln occupy in the US. The truth is in the myth, not in the history.'

We drive west along the Gibb River Road, which, given the rugged history of the Kimberley, is surprisingly devoid of dots on the Map of Misery. There is, however, a solitary red spot in the middle of Lake Argyle, near the Northern Territory border. Mount Misery, in fact. We've arranged to meet someone next week who can take us there, because Frank sure won't be able to do the job.

So with five days to get there, we amble along the 701 kilometres of road that has become a four-wheel driving Mecca, full of gorges and waterfalls, and cattle stations that would go broke but for the tourism dollar.

CHAPTER 12

A WITCH'S GARDEN

Lake Argyle, Western Australia

MARK As Steve Sharpe's boat noses in to shore, he advises us that what we can smell is dead insects trapped in the basket-spider webs that thickly cloak all the trees and bushes. It's not entirely unpleasant, almost sweet, and quickly fades from our senses.

Steve also advises us not to tread on the dead catfish; their plump, dried bodies are scattered all over the pebbly beach. 'What happens is they gorge themselves during the wet, there's so much food about, and basically just eat themselves to death. Their spines still have poison in them, though, so they can really hurt – you get up in the middle of the night and tread on one, and it'll ruin your stay.

'You might see some cattle, too. They're wild. Been here since the seventies and it's been too much trouble to get them out. They're shorthorn crosses from the Durack station. They live on the seaweed.'

He points at the bok-choy-green mat on the shoreline pocked with cow and roo poo. The euros, large wallabies, live on it, too.

He backs the boat away from the beach to leave us here until tomorrow afternoon. 'And by the way', he calls out 'if you hear any strange growling and grunting kind of noises at night, don't worry, it's only the crocodiles. Coming up to breeding season they start to stake out territory on beaches like this. The last couple we dropped out here didn't get any sleep. They were terrified.'

We met up with Steve last night at Lake Argyle Village after coming across the Gibb River Road to Kununurra in our five-day time frame. The track had been freshly graded.

We sped out here before dawn, across the sea that now covers the black soil plains of the pioneering Durack family's old station, Argyle Downs.

Now Steve pulls away. We're alone.

Mount Misery is glorious. Orange rock framed by blue water that laps a few metres below our camp. The basket-spider webs form a thick white sheet through the surrounding trees – a witch's garden, says Amy – backlit by the morning sunshine.

Mount Misery is now the highest peak of Hagan Island in Lake Argyle – aka the Ord River Dam. R. Hagan was a farrier for the surveyor H.F. Johnston, on a mission up the Ord in the middle of tourist season, 1885. One morning, Hagan was riding a barebacked runaway when it struck his left leg against a tree, breaking it just above the knee. Johnston still had surveying to do. He wrote: 'It was impossible for Hagan to travel with his broken leg, so I had a stockade built as protection for the party of three men that were obliged to remain with him.'

It was the same year the Duracks turned up to set up their station. Mary Durack, in her family history, *Kings in Grass Castles*, wrote of Hagan's 'long, uncomfortable camp, besieged by blacks, plagued by mosquitoes and flies'.

Happy campers that they were, they called it Mount Miserable, later shortened to Misery. To make it even more fun, Hagan slipped on his crutches the first day he got up, hurting his leg again. A few days later he began a journey of more than

160 kilometres on horseback to rendezvous with a steamer and the main surveying party at the coast.

'It must have been a time of great suffering for the invalid, who, on arrival, looked very ill and reduced,' Johnston wrote.

Hagan had camped somewhere near our spot. Stockade Creek is now deep below the waters of Lake Argyle, which flooded out the Durack property when the Ord River Dam was completed in 1972. Mount Misery is still no mean hill at 240 metres above the water.

Here for two days, there's not much to do other than try to climb it. Steve said he had done it by moving up the spine from the southern tip, but we are camped several kilometres away from that, so we have to walk around the shoreline towards the ridge. A croc and a euro flee before our heavy plodding. We scoot up a side ridge as a bit of a shortcut. The loose stones and fresh green spinifex prove tough going. And don't mention snakes. We don't, the whole way up, but both of us are thinking about them. Steve hadn't mentioned them, but we both sense that they are here. (Only after we return does he tell us the place is crawling with them.)

It feels like we are about three-quarters of the way up when Amy starts to get stressed by the unstable, crumbly rocks. You can crack them with your fingers. Every step is uncertain, sending little landslides down the steep slope to the water behind us.

'Okay, we'll head back,' I offer.

'No.'

We go a bit further and her state is deteriorating.

'Come on, let's go down,' I say.

'No. I'm not going to have you blame me for stopping you going to the top.'

'But babe, it's clear you don't want to go on.'

'I do,' she says through gritted teeth.

And so it is that while I do want to go on, I argue to go down, and she wants to go down but argues to go up. Ain't love grand.

We get high enough to look down across the purple turkey bush, or Kimberley heather, and out to the distant mainland. A quite different view from the one the Duracks saw when they brought visitors to the top of Mount Misery to see Johnston's peg, 'and to point out the charred stumps of his stockade on the creek below', Mary Durack wrote. 'From the dome-shaped mount, the vista of the sweeping Mitchell grass plains, dotted with grazing cattle, and the misty blue of the O'Donnell Ranges tumbling into the Ord River gorge has always seemed to me one of the loveliest on earth.'

Now, it is like the deep blue of the Mediterranean.

The scale of the lake is awesome. It has been classified as an inland sea since a couple went out on it on New Year's Eve 1972 and were hit by 105-knot winds. Their boat flipped in the two-metre swell, trapping them inside, fatally. Boats using the lake now have to carry all the safety gear required to put to sea.

Above us, the climb looks even more difficult. So I at last convince Amy that I really do want to turn around now. The descent proves tougher than the ascent, but we manage with Amy only going onto her arse once and both of us covered in spider webs.

We fall asleep on our mattresses faster than characters in a Shakespearean comedy. It is 11.15 am.

During the afternoon we realise that there's a little freshwater crocodile watching us just fifteen metres away. We call him Johnno. We have come without any reading material, so watching Johnno becomes our main entertainment. The highlight being when he catches a fish. The next twenty-four hours pass without event. We catch a few catfish and eventually have a go at eating one, after trying all combinations of shoes, rocks and pliers to break off its spine. Unsuccessful, we throw it whole into the coals. It eats okay.

We are picked up next afternoon by the boat that carts a mixed bag of about twenty tourists up the huge lake. At one point our guide, Scotty, stops the boat in the middle of a huge expanse and explains that directly below us is the old Durack homestead, or what's left of it. He tells how some locals had painstakingly started to dismantle the place, numbering each brick as they went so it could be reconstructed as a museum above the high water mark. They thought they had a couple of years to do it. Not so. One night the water came up over them and all their equipment. They had to swim to shore hundreds of metres away, returning with diving gear a few weeks later to float their trucks and equipment out.

So now the top two-thirds of the Durack homestead near Lake Argyle Village is the real thing, but the bottom third is a replica.

Everyone on the tour is supplied with binoculars and Scotty talks us through the birdlife with such enthusiasm it has a dire effect on me and the rest of our trip. I become a birdwatcher. Scotty could not have known how many morning cuddles this cost Amy, as I would rise at dawn to go 'twitching', ticking off all the new species in my Simpson and Day field guide.

Anyway, even Amy loves Scotty's tour, which ends with complimentary drinks at sunset as Mount Misery, a few kilometres to the north, turns deeper and deeper orange.

We get talking to a guy we'd met earlier in a Broome caravan park, John Duffy. Going through the usual traveller banter with John, a talkative redhead, we learn that he's been to the El Questro Station and might be going back there to work. Or maybe Broome.

'There's 600 horses need shoeing.'

'Oh yeah, are you a blacksmith?' I ask.

'Farrier.'

'How bizarre. The guy who broke his leg and had the miserable time at Mount Misery, Hagan, he was a farrier.'

'Shit. That is bizarre. I'm here because I broke me leg. A horse kicked me in the knee.' John's insurance company figured it was cheaper for him to have eight months off than to have his knee reconstructed and have a possible eighteen months off recovering from it.

Old Hagan would be pleased to know the farrier business is booming. Especially around John's area of Geelong/Torquay in Victoria. All the hobby farms with two ponies have meant an explosion in horse numbers.

'I knock back thousands of dollars worth of work every week,' he reveals.

Life should be so tough.

It's hard to remember the real world out here, but we've got one annoyance that keeps dragging us back to it. The fridge. We've rung the manufacturer and they've told us they've got a place to get it serviced in Kununurra, so from Lake Argyle we drive the seventy kilometres north to get it looked at. The fridge mechanic tells us there's nothing wrong with it. Frank's wiring is to blame. We need an auto electrician.

But not even the prospect of the Olympic torch coming through town can keep us for another day. The road east takes us into the Northern Territory along the winding red valley of the Victoria River.

We cross Stokes's Whirlwind Plains and pass Hopeless Reach, where he decided that the Victoria River was not going to be the one to take him to the centre of the continent. He looked at a mountain in the distance and lamented that he would not get there, so he named it Mount Regret and headed back to the *Beagle*.

We travel north and spend a few days in Darwin, where an auto electrician tells us Frank's wiring is fine and that it's our fridge that is crap.

So, we have more mouldy tomatoes to look forward to as we return to the Map of Misery. A couple of dots on the Northern Territory–Queensland border beckon, announcing a new stage in our journey – the tough way into Queensland.

CHAPTER 13

IT MADE *a* JACK RABBIT FIGHT *a* BULLDOG

Roper Bar, Northern Territory

AMY ▶ Either side of us, termite mounds poke through the long, dried grass, pale and tall like unmarked headstones in an overgrown cemetery. Occasionally, a clump of wattle trumpets its yellow, or the grevillea its iridescent orange, through the thin trees. We pass signs to stations with names like Lonesome Dove, Chatterhoochee and Big River as we make our way along the rough Gulf track to Hell's Gate. But first we cross a bridge over Fizzer Creek and rattle into the small 'town' of Roper Bar.

Standing down by the Roper River we notice what looks like a ruin. Gum trees frame four water tanks on stilts and a couple of tin sheds. There's no-one around and so we wander up for a look. Sheets of corrugated iron are strewn through the long grass, there's an animal pen, empty tobacco tins, mounds of green beer cans, old campfires.

Tucked away in the scrub is a curious headstone: a rotten old piece of wood supported by cement rendered into its cracks. It is difficult to read, but after looking at them for a while it becomes apparent that the letters, some still visible in the wood and others carved into the cement, form the words 'SPEARED BY BLACKS'.

We pitch the tent at the little campground by the river, and before heading out of town the next morning, revisit the ruin to take a photo. This time we notice a large sign:

'Ceremony country. Beyond this point lies sites of traditional significance to Aboriginal people. Please respect the sanctity of this area. Penalty for unlawful entry up to $20,000.'

We back off and instead drop in at the Roper Bar store to ask about the ruins. Standing out by the petrol bowsers, a lined old bushy pulling on a cigarette says it's the old police station, but he's not sure about the mystery headstone.

'There are gravestones like that all over the place around this area.'

Borroloola, Northern Territory

AMY When legendary bushman Nat Buchanan took up the first two cattle runs in what is now the Northern Territory in 1881, he carved a track from the Queensland frontier along the Gulf of Carpentaria. The drovers and gold diggers who followed him into this no-man's-land relinquished police protection just inside the Queensland border – at a gap in the escarpment christened Hell's Gate. For almost a thousand kilometres from Hell's Gate until they reached Katherine in the Territory, the trigger-happy settlers had no safeguard against the spear-wielding Aborigines. It was a free-for-all.

In the heart of that free-for-all country is present day Borroloola. Its outskirts are blackened from recent burning. We drive into town past a fearsome looking pub: a concrete bunker caged behind a fence. We are heading for the town's museum, housed in the old police station.

The former cop shop is jammed with stories and relics of wild pioneers and recluses, drunken brawls and gun battles. On a board in the middle of the front room is an article that captures the lawlessness.

C.E. Gaunt was a drover with one of the first mobs into the area. He wrote in the article 'The Birth of Borroloola' that there were 'blacks as thick as the hair on a dog, on the route, burning the country behind and ahead of us'. By the time Gaunt reached his destination on the McArthur River, Borroloola, he had lost six horses. 'Found four killed and butchered and two so badly injured that we shot them.'

With no police around, the settlers took the matter of punishment into their own hands. Aborigines caught in the act of spearing were branded 'with a lead brand that never came off'. When a cattleman was killed by Aborigines on Broadmere on the Parsons River, 'we formed a party, followed the blacks up, found his head untouched where he was speared and . . . found his bones where they had eaten him, and in a dilly bag got a gold ring he used to wear. We followed them up for several days and at last surprised them at the head of Malakoff Creek and dispersed them.' Gaunt doesn't say what was meant by the commonly euphemistic 'dispersal', but their naming of the creek Malakoff was a clue. It was a bloody Crimean battlefield.

The settlers inflicted plenty of damage upon themselves, too. A few days after Gaunt arrived in Borroloola, a schooner called the *Good Intent* turned up, skippered by 'Black Jack' Reid. Reid was a renowned blackbirder, having made a career of raiding South Sea island villages for labourers to man the Queensland sugar plantations.

Fearing a night raid on his boat by the local Aborigines, Reid had stocked up with whisky – 'square bottles, with green labels named "Come Hither"' – as an inducement to the settlers to help him unload quickly.

Reid had no trouble recruiting men to unload his cargo, 'and then the orgie started. What a christening Borroloola got! I, being sane and sober, can vouch for all these details not being Come Hither dreams,' Gaunt wrote. 'Good God what havoc that terrible stuff did. It made a jack rabbit fight a bulldog. A man got a few shots of that stuff under his belt would charge hell with a bucket of water.

'When the "Come Hither" had got to work, The Orphan and Big-Eyed Billy had a fight; The Orphan pulled out his revolver and with one hand over the muzzle of the gun fired at Big-Eye and blew his own thumb off and shattered two of his fingers. "Come Hither" was poured over the wounded member, bandaged up, and forgotten. Johnnie Mooney tried to jump his horse over an obstacle with the result that the horse fell and a splinter ran into Johnnie's throat, getting a big gash in it. A bottle of pain killer was obtained at once, and Johnnie holding his head on one side, the whole contents of the bottle were emptied into the wound. A great part of it ran into his ear, and if Johnnie had been dancing an Apache war dance in a camp of Indians he would certainly have been proclaimed champion. The crowd roared with laughter.'

Another bloke, crazed with Come Hither, rode over the bank of the river and drowned himself, pack horse and riding horse.

And while all this was going on, a detective arrived in town looking for a man wanted for 'lifting horses', Jack Sherringham. But Sherringham had moved to a creek further up the coast. So the detective instead succumbed to Come Hither and, full of booze, jumped into the river and was taken by a crocodile.

When, a week later, news reached Sherringham that a detective was on his trail, the horse thief 'blew his brains out'.

Hell's Gate, Queensland

AMY Bill Olive is at the barbecue turning steaks and sausages, a hand-rolled cigarette hanging out of his mouth. His wife Lee is organising salads and serving drinks behind the outdoor bar, impeccably dressed in a suit jacket. Sparkling earrings swing below her greying curls.

We drove in from Borroloola yesterday. The potholed, rusty red road still passes through that fateful gap in the escarpment from which Bill and Lee's roadhouse takes its name. Out the

front a huge diesel drum declares 'HELL'S GATE ROAD-
HOUSE' in metre-high red and black.

Bill sent us off for the night to camp by a dam on his property,
Cliffdale Station, with a tattered old book he thought we should
read, *Bagmen Millionaires* by John Andersen, about the station
owners in the Gulf country. So, sitting by the dam with the cattle
and wild pigs for company, we read the chapter on Bill. It began:
'Every three or four months Bill Olive of Cliffdale Station,
between Doomadgee and the Northern Territory border, packs
up the four-wheel drive and heads into Burketown for a bender.'

And it ended with Bill's life goal: 'When I'm ninety years old
my ambition is to chase a topless barmaid around the bar of the
Burketown pub.'

It was with this image of Bill in mind that we returned to
Hell's Gate Roadhouse for the barbecue which he and Lee put
on every Sunday night. We're keen to find out if he really has
inherited some of the frontier madness of the original Hell's
Gate brigade.

We are ordering a drink when a young couple turns up at
the bar, faces and arms crudely blackened with charcoal. The
young guy is carrying a didgeridoo, and gibbering about Toyota
Dreaming.

'What you eatin', whitefella? Witchetty grub?' Charcoal Face
says to a man at the bar picking at a sausage.

It is meant to be a joke. Nobody is laughing, just standing
around uncomfortably. Much to everyone's relief, the couple
soon disappears, returning a little later scrubbed up.

We sit at a communal table with our plate-sized T-bones and
salad. Over at the other table, things are getting a bit rowdy as
Jack, the old truck driver, starts arguing beef quality with the
dapper grader driver.

Leaning up against the bar is a chubby tourist, Foster's T-shirt
straining against his protruding belly. He awkwardly pushes his
large, tinted glasses up his nose with his middle finger as he bores
a local station manager with stories of the places he's been and
the wide variety of beers he's drunk.

Dinner served up, Bill and Lee relax behind the bar, chatting away to their guests. Bill looks disturbingly like H.G. Nelson with his straight, dark hair swept across his forehead. His face is open and friendly, deeply lined around the eyes, but still not looking his fifty-nine years. He has a sharp, dry wit and the couple laughs often.

We finish off our T-bones and take a seat at the bar to chat with Bill and Lee. Bill is talking about his barramundi fishing days when he and a mate bought a three-horsepower outboard to go up the creeks. They'd catch a thousand pound of barra fillets in three or four days, then drive to Cloncurry, sell them for a thousand dollars, buy a drum of diesel and spend the rest on beer.

'It was a great life,' he says. 'When we first came to Burketown, you only knew people in the pub as Tom or Jack or Bob . . . '

'You never asked their last name,' Bill and Lee finish together.

'Everyone was running away, hiding from an old woman after maintenance, or on the run from something,' continues Bill. 'Even the coppers with a summons, they'd say, "you're not here, are you", and send it on to the next place.'

Bill bought Cliffdale in 1973. His dream was always to have his own station, and this was the only place he could afford. Feral cattle and brumbies had the run of the joint. There were no fences or buildings, just wild, open country. Beef prices, however, were high.

'We had enough cattle mustered that we could have paid our mortgage, paid our wages. Had thirty grand worth of cattle no worries,' Bill says. But by the time the cattle had been dipped and transported to Cloncurry, their value had dropped to 3800 dollars. 'The American market had closed up overnight. Some buyers lost hundreds of thousands. Friend of mine lost nearly everything he had. Took his house and everything in the end.'

With prices at an all-time low, Cliffdale wasn't viable. Bill turned to professional fishing and left the cattle on Cliffdale to run wild.

Bill and Lee met when Lee was married to a former rodeo professional, John Culbert. Lee, John and their young son Alan were living on their boat, the *Sea Marie*, fishing the Gulf. In the late 1970s, Bill spent six months fishing with them around Morning Inlet, Disaster Inlet (another Stokes name) and the mouth of the Leichhardt River.

Later that year, after Bill had left the boat, John and Lee were fishing the Gin Arm west of Burketown when their little boy Alan fell overboard in rough water. John dived in after him and Lee jumped in the tender. She couldn't start the outboard motor and by the time it revved into action she had lost sight of John. She dragged her son out of the water, but John's body wasn't found for another ten days.

Bill and Lee got together after that.

In 1980 one of the original partners retired from Cliffdale and a new partner was taken on. With an injection of capital, work could begin again: clearing, building fences and constructing dams. Bill did a bit of fishing through the wet. They'd muster enough cattle to pay some wages and he'd keep his head high enough above water to do it all again next year.

They opened the roadhouse in the 1980s and got the cattle back to a viable situation. Now they've had enough of Hell's Gate. Bill and Lee tell us they're getting ready to move south. Their bones are tired. They've got a place further south-east between Hughenden and Muttaburra.

'What have you got there? Sheep?' Mark asks.

'No!' they both shudder.

'Even our dog doesn't like sheep,' says Lee.

Next morning, Bill puts Frank over the pits to have a look at our rear diff, which is spewing oil. He declares the truck will be just fine, for now, and won't accept any money for his efforts. Before we leave, we've got to ask him if those Burketown benders are still part of the schedule.

'Nah. Don't drink hardly much at all now. I settled down when I got to thirty-five . . .' he pauses '. . . forty. When I was a young fella I used to go into town just to have a fight and a beer.

Liven the place up a bit. Nearly always used to get into a blue. Mainly because I was a cheeky bugger. I'd walk up to a copper and put me arm around his wife and say, "Gee, you're not a bad sort. What are you doing with an ugly bastard like him?" That was life, you enjoyed yourself. Only for a week, then went bush.'

'How about that ambition to chase a topless barmaid around the Burketown pub when you're ninety?

'If I can catch one. That might be when I die. If the missus don't kill me, the shock will.'

CHAPTER 14

GOT HIM RIGHT *in* *the* PIG

Wollogorang, Northern Territory

MARK On the dining room wall at Hell's Gate is an article about an incident at neighbouring Westmoreland Station some unknown time ago. It read: 'A renegade bunch of Aborigines raided the Homestead while all the station men (Aborigines and Europeans) were mustering. The renegades killed all the inhabitants except for one old Aboriginal woman, who, being badly wounded, managed to track down the station men and relate the horrifying tale. The men returned to the station, buried their dead, tracked down the culprits and shot all the renegades at a place now known as Massacre Inlet.'

Massacre Inlet is the only place for hundreds of kilometres on the southern shore of the Gulf of Carpentaria accessible by road. While the inlet is thirty-two kilometres inside the Queensland border, the station where you get access, Wollogorang, is in the Northern Territory. We rumble back over the border.

Wollogorang, like Hell's Gate, now has a roadhouse, too. Cigarettes cost over eleven dollars a packet. We are sitting there, drinking XXXX Gold, watching *Who Wants To Be a Millionaire*, when the resident hunting guide, Tod, comes in with his latest client.

'You do the pig shooting, eh? Any chance of going out with you?' I ask.

'No, mate, not until September. I'm booked solid.'

'Damn. How'd you go today?'

'We got nineteen. We only went out at two-thirty to have a look around.'

I see Tod and his client again next morning drinking coffee and ask if they've got room for a passenger. They do. How about two? Alright, in a couple of days. Cool.

In the meantime, Amy and I pay our fifty dollars to the station owner and head the eighty kilometres down the slow track to Massacre Inlet, getting slower as it passes wetlands. I stop the car every ten minutes to look at birds.

Hitting the beach, we turn right and drive on the sand for three kilometres. The track cuts back inland for another five kilometres across reddish-purple heather and through white gum forests before bursting upon the inlet, a seventy-metre wide stretch of blue-green water with mangroves thickly lining the opposite bank.

We drive along the inlet looking for a camp, past scattered crab shell, empty fuel drums and a dumped crab trap, which we snaffle. Selecting an abandoned fisherman's camp, we have upturned carpet for flooring, drums and rubbish for decor. Out back, behind a tree, is the previous occupants' toilet paper. Used. But it is shady and they left firewood for us. It really is a good spot.

In the afternoon we drive from the inlet to the nearby beach. It's a 500-metre wide stretch of almost white sand covered by millions of shells. Strangely, none of them are broken. Even those corkscrew ones that always seem to have the tip broken off are in pristine condition. Amy goes berserk with the camera while the sun sets over the sandy plain. 'I want to live here,' she says, beside herself with joy at the wonderland of shells.

'Is that what I think it is?' she points at a large white lump in the sand.

It is. A perfectly intact conch shell. First one either of us has ever found.

As we drive back to camp in the dying light, agile wallabies scamper about everywhere.

The night is far from quiet as crickets set up a racket. There are thumps in the bush behind us and strange cracking noises waft over from the mangroves. Yet it's terribly peaceful. We know there are birdwatchers camped about ten kilometres north and another group somewhere north of them. It feels isolated now. How far from the world must it have seemed in the bad old days? To the doomed mob of alleged murderers and to the posse who knew they could get away with murder?

The massacre is, of course, another world away. The screams of women, babies and men. The dull thud of horse hooves on sand. The crack of rifle fire, perhaps stockwhips. Not here. Not possible.

Two nights later, we've pitched the tent on the grass beside the Wollogorang Roadhouse. As I make my way to the toilet, a blackfella is going too, and we meet as we enter the door.

'G'day,' I say.

'How's it going?'

'Good, good. Just been down to the beach, it was great.'

We do our business and while he is still at the trough I ask, 'So do you know who's got the story to Massacre Inlet?'

'Yeah. Where I live there is an old lady. She's got all the story for this place. Her people belong on this place. You know the border grid where all the signs are? Just there. Go there and she can tell you. You really want to know?'

'Yeah, I'm researching a book.'

An old man approaches in a sleeveless cowboy shirt. His naked gums protrude from his mouth and his eyeballs hide deep in his head.

'This is my dad,' says the younger guy.

'How you travelling?' he croaks.

'Good. Good,' I say. He repeats the question and I repeat the answer.

'No, how you travelling? What you driving?'

'Oh, a troopie.'

He starts to say something about me driving somewhere and coming back with someone.

'Don't worry about him. Drunk,' says his son, who introduces himself as Bobby. The old man is Tolby.

'How about a beer?' asks Bobby. I pat my pockets and say I'll be back in a tick.

I buy Bobby a beer, which he takes without acknowledgement. He's being monopolised at the pool table by another couple of campers, so we don't get to talk much, but he tells me the old lady we want is called Phyllis.

Warwick behind the bar, however, says that Phyllis won't tell us anything. 'It took me six months before she told me anything. And you better get her sober.'

First, we've got to go a-hunting.

Next Morning

Poor Amy. She's in a car with three men, all facial hair and khaki shirts. Two of them are armed. We drive quickly over rough bush tracks. It all happens at pace. Suddenly, Gary Richards, the client on this Gulf Wilderness Safari, is out of the vehicle, gun in hand and ammo belt around his waist. I hadn't even realised he had his gun up there in the front seat, let alone the cowboy clobber.

Boom. Boom.

Tod has his knife at the throat of a black sow, whimpering in its last moments. I grimace.

Boom. Boom.

Gary has disappeared. We try to follow, looking for a blood trail from the brindle pig that has disappeared too. Tod points to luminescent red traces on the grass. 'Lung blood. See how it's all sort of bubbly and bright? She hasn't gone far.'

We follow the splatters, which lead to a pig, then follow the forensic trail back to where she was shot. There's a piece of bright goop a metre or so up a tea-tree and splatter marks on the trees all around. We are detectives at a murder scene.

'Got him right in the pig,' as Tod, who is thirty-three and precise, likes to say.

This becomes the rhythm for the day.

Gary is a carpenter from Sydney's west, pushing fifty, with a mean eye. Heaven help us if he ever runs amok in a shopping mall. Fortunately he is charming and pleasant company. Loves telling stories about his kids.

This time last year Gary was in hospital with a broken back from falling off a roof.

'Did you have insurance?'

'Yeah, but you can't get insurance for depression. The body has come back. I'm working three days a week and the mind's just starting to fall into place. This is all part of that.'

We have trudged through swamps and waterholes and seen the chaos that pigs leave behind when they dig through these places. Trudging through one swamp, the reeds flattened and muddied by pigs, we see forty brolgas take off with their huge, slow wings and we all stop in awe.

'In the five years I've been coming here,' says Tod, surveying the damage caused by the pigs, 'the waterholes have got smaller because every wet, a bit of that mud gets washed into the holes.' By sunset Gary has killed thirteen pigs. Most of them with little crimson holes right behind the shoulder blade.

'Is that where you're aiming for?' I ask.

'I'm just going for the black bit,' he says modestly.

Now we're driving madly on a track which to my eyes doesn't exist. Tod assures us it does: where the saplings are higher than the windscreen, that's not it; where they are lower, that's it. He's flying along but abruptly halts for no apparent reason. Gary gets out.

'Walk up to 'em slowly,' advises Tod, and we see that Gary is approaching the carcasses of two brumbies, their legs pointing skyward. Pigs have their heads deep in the horses' guts, and with their noses full of long-dead horse, they are oblivious to the hunters.

Gary opens up from fifteen metres. There is mayhem. Pigs flee, then come charging back, honking and squealing. They don't know what's going on. Boom boom boom. His tally for the day doubles.

As we walk back to the car, the sweet and ghastly smell of death all around, Amy comes over. 'There was a little one came squealing under the car when you shot the others. It's over there now.'

Tod picks it up, a little week-old black ball of cuddles. Whack. Whack. We walk back to the car.

The blood and guts don't seem to bother Amy. She usually can't even put on a bandaid without a blindfold and a cigarette, but she's having a ball. It is all a matter of acclimatisation. Of rationalisation.

We pause, next morning, at the gate to Jungalina. We'd been told we'd find Phyllis here, the woman who apparently has the story for Massacre Inlet. A red painted sign tells us it's private property, to keep out. Next to the sign, a bin has overturned, a few green cans spilled out. Next to that, a more official sign threatens us with a thousand dollar fine for entering without a permit. We drive through and see Tolby sitting under a rough shelter by the side of the road. Alone, still in a spaced-out state, but better than he looked the other day. When we were out hunting, Tod told us that Tolby's voice was so croaky because he used to drink brake fluid and spray Mortein down his throat for some sort of high. Burnt out his vocal chords.

A few hundred metres through burnt-out country we come to two tin sheds. A dog is chasing a cat up a tree. Two men and two women are sitting around. A kid is wearing US-flag boxing gloves.

We ask about Phyllis and another woman comes over to us. She extends her hand over the barbed wire fence and we shake limply. We explain what we're doing.

THE ROAD TO MOUNT BUGGERY

'Language,' she says.

We presume she means she can't understand us, so we say it again more slowly.

She answers. 'I don't go down Massacre land. White man. This our country Jungalina. Haven't been there since I was little girl.'

'Do you know the story? How it got that name?'

'My grandfather he been dead before me.'

She continues on and we can't understand most of it, but we do hear, 'Grandfather . . . Chinese man . . . white man . . . one gun one spear.'

It sounds enigmatic and significant, but we leave none the wiser. We thank her and drive out, suspicious that maybe Warwick the barman was right. It's not our story.

CHAPTER 15

A SUCCESSION *of* TAPERING SPIRES

Burketown, Queensland

AMY Somewhere east of Hell's Gate and before Burketown, Mark does a count of VB cans littering the road. Over one random kilometre, he counts 125 on the left side only. Theoretically, that adds up to 25,000 green cans over a hundred kilometres. Strangely, there is virtually no other litter, nor any other brand of beer.

As we approach Burketown, the land suddenly opens up to vast grassy plains full of healthy, fat Brahman cattle. This was what our mate Stokes called the Plains of Promise, and you can see how he could have believed it.

In August 1841, some three and a half years after he discovered the Fitzroy and Victoria rivers, Stokes was in the Gulf of Carpentaria still looking for that magical river to the heart of the country. In the meantime, he'd named Port Darwin as an 'opportunity of convincing an old shipmate and friend, that he still lived in our memory'.

Stokes had been speared through the shoulder by Aborigines at what he called Treachery Bay (south-east of Darwin), but he was chipper as ever as he and his crew followed a new inlet southwards. They found the water to be fresh and were sure they were onto something important, so Stokes named it the Albert River, for Queen Victoria's 'noble consort'. And as the river continued wide and deep, Stokes began congratulating himself on finally finding a waterway to the Centre: 'To this part of the Albert that had given rise to such expectations we gave the name of Hope Reach.' The extensive plains stretching away from either bank he called Plains of Promise.

Actually, he thought the plains rather dreary, and longed for some important mountain to discover. Even so, his imagination ran wild with the prospects for 'future prosperity', which he was sure would justify the name he had bestowed. He gazed around 'and could not refrain from breathing a prayer that ere long the now level horizon would be broken by a succession of tapering spires rising from the many Christian hamlets that must ultimately stud this country.'

Wrong.

The sign pronounces 'BURKETOWN – Barramundi Capital of Australia'. It is flat and bare and muted, like there used to be more to the place than all these demountable houses. It has a population of around 230. Brolgas walk the wide streets. The backyard of the post office is full of squawking chooks, geese and wallabies. There's a rodeo ground and a wharf, but the centre of town is elusive. Must be the hotel: 'Australia's Greatest Outback Pub'.

No sign of any church, sorry Stokesy.

We wander into the pub to watch Sydney get flogged by Richmond in Aussie Rules until we strike up a conversation with a couple of locals.

'What should we do while we're here?' Mark asks.

'Fish, or drink,' says one of them. 'Or fish *and* drink.'

'You *have* to drink when you're fishing,' drawls the other, whose eyelids are dangerously droopy. 'It's compulsory, actually. If they catch you fishing without a carton they fine you. Other places it's illegal but here they bust you if ya don't.'

The footy ends and we go and check in at the caravan park. Out the front is a pond with a dummy sitting in a tinny, drinking beer, dangling a fishing line. Okay, we get it. Fishing and drinking.

'Watch out for the brolga,' warns the four-year-old playing nearby. 'It'll poke your eye out.' The brolga approaches and its beak does look sharp as we settle into our camp chairs to read the loose-leaf folder containing Burketown's history, lent to us by the woman who owns the van park. She also wins a place in our hearts by giving us some frozen barra fillets.

 Stokes's Plains of Promise was renamed the Province of Albert in 1853. Eleven years later, a port was established at 'Burkesland', named for Robert O'Hara Burke who hit saltwater 130 kilometres east of here. Slowly, it grew into a tent settlement where grog and rations were plentiful, everyone carried a pistol and dreams of limitless Asian cattle markets were rampant. By 1867, more than 1600 people had moved to the area.

Within a year, however, Burketown was deserted. 'Yellow Jack' fever had arrived on the *Margaret and Mary* from Batavia. The explorer William Landsborough led some of the 550 survivors to Sweers Island in the Gulf, where they stayed for eighteen months. Others simply left. The romance of those limitless markets had died. Surplus stock and bankruptcy forced men off their runs.

By 1870, the little town had gently rustled into life again. There was a policeman and a bank. A meatworks was up and running. When all was humming along, a big wet wiped out stock, and the Fever raged again. A mass grave was dug for the 150 victims, and the survivors were again evacuated to Sweers Island. This time the port wasn't re-established until 1875, but over the following decade, Burketown managed to get back on its feet.

By 1886, the town boasted four pubs, a telegraph office and a Chinese market garden. In January the following year, a furious cyclone hit. The wind and tide pushed a surge of water over the Plains of Promise, thirty kilometres from the nominal coast, sweeping away two of the hotels and wiping all the humpies and shacks off the face of the earth. By the time the water receded eleven hours later, ninety-eight per cent of the town was gone and seven people were dead.

Burketown's agonising birth wasn't exactly the dreamy tide of civilisation Stokes imagined. The early 1900s marked a better start for the town, but devastating wets and cyclones still punctuate its recent history.

AMY ▶ Sitting here in the caravan park reading the last of the timeline, we're happy to see – for Stokes's sake at least – that a church was finally opened in Burketown in 1979. For the life of us, we can't find it, though, so we wander into the Burke Shire Council to ask if it's still around.

'Yeah, I can show you,' the woman behind the counter, Sandy, says, walking us outside. She points behind the basketball court. 'See that building with the green beams behind the court? That's the old church. It's for all denominations.'

It's closed now. The Catholics used to visit annually but people just weren't that interested, so even those meagre house calls dwindled. If there is ever a service, it's held in the Shire hall.

'What about weddings and funerals?' I ask.

'Oh, God, we haven't had a wedding here for a hundred years. Oh, sorry, yes we did, but he got married out at Escott (a nearby station). But usually if we have a service we have to get the padre in. Doug from Doomadgee usually comes out.'

As we walk to the church, a brilliant blue ute revs past, cowboy at the wheel in his ten-gallon hat, a large sticker emblazoned across the back: 'All for rum and rum for all.'

The building looks more like a barn than a church. A thread of bougainvillea climbing one wall does little to hide the neglect. The louvre windows and flyscreens are sticky with cobwebs. The closest thing it has to a spire is a bit of piping sticking up on the roof.

We spend a day fishing on the banks of the Albert, but we don't even get a bite. Must have been using the wrong type of beer. We head east of Burketown to Karumba, where we fill the tank with diesel and ask the attendant which route he would take out of the mish-mash of station tracks and dirt roads to head up the Cape York Peninsula.

'Well, the Mitchell River's been a bit dodgy. But I sent a group up that way last week and I haven't seen them since, so they musta got through. I heard someone got into town yesterday that way.'

We're none too clearer on the state of the roads, but the basic thrust of what he's saying sticks. Take the adventurous route. So rather than following the blacktop east, we churn north-east through bulldust and corrugations, to the coast north of Cairns and perhaps the most famously turbulent name in Australia. A permanent reminder of the tribulation and hope that marked James Cook's Pacific adventure.

CHAPTER 16

HERE BEGUN ALL OUR TROUBLES

Most on board HMS *Endeavour* were in bed when the ship hit coral. Lieutenant James Cook, wrenched from his dreams, was on deck in his drawers by the time a second blow shuddered through his vessel. She began beating violently.

Men ran up on deck to learn they were grounded. Cook, cool and precise, delivered orders. Sails were taken in and boats hoisted out to sound round the ship. Their findings looked bleak.

When the obscure naval lieutenant, thirty-nine-year-old James Cook, set sail from Plymouth in the *Endeavour* in 1768, his destination was Tahiti. His goal: to observe the transit of Venus. However, Cook was also carrying secret orders from the Admiralty instructing him to search the uncharted waters of the south.

And so from Tahiti, Cook – the son of a Yorkshire day-labourer who had begun life with no formal education – circumnavigated the two main islands of New Zealand and headed west. On 19 April 1770 he sighted the east coast of Australia and began charting the land he awkwardly called New South Wales. In his northward course, Cook, ever the diplomat, named major landmarks after his superiors back home, or occasionally noted descriptive names, like Pigeon House Mountain and Mount Warning. But suddenly, north of Cairns, Cook's chart breaks into melodramatic song: Tribulation, Hope, Flattery and Providence.

The objective young lieutenant had discovered passion, quite literally overnight.

The sail had been shortened and the *Endeavour* was sailing north-west. Cook's intention had been to stretch off the coast all night to avoid any rocks. He was puzzled by the lack of swell, but didn't connect it to there being a protective reef seaward. It was high tide on a clear, moonlit night. The leadsman sounded seventeen fathoms, and before he had time to make another cast, crash.

Up on deck, watching the chaos unfold, was a paying customer, young Joseph Banks. While the fashion in London was for men of his standing to take the grand tour of Europe, Banks was alleged to have said, 'Every blockhead does that, my grand tour shall be one around the whole globe.' He had a passion for natural history, and had paid for naturalists, artists, servants and dogs to accompany him.

As Banks struggled to hold his balance on this lonely night, watching Cook fire off orders, the twenty-seven-year-old must have wondered if it had been such a good idea.

Cook realised they had no choice but to lighten the ship's load immediately. Guns, iron, stone ballast, casks, hoops, staves, oil jars and decayed stores were all thrown over in the hope of lifting her off. By 11 am, forty to fifty tonnes had been tossed. It was high tide – their opportunity to heave off. But Cook was stunned to see they were nearly two feet short. They would have to try again at midnight. At least the ship wasn't taking on much water.

So the lightening continued and, as the tide dropped, the sound of the battering waves was replaced by an ominous scraping. She began to take water.

The *Endeavour* had four suction pumps, but one was found to be useless. Every man on board, including Cook and Banks, took fifteen-minute shifts pumping out the water, barely containing the flood.

Banks wrote, 'I entirely gave up the ship and packing up what I thought I might save prepared myself for the worst.'

Cook looked landward and saw two small, low islands, barely sandbanks with a bit of bush. If they couldn't get the *Endeavour* off the reef in one piece, these were his last hope.

At 9 pm, with the tide rising, the ship righted, bringing on a deluge of water that overpowered the three pumps. Cook feared 'immidiate destruction to us as soon as the Ship was afloat'. Despite the risk of sinking, he heaved the *Endeavour* off into deep water at 10.20 pm. The crew, exhausted, pumped for their lives.

By morning, a stuffed sail dragged under the hull had been used to plug the leak. One pump was handling the bilge. 'We were in an instant raised from almost despondency to the greatest hopes,' wrote Banks.

The re-invigorated crew now thought only of repairing the damage and moving on. As they sailed past the two nearby low islands, Cook named them Hope Islands, because 'we were always in hopes of being able to reach these Islands'. He named the reef Endeavour Reef. The point north of Trinity Bay he called Cape Tribulation 'because here begun all our troubles'.

Cape Tribulation, Queensland

AMY Emerging from our dusty route across the peninsula, we hit the east coast and trace it north along the Captain Cook Highway, threading our way through thick, green cane fields. The skinny cane railway runs alongside. The road narrows and coils its way up into the hills. Barefoot hitchhikers wait by the road.

The reception area at PK's Jungle Village is vibrant and chaotic, busy with accents, suntans, bikinis, sarongs, tattoos and piercings. On the beach a guy plays a banjo. In the evening a young Australian surfie serenades his beautiful Nordic girlfriend. This is Cape Tribulation.

For a while the next morning, it looks like our troubles might begin here, too. Mark and I have a domestic, and then while he is up on Frank's roof-rack tying down the spare tyre, Frank rolls straight into the path of another car. Someone forgot to put on the handbrake. It's no Endeavour Reef, but it feels a little ominous. We break camp and head north, just in case.

Up the road, at the end of a rainforest boardwalk, we look out over quandong trees to the Coral Sea and the tip of Cape Tribulation. To our left, pale yellowy-grey sand loops around the bay, below jungle-covered mountains.

We continue north and by late afternoon are driving along the sandy track behind another place with a name courtesy of Cook: Weary Bay.

Having escaped Endeavour Reef, Cook sent two boats ahead in search of a harbour. They rowed in here to check it out but found it wasn't deep enough for a ship. The bay earned its name on account of the crew's fruitless exhaustion.

Armed with handlines and frozen pilchards we follow the sandy track. A four-wheel drive is parked by the road. We turn our heads to see a mop of blonde dreadlocks, and a smooth, tanned bottom in squatting position, the owner doing a wee.

The last of the tide is draining out of a wide, mangrove-lined creek into Weary Bay. By the time we reach the mouth of the inlet, the tide has turned and we toss our lines in from the steep sandbank. The sun sinks pink behind the mangroves. Before long I have caught a whopper flathead, and then another. Dinner and breakfast. Mark gets cranky because I still can't get fish off the hook and he has to spend all his time doing it for me.

It's a short drive the next morning to Cooktown, where Cook found a river to haul the battered *Endeavour* ashore and set up camp. The carpenters and metalsmiths got to work. They stayed six weeks.

We drive straight up Grassy Hill, which Cook and Banks had climbed for its 360-degree view. For them, the prospect was frightening. All around lay 'innumerable sandbanks and shoals'. Impatient as they were to leave, Cook didn't know how the hell they would get out. The only possibility was a gap to the north. 'To return as we came was impossible, the trade wind blew directly in our teeth; most dangerous then our navigation must be among unknown dangers. How soon might we again be reducd to the misfortune we had so lately escapd! Escapd indeed we had not till we were again in open sea.'

There was a further risk in Cook's decision to continue north. He had no proof that there was a strait between Australia and New Guinea. Torres Strait was only a rumour in 1770. Luis Váez de Torres had sailed through in 1606, but the Spanish had kept it to themselves. Cook's map had it marked in, speculatively. But he believed in its existence and was desperate to find it.

Our bakery pies come in brown paper bags with Cook's head printed on them. He is everywhere in Cooktown: Endeavour Farms Trading Post, Endeavour Butchery, Endeavour Cargo Hold, a memorial to Cook, a statue of Cook, Cook's Landing Kiosk, the James Cook Museum. But it is a sign outside the tourist office – Cook's Tours – that grabs us.

We are greeted – 'What ho' – by Geoff Wordsworth. Tall, tanned and lean, he is the pilot/mechanic/cleaner/receptionist/ ship's captain for Marine Air Seaplanes. He quickly mentions, and mentions often, how seaplanes are boats that fly and not planes that float.

Sitting in his cramped office, he recounts his version of Cook's tribulations, pointing to the wall map as he goes. His finger lands on Weary Bay: 'They still had a bit of fuel left for the outboard motor, see, so a few of the blokes went in to check it out, and they came back and said, "Listen Jim, there's good water, GST-free wood, no sales tax, only problem is there's a big sandbank. The boat won't be able to get in".'

We're sold.

It seems somehow incongruous to have a paddle strapped to

one's aeroplane. An anchor, too. Geoff, wearing a huge straw hat skew-whiff, looks ready for a boat trip as he lifts the little plane into the sky. We pass Grassy Hill and then we are at sea, flying low over the Great Barrier Reef Lagoon. The mainland is a mountainous silhouette swathed in soft white haze. Geoff points to Cape Tribulation in the distance. We are tracing Cook's path, backwards.

Approaching low tide, the shallow water over the reef is green. Geoff circles sharks, and swings the little plane from side to side over turtles, manta rays and stingrays sweeping through the sand.

Then Endeavour Reef is in front of us. The occasion feels unexpectedly momentous. He drops the wing. A sharp turn. My stomach lurches and we hang over the left to admire Cook's nemesis.

Geoff points out two round bits of coral jutting slightly above the water. One piece is yellow. This is where Cook hit. 'The six cannons tossed overboard were recovered there, marking the spot of the collision to within a metre. After the cannons were removed a piece of railway line was laid down to ensure the spot would always be marked.'

The brown and yellow shadows of the reef melt into turquoise, then thick, inky blue.

Below us now are two wooded coral cays – Hope Islands. They are tiny. West Hope is flat, a green pancake poured onto the water. East Hope is a fantasy island. It's more like an egg: raised green yolk with a white rim. A small Gilligan's Island. Six yachts are anchored off it.

We touch down on the water fast and smooth, pulling up just short of the East Hope beach. It feels seriously luxurious.

'Oh, yes, we always go to the beach like this,' says Mark.

A couple of men from the yachts watch from the sand as we climb out of the plane into shin-deep water.

The water is warm as we don snorkels and goggles to slide in above the coral, drifting with the current. The silent, vibrant garden sways in time. The purple velvet clam lips suck in quickly. Orange spaghetti coral dances, and tiny fish dart into hidey-holes.

Back up on the crunchy sand we walk around the island. There's a constant swishing noise from the stream of Torresian pigeons flying in from the mainland to roost. Their soft coo-woos crescendo through the afternoon, a baseline for the screeching bats hidden in the thick green yolk. Even stopping for Mark to watch the birds it takes just fifteen minutes to circumnavigate. It's heaven, but if this was Cook's last hope, heaven help him.

Chatting with Geoff, we learn he's also the 'high speed asset' for the local coastguard. Just a few months ago a fishing boat with two men on board went missing.

Geoff went searching up around Cape Flattery, Lizard Island and Rocky Island. The sea was calm. Around Eagle Island, about eight kilometres west of Lizard, he saw something.

'They were standing on the beach waving a big stick like mad.' Geoff was too heavy to land, so he went back to Lizard Island to lighten up. He also picked up a platter of fruit and some bottles of water from the resort there, before flying back. He cruised up to the beach, imagining what horrible privations the stranded men must have gone through. One was clad only in his bright red jocks, the other in board shorts.

'G'day, fellas,' he said, climbing out onto the plane's float, producing the platter. 'Want something to eat?'

'Nah.'

'Want something to drink?'

'Nah.'

It turned out they had been living quite nicely on oysters and coconuts.

Maybe Cook and his crew would have had a chance of survival here.

'That's one of our happy endings,' says Geoff. 'Unfortunately not all of them are like that. A lot of fishermen just disappear and are never seen again. There's one missing right now off Townsville.'

The return flight in the slanting late-afternoon light is warm and golden. From the mainland we trace the Endeavour River as far as the airport. Before landing, Geoff points inland: the old route to the goldfields and another Hell's Gate, where we are headed next.

CHAPTER 17

ONE CAME BACK
REAL DARK *on the*
WORLD

Cooktown, Queensland

AMY ▶ Browsing through the local history section upstairs in the
James Cook Museum, our attention is drawn to the story of the
Palmer River gold rush, from which Cooktown grew. It was the
1870s. Boom time. The population hit 30,000.

One sentence on the wall in particular sparks our interest:
'There were numerous skirmishes with the Aborigines and
Chinese, and the area surrounding Cooktown is studded with
such places as Murdering Gully, Rifle Creek, Cannibal Creek,
Revolver Point and Battle Camp.' There's also a Hell's Gate,
which has much the same story as the one in the Gulf.

Leaving Cooktown, the track west into the Battle Camp Range
roughly follows the diggers' path up into the goldfields. We
figure Battle Camp Station is a good place to start poking
around, but a padlock on the front gate prevents us from driving
in. Intrepid travellers that we are, we push on the fifty-odd

kilometres to the nearest pub to watch the AFL grand final between Essendon and Melbourne.

The mercury is pushing forty and from outside the Quinkan Hotel in Laura we can already hear the frenetic voice of Bruce McAvaney calling the opening minutes of the game.

'Where are you from?' A man at the bar accosts us before we've even come through the door.

'Sydney,' Mark says.

'Bullshit,' the man spits out. 'Victoria! It's the AFL grand final.' As if somehow everyone should be Victorian on grand final day.

A little reluctantly, we join the four men lined up on their bar stools. On the bar in front of them are four brown stubbies in white stubby coolers, next to packets of Winfield blue and red.

The man sitting next to Mark wearing a dirty white cowboy hat turns to smile at us and with horror I see he has a hideous cherry scab covering most of his nose. His left eyelid is purple. I presume he was in a blue, but it turns out he got into his car last night full of booze and wrote it off in a ditch.

Next to him is a middle-aged man with a short brown ponytail, hunched slightly over his beer. He doesn't say much. His friend – the one who accosted us when we walked in – is still talking and swearing and running his own commentary of the game.

'It's a sausage roll!' he cries as a Melbourne player boots a goal. He turns to us. 'Sausage roll – get it?' Not being Victorian, after all, we may have trouble rhyming sausage roll with goal.

He wears his long, grey hair in a ponytail, too. His arms are strong and tattooed. His belly bulges under his T-shirt.

The last man is sitting in the corner. He's small and all except for his protruding black moustache is hidden beneath a ten-gallon hat. The vivacious young barmaid with her pale lion's mane sits very close to him and they whisper.

Grey ponytail introduces himself.

'John,' he says to Mark, before turning to me. 'And what's your name, sweetheart?'

He wanders off, but soon returns to introduce himself. Again.

'Yes, John. We've met.'

Essendon cements its claim on the premiership and John, bored with the game, introduces himself a third time from down the bar. He and his mate Cliff look like extras from *Born on the Fourth of July* and it turns out they are Vietnam vets.

Cliff tells us he came back in 1967 and spent two months in a psychiatric hospital. He's quiet and sincere when he says he didn't cope too well – he lost a two-million dollar business and has had more than one readmission to the psych ward.

John, although he has a certain charisma, is right on the edge. Manic, knocking back beers, darting up and down the bar, fuck this and fuck that, bullshit! Have I introduced myself? It's a sausage roll!! His medication seems to be kicking in.

'Journo!' he yells out to Mark. 'You wanna beer?'

'No thanks, mate,' says Mark for about the third time.

'How about you, journo-ess?'

He goes to pay for his round and hands the barmaid a card.

'Do you want any cash out?' she asks.

'Yeah, give us a thousand dollars,' he says with a sweeping wave, then a wink to the audience.

'How about fifty?' she counters, before looking up, confused. 'It says, "Card Not Accepted".'

'Bullshit!' booms John. 'Try again.'

The rest of us are laughing. We all know he has given her his pension card. TPI. Totally and permanently incapacitated.

Three-quarter time rolls around and the three battle-scarred men grab one for the road and head off together. They're actually *driving* to Cairns.

The publican, a slim, neat man with his own thousand-yard stare and missing the index and middle fingers on his right hand, comes over for a yarn.

'Yeah, I tried to join up for Vietnam,' he says, 'but they wouldn't let me. Said I was too old. It seemed unfair to me. All me mates were going and I wanted to go.'

'Oh well, you probably got lucky in the end, then,' says Mark.

'Why?' he asks, staring through us like the thought had never once entered his head.

'Your mates got out of it all right, then?'

'Nah. One of them came back real dark on the world. Still is. Like he might do himself some harm at any moment.'

We tell him we've come past Battle Camp, and mention the other violent names in the area. One that struck us in particular was Cannibal Creek – not the only placename relating to cannibalism up this way, and the references don't sit comfortably with a lot of indigenous people.

Mark was up this way once before, though, when one of the local elders, George Musgrave, a custodian of the famous Quinkan rock art, told him stories about his grandfather attacking and eating Chinese miners. They preferred the taste of Chinese, George had said with no great fuss.

We ask after George and the publican tells us he isn't about. Instead, he takes us out the back into the dining room. Covering one wall is a painting by well-known local artist Percy Trezise that depicts the scene of an attack at Battle Camp. Hundreds of silhouetted Aborigines armed with spears surround a party of diggers, who are hiding within their makeshift barricade. It is early dawn, the colours all brown and yellow.

A book we'd bought in Cooktown, *River of Gold* by Hector Holthouse, had the story behind this painting. It was November 1873 and the first wave of diggers were making their way from Cooktown to the Palmer River goldfields when a number of Aborigines were shot following some forgotten confrontation.

Fearing retribution, that night the diggers stacked saddles and packs in a circle around the camp. Fires were put out, and the uneasy men took turns to stand watch. At dawn, the Aborigines – an estimated five hundred of whom had been hiding throughout the night – attacked. Like trained soldiers, waves of maybe forty or fifty men, screaming and wielding spears, charged the diggers. From within the barricade the miners fired on each new wave of Aborigines, ripping through their ranks.

It seemed to the diggers that the Aborigines couldn't understand how their comrades were dying. They had maybe five times the number of the diggers and no understanding of guns. After a last-ditch effort to throw their spears from behind bushes, they took off. Some of the miners followed and the slaughter continued.

It was not the first attack at Battle Camp, as the site became known. Indeed, various conflicts between settlers and Aborigines there make it difficult to decide which battle actually inspired its name. And those other names, Murdering Gully, Rifle Creek, Revolver Point, tell much the same story.

CHAPTER 18

For We Were Restored *to* Fresh Life

Iron Range National Park, Queensland

AMY ▶ A soft rain slides down the windscreen and we wind down our windows to inhale the moist air of the rainforest. Trails of vines hang suspended above creeks. Our wheels slip on the muddy track. The rainforest is dark and damp, full of unseen birds making mysterious noises. Hidden riflebirds, palm cocka-toos and wompoo fruit-doves. Mark, whose birdwatching has become obsessive, is like a child before Christmas at the prospect of spotting a cassowary.

We've been driving for days up the Cape York Peninsula from Battle Camp. This morning we finally turned right onto a wickedly corrugated road into this new world of Iron Range – probably the closest thing you can get to New Guinea and still be in Australia. It's oppressive after months of wide-open space.

We camp beneath a huge fig. It's muddy, despite the carpet of large, dead leaves. Everything feels damp and it's dark long before the sun goes down. The birds continue their mysterious noises throughout the night.

Next morning, I desperately need to go to the loo but a car parks right outside our camp, the occupants hanging around doing we don't know what. Eventually, I am so busting to go I don't have any choice but to take the steep track down towards a creek for privacy, leaving Mark to guard me.

It takes ages to dig the hole; the ground is a thick tangle of roots. Finally it's done and I am just finishing up when I hear Mark talking loudly. I start hurrying. It goes quiet and I look up. There is a man standing at the top of the hill looking straight down at me. Oh, shit. I look down, pretending to be invisible, expecting him to politely go away. But when I look up again there are three people looking down. Oh my God. Not since I was eight, when I inadvertently bared my bottom to the swimming class, have I been this humiliated.

The trio finally slips away and I slouch back up, hoping they are gone, unsure whether to laugh, cry or scream.

By the time I get back up the hill, the urge to scream has won: 'You were supposed to guard me,' I shout, tears spilling.

Mark's feeble excuses don't wash.

'Come and have a lie down,' he says.

'I don't need a lie down.'

'Well I do.' And just as he disappears into the tent, the trio returns and I dive for cover, landing on top of him. We start to laugh. Really hard. Of course they were bloody birdwatchers. So desperate to see a cassowary nothing was going to get in their way.

A few hours later, we're driving out to the Lockhart River Aboriginal community when Frank's wheels hit a ridge of mud and we slide. We are hurtling sideways. A shot of adrenaline explodes through me and I'm sure we will roll. I grip the bar in front of me. Brace myself. It takes forever. We skid off the track. Down a ditch, heading straight for the trees to the right. The wheels hit the opposite side of the ditch. Mark corrects left and we are suddenly running back onto the track like nothing ever happened, except my arms are shaking and Mark looks apologetic. Again.

Iron Range National Park takes in part of Restoration Island, just off the coast. Lieutenant William Bligh named the little island when he and his men washed up there following the *Bounty* mutiny. The idea of visiting their tropical salvation is alluring.

At the ranger's station, Claire Blackman tells us a bloke called Dave lives in a humpy on the leasehold side of 'Resto', on the beach where Bligh probably landed. Perfect.

'What's Dave's surname?' Mark asks.

'I dunno . . . Dave from Sydney. We don't ask people's last names up here. I just call him Moses. He can talk the leg off an iron stove.'

That's funny, because when we ask John Hardaker, who runs the Lockhart River airport, about Dave, he says he can talk the bottom out of a cast iron stove.

We have been warned.

We call Dave and our delicate plan to invite ourselves onto his island never even gets a run. His voice is energetic and friendly and he jumps straight in with the offer to pick us up next morning at Portland Roads.

'I've got white hair and a white beard,' he says, in lieu of a carnation in his lapel.

So we head back through the slippery rainforest, north towards Portland Roads, and camp the night at Chili Beach. Coconut palms hang over the beach, which is thick with seaweed, coral and mounds of flotsam. The easterly trade winds have turned the ocean into a raging sea of dirty dishwater that seems to dump every thong ever lost in the Pacific on this beach. We hear a story from one of the locals that a couple of years after the space shuttle blew up, someone here found a boot with NASA written on it.

Next morning we drive into Portland Roads, leaving the dreary weather behind. There are a handful of houses on the slope overlooking the water. It's a picture-book village of fishing trawlers, palms, hibiscus, frangipani and bougainvillea.

Sitting – rather foolishly – under a coconut tree, we see a tinny putting toward us, its only passenger a man with white hair and a white beard. The boat stops a hundred metres offshore and Mark puts the binoculars on him. 'I think he's naked . . . he's putting some shorts on now. I think his pubes are white, too.'

Dave comes into shore and beneath the wild white beard and hair is an even whiter set of teeth and watery blue eyes. He is in his late fifties but his body is lean and deeply tanned.

He collects his mail from a neighbour and tosses some rubbish out before we pile into the boat for the short ride to the island. He's chattering away but it's impossible to hear him over the motor as we bump into the easterly wind.

Soon we nudge onto a sandy beach, leading up to a lawn littered with palm trees. There is an old dinghy on the grass, and seated in it is a blonde dummy wearing nautical stripes.

'That's Miranda,' Dave chuckles. 'You've got to have a good woman on an island.'

It's not yet midday, but Dave goes into his open-plan shack and grabs three bottles of home brew from the fridge. We sit drinking the cloudy beer on the patio, surrounded by giant clam shells and buoys that have washed up over the years. Off to the side is the vegie garden filled with corn, radishes, spinach and pawpaws. And Dave talks.

'Most of the corporate cats I know are still living a life about how many more millions they need before they can do anything. I keep saying, "Well why can't you do it now?" Why does money change your ability to do anything?'

Flipping through his photo albums, we stop at a picture of a middle-aged man; slick suit, slicked hair, thick briefcase, thicker waist.

'Who's that?'

'That's me.' And out pours Dave's story.

David Glasheen was a corporate cat. Private school-educated from a family of lawyers. Life was about business trips, takeovers and martini-drenched lunches, and getting home to the plush Sydney suburb of Church Point too late to tuck his two girls into bed.

Somewhere amidst the adrenaline and indulgence things started to fall apart. It started in the early 1980s when he lost 200,000 dollars attempting to establish a family business in the United States.

Hobbling back to Sydney, a mate showed him what looked like a pirate map on parchment, marking gold deposits in Papua New Guinea. It was like it belonged in a museum but the guy reckoned the gold was fair dinkum. And so he entered the speculative business of goldmining. Gung-ho Glasheen took charge and hired geologists to peg out plots in PNG. Money was easy. They raised a couple of million dollars from investors and set up a company, which they floated on the stock market. Glasheen was chairman.

'It was all going gangbusters. Then the crash arrived, and bang. The bells were ringing and nobody was home. It was just doom and gloom and blood and guts.'

The shares went down from about $1.40 to sixty cents, seller, no buyer. The next buyer was at twenty cents and the share price kept falling.

The bickering started and Glasheen stepped down. His marriage was falling apart. His wife kicked him out.

That's when he met Denise, an African beautician dazed after the break-up of an eighteen-day marriage to an Australian. They started a life together and he changed her name to Denika. It was a new start. 'Denika' suited his passionate, exotic woman way more than a 'Denise Agnes' could. His 'wild creature from Africa' wanted to escape.

I want an island, she told him.

He liked the idea: Adam and Eve leaping around in paradise. He called his real estate agent mate, Bluey, in Queensland, and the couple started island shopping with the little bit of money he had left. The brief was simple: primitive, uncomplicated, surrounded by water.

The name Restoration Island popped up. 'That's it, when can we see it?' When he stepped off the boat to check it out at the end of 1993, 'Resto Dave' was born.

'Most people are bloody packing up and going wheelchair shopping by my stage. But you know, this is what it's about here, you throw away the wheelchair, mate.'

Dave formed a partnership with three other blokes to take up a commercial lease on the island from the head lease company. None of the others seem too interested in living here, he says. They write the cheques and just like the idea of being able to fly their mates to their own tropical island.

They have approval for a sixty-bed concrete resort in the 'airport terminal' manner of design – which doesn't appeal to Dave at all. He wants something more conducive to the Adam and Eve thing. He's had an old girlfriend and her partner draw up alternative plans with bures, a long house and a swimming pool. It's been in the pipeline for so long, though, any development seems way off.

Dave busies himself trying to make decent soil for the garden, getting rid of all the junk left by the previous caretaker and turning the shed on the beach into a nice bar.

In the end, though, he's here alone. Denika moved to Cairns and has been up three or four times, but Dave says she's not really too sure about where things are headed. She got pregnant and they have a two-year-old son, Kye. Dave says the name is Hawaiian for ocean, Japanese for ocean or shell, and a variation of the Swedish word for port.

A few beers later, whirlwind Dave has barely paused to draw breath. Sentences merge and words get dropped as he takes us through his life; his corporate war stories, his grand business ideas for Restoration Island, his philosophies on spirituality, drugs, sexuality and health. Forunately it's all quite entertaining, but we quickly learn that a conversation with Dave is a one-way street. I start out participating with the odd nod, 'Oh yeah', 'Mmm', but soon realise that even these signs of engagement are unnecessary.

Eventually, we leave our perches for a tour of the island. He walks us past the compost heap, the old pig pen. 'The pig's in the freezer. I couldn't kill it. I had to get one of the fishermen to do it.' Up a rough track on the side of the hill, he shows us where he plans to build the bures.

Returning to the shack, Dave takes an enormous painted crayfish out of the freezer for dinner. (He swapped it for some of the pig. Fishermen hate seafood.) He cooks it up over the fire pit, which he stokes with old coconuts. Wood is too valuable a commodity here. He plies us with wine and talks and talks. This island life is oh so enchanting, but we're falling asleep at the table.

Next morning, we wake to see Dave wandering around the kitchen wearing nothing more than a lap-lap. It suits his image well, although it is a little disconcerting when he bends over and his tackle flops out.

It didn't take long to abandon clothes when he first came to the island. Washing them was a waste of time so he made lap-laps out of old Chinese-restaurant napkins. He washes them under the shower.

Some of Dave's partners are coming up in a few days and he's got work to do so we leave him to it. Poking around the book-shelf, we find a copy of Bligh's account of his hellish journey after Fletcher Christian and the Bounty mutineers set him adrift off Tahiti.

Bligh's twenty-three-foot longboat had just seven inches of freeboard after eighteen men were loaded into it and some food and water were tossed aboard. It was 30 April 1789, and while Bligh was aware a fleet of convict ships had sailed for New South Wales two years earlier, he knew nothing of its fate. So sailing to Botany Bay would be risky.

He was familiar with Captain Cook's charts. Cook was his mentor and he knew the way to Timor off the top of his head. Ten years earlier, Bligh had watched from a distance as Cook was slaughtered by Hawaiians. And a few days into this desperate voyage he watched close up as one of his men was clubbed to death by Tongans as the castaways tried to flee a beach.

He was scared as all hell of meeting more natives, so he hooked the longboat into the south-easterly trade wind and he rode it like all those washed-up thongs on Chili Beach. It rained often and the store of twenty-eight gallons of water actually increased during the following weeks, but they were constantly wet, cramped with cold. No-one needed to drink much, anyway. 'That desire, perhaps, being satisfied through the skin.' The strong winds constantly heaped waves over the gunwales, keeping the cold, weak men bailing through sleepless nights.

They had on board 150 pounds (sixty-eight kilograms) of bread and twenty pounds (nine kilograms) of pork. In the evenings, Bligh might issue each man a teaspoon of rum against the cold, from the six quarts (6.8 litres) they had on board. Each day, he would give out one ounce (twenty-eight grams) of sometimes rotten bread – the equivalent of half a slice of wholegrain – and most days, an ounce of pork, which is less than half a rasher of bacon.

After three weeks in the longboat and another night constantly waking from cramps and pains in their bones, he wrote: 'At dawn of day, some of my people seemed half dead: our appearances were horrible; and I could look no way, but I caught the eye of some one in distress.'

As they neared New Holland, some seabirds – boobies – landed on their boat and were quickly grabbed, killed and divided into eighteen equal parts by Bligh, entrails and all. The men's spirits were on the rise as they broke through the as yet unnamed barrier of reefs to calmer waters and the New Holland mainland, thirty days after leaving the ship.

Bligh sighted the Australian coast at Cape Direction, but was scared of the natives on the mainland. The little island nearby was perfect.

It was 30 May. He called it Restoration Island: 'This day being the anniversary of the restoration of King Charles the Second, and the name not being inapplicable to our present situation, for we were restored to fresh life and strength.'

There were no inhabitants on the island, but signs of Aborigines having been there: 'Saw two wigwams. Weather side only covered.'

Bligh set the men to work digging for water, which they found in good supply. He had them gathering oysters. They tried palm tree tops and found the 'part next to the tree good eating'. They mixed it with the oysters and made 'a good Stew for Supper & issued full one and a half pint of it to each Man and everyone found himself vastly better – the general complaints were a great weakness & some few of a dizziness in the head.' They also ate wild berries. The results were racking diarrhoea, 'most having had no evacuation by stool since we left the ship'.

It was a fine day and they slept, rested and shat. In the morning, Bligh 'directed the oystering party to go on for our last good dinner . . . By noon I offered to everyone as much as before. They now began to complain of gathering their food. I therefore prepared for Sailing . . . The little pork I had when we sailed we have found frequently to be stolen & found it so now, but cannot discover the Wretch that did it.' So Bligh 'resolved to put it out of temptation's way' by issuing the last of it for dinner.

'Kind providence protects us wonderfully but it is a most unhappy situation to be in a boat among such discontented people who don't know what to be at or what is best for them.'

Far from restoring the men's peace of mind, the stay on the island seems to have heightened their discontent. The day after leaving, Bligh had to draw his cutlass to put down a minor insurrection. But he proceeded to navigate them through the Torres Strait, only the third European to do so, suffering badly from malnourishment and dehydration. Even when they could see Timor, twelve days after leaving Resto, Bligh still wouldn't let them eat the remaining week's rations. The guys didn't like him. But the forty-four-day, 5800 kilometre journey from Tahiti to Timor without a map remains an extraordinary feat.

Restoration Island, Queensland

AMY ▶ Dave's corporate cat mates think he's lost the plot and keep asking him when he's coming back to the real world. But he's got plans up here. He's always been a big believer in the untapped healing resources of the ocean, which was why the name Restoration Island grabbed him in the first place. Not only would it be a new start for him and Denika, but after having lost four family members to cancer within five weeks of diagnosis, he wants to develop shark cartilage as a treatment for the disease. Save the world and make money. 'They haven't even started to explore what this stuff can do for people.'

His grand plan is for shark cartilage to be added to food, 'like riboflavin'. Dave raised a bit of dough and put a business plan together, but he ran out of money and now the thing's sitting on his shelf gathering dust.

'Restoration Island is the place where we can restore people's life, and spiritualism and sexuality – everything, their sensitivity to everything. Why can't it be this place? It worked for Bligh.' The idea apparently grows on him as we speak.

'I've seen people come here who are either a bit crook or have personal problems or whatever, and it's a powerful area here . . . Kye wasn't a planned arrangement, and Denika reckons that the odds of that happening was amazing. She figured she couldn't have children. So there's something going on here in that area – fertility.'

It all sounds great, but as our stay drags on a second night, Dave's corporate war stories flood the rest of the conversation – apparently still uppermost in his mind.

On our last night, we say our goodnights and tuck ourselves into separate beds. Dave pulls a chair up between us, pours another beer and continues talking in the darkness.

Next morning, we're up early and head around to the rocks to get some oysters for breakfast, like Bligh and his men. But we aren't feeling restored at all. We're exhausted. It's time to get some rest back in the real world.

CHAPTER 19

FINDING NO GOOD
to be DONE THERE

Weipa, Queensland

MARK The drive across to the west coast of the Cape York Peninsula from Iron Range to Weipa is more rugged than expected. There's nothing like river crossings with water over the bonnet to test a vehicle and a relationship. Frank bobs over boulders hidden by the fast waters of the Pascoe River, gurgling and steaming, then roars up the opposite bank to save the day. Then we dance through corrugations, our bodies swaying like awkward people on the edge of a disco floor, all the way to Weipa.

We want to explore the place with Australia's oldest extant European placename, but the importance of that pales in comparison to our appetites after a hard day on the edge of the dance floor. Arriving in town late, we head to the golf club in search of dinner, only to get caught up in bingo. It being Tuesday and all.

Twelve dollars finds us with six different sets of numbers to keep our eyes on. My great fear is that we'll actually win and I'll have to call 'Bingo'. I know Amy won't do it.

The room, lined with honour boards, is full of fat people drinking Diet Coke. Every time the caller says, 'Twenty-two, two little ducks', someone behind us says, 'Quack quack.' Like it's funny even after the sixth time. And every time he calls 'Lisa's legs, eleven', the same person gives a cat call. This is very real. Right down to the two lovely women beside us who are on a roll: 'We only came because we've got a birthday coming up and we want to have a party, so hopefully this will pay for the DJ and alcohol.'

At nine dollars per win, the roll better be a big one.

Every time we get close, I get nervous. Fortunately, someone always beats us to the punch. Then, on the second-last game of the night, we stay stuck one number from victory forever. I'm nervous and excited, fully psyched now to make that call.

There it is: 'Forty-two.' I pause briefly: 'BINGO!' in my most assertive voice.

Amy is nudging me. 'No, it's not, we've got one to go.'

My eyes find the thirty-nine straight away. How could I have missed it? This explains all the Diet Coke. 'Sorry,' I say, waving my arm at the caller, not sure what the procedure is for a false alarm. Of course no-one else has done one all night and they're all staring at us. Smiling.

'That's so embarrassing, I want to die,' says Amy, like I need telling.

The game proceeds for an eternity with no-one winning, and then, 'Thirty-nine'.

'Bingo,' I say meekly.

'Bingo!' says one of the big women with the birthday party. We win $4.50 each.

In about March 1606, Willem Jansz (sometimes referred to as Janszoon and Janssen) was the commander of a small Dutch ship, the *Duyfken*, which landed on the west coast of Cape York. In so doing, he discovered Australia, and if few Australians know this, they can be heartened by the fact he didn't know it either. He thought it was a southern projection of the wild, mysterious land of Nova Guinea.

While it is probable that other Europeans had previously gazed upon Australia, there is no direct evidence for who they were. Jansz is the man. And so overwhelmed was he by his experience at what we now call the Pennefather River, he marked on his chart 'river with the bush'.

He sailed south, and not until he reached what we today know as Albatross Bay at Weipa did he bother to bestow a name. He called it Vliege Bay, or Fly Bay, presumably for all the sandflies. He continued south to a point he marked as 'Cabo Keerweer' – Cape Turn Around.

Matthew Flinders was carrying a copy of Jansz's chart when he did his more definitive survey of the area almost two hundred years later and thanks to him the name Keerweer lives on as the oldest European name in Australia.

No first-hand accounts of the *Duyfken*'s voyage survive, but the agent for the English East India company, Captain John Saris, was keeping an eye on the competition at the time. He talked to the Indian skipper of a Java junk laden with mace and nutmeg who told him that the Dutch boat that went off exploring to 'Nova Ginny' had returned, 'but in sending their men on shore to intreate of Trade, there were nine of them killed by the Heathens, which are man-eaters. So they were constrained to returne, finding no good to be done there.'

The instructions given to Abel Tasman when he went off exploring in 1644 told him the *Duyfken* only found out 'that vast degrees were for the greater part uncultivated, and certain parts inhabited by savage, cruel, black barbarians who slew some of our sailors'. Tasman was told they got no information on trade goods available there, and, running out of provisions were forced to return, 'only registering in their chart the name of Cape Keerweer, the extreme point of the discovered land'.

Weipa, Queensland

MARK By extraordinary coincidence, a *Duyfken* replica vessel built in Fremantle is landing at the Pennefather River the day after our night at the bingo. It turns out to be a big occasion. At the beach there is a large contingent of men in chinos and long-sleeved blue shirts. We bemoan the decline of shorts and long socks as the corporate uniform of the tropics.

The *Duyfken* is out in the bay, maybe a kilometre away, flapping with a generous array of flags and banners. Helicopters buzz around and a group of Aborigines sit in the shade. Half a dozen Aboriginal soldiers in Ozcam and carrying Steyr assault rifles sit quietly off to the side.

One of the helicopters lands and the Queensland premier, Peter Beattie, jumps out wearing his blue shirt and chinos. He beams as he moves through the crowd with his boof head and easy manner, heading straight to the indigenous tent. He clearly makes quite an effort, but one of the old women turns to the woman next to her and asks, 'Who this fella?'

After we've stood in the sun for what seems like forever, a small canoe starts towards shore from the *Duyfken*. There's some blackfellow ceremony business and some whitefellow ceremony business. There is dancing by bare-breasted women and then we see another man in chinos and blue shirt. It's James Henderson, who wrote a book about the *Duyfken*.

According to his book, which we bought back in Broome, the Wik people of this area have maintained an oral history of the *Duyfken* landing at Keerweer. I mention to James that we're going to the Aurukun community to follow it up. Unfortunately, he says, the Yunkaporta brothers who he had spoken to, have died.

'Last year, a fortnight before he died, I rang Francis to see how he was going. "Not much good," he said. "What's the trouble?" "The leg's givin' me lots of pain." "The one the croc bit?" "Yeah, that one." '

That night in Weipa we catch up with some newspaper friends, Anna Rogers from *The Courier Mail* and Cathy Pryor from *The Australian*, in town to cover the *Duyfken*. Coincidentally, Cathy is going to Aurukun tomorrow too, to do a story on Aboriginal health.

Overhearing our conversation, the chatty bar person chips in: 'Aurukun's, like, the murder capital of Australia. There's been something like eight murders out there this year.'

'They had three in a month,' says Cathy, not wanting to directly contradict the woman. 'And the last two were at the wakes for the previous one.'

'Be careful out there, eh,' says the bar person.

Aurukun has a great uniformity of housing. Lolly pink and lolly green are the most popular colours. Of all the Aboriginal towns we've been to, this one seems to have the most people running around in overalls doing council work.

We spend two hours in the council office waiting for someone to tell us who to speak to about Keerweer. Linda, the secretary, whispers to us that Clive, Francis and Annie Yunka-porta all died within ten months of each other from October to June this year, and so the family is still deep in mourning and not quite as settled as they might be. 'That's why Keerweer is closed at the moment.'

She isn't sure that Bruce Yunkaporta will be able to talk to us. He's seventy-five. 'His wife passed away two weeks ago,' she says.

But the mayor, Jacob Wolmby, is part of the other family with connections to that country. We eventually find him driving through town in his Landcruiser – a middle-aged man, neat and handsome, with coiffed grey hair and bare feet.

We explain what we're doing and the mayor says, 'Not me. You got to talk to my uncle, Reverend Silas Wolmby. You have to go to the green house . . . he got the whole story.'

He takes us there but the Reverend isn't home, so we follow Jacob to his aunty, Peggy. We pull up outside a dingy yellow, brick house. A woman with fuzzy white hair and wearing a bright dress is sitting in a plastic chair under a tree. She pulls up some other cracked plastic chairs for us. She's an attractive woman, obviously old. Her tobacco and rollies come out of a black handbag that wouldn't be out of place on the Queen Mum. As she rolls, I notice she has a prosthetic left leg.

'Are your keys in the ignition?' asks Jacob.

'No,' I say, feeling my pockets.

'Good, some of our bright young kids might want to go for a drive.'

They'd have to be bright. It is parked ten metres away, in full view of us and their mayor.

Jacob tells us: 'My great-grandfather his name was Pumpkin. Captain Jansz called him Pumpkin because he couldn't say his real name. He was a big man.'

'A very big man,' adds Peggy, jumping in.

Their version of the story is that their ancestors were happily employed digging a well for the Dutch, until 'they found some women were missing. That's when old Pumpkin changed his mind about them. Someone ran to tell my grandfather, "Our women are missing. White pella, different colour to us he took them. They in that boat now."'

While Jacob is telling me of the ensuing fight, Peggy leans over to Amy conspiratorially: 'Because they were young. They were looking at these ones.' She grabs her breasts and jiggles them.

Jacob resumes: 'Both the *Pera* (a later Dutch vessel) and the *Duyfken* sailed down together. They came ashore in the whale-boat. And Pumpkin planned the ambush. First they burned the whaleboat then they jumped down on the men when they were in the well. They were fighting and spearing.'

'The Dutch had powder guns,' Peggy joins in.

'Muskets,' says Jacob. 'That's why they called it Keerweer because they turned back after that.'

The pair continue filling in detail with verve, like it only happened a couple of years ago. One remembers a bit of the story and gets excited, the other jumps in with more.

Fifteen minutes in, Peggy leans over and says quietly to Amy: 'I'm Peggy Kelinda.' Like it's okay to introduce herself now. They shake hands softly.

'Are you Dutch?' she asks, pointing at Amy's hair, looking confused.

'My mum's from Scotland.'

That seems to satisfy her. 'What about him?'

'He's got family from Ireland.' Sure that was 150 years ago, but that gives me context.

Jacob mentions how both his parents died when he was a young boy, and he was grown up by various aunts and the missionary's wife. 'I was a radical. Used to sabotage the market garden. But I've mellowed now.'

While they give us something of the *Duyfken* story, they make it clear it is not theirs to tell and we must return on Saturday to talk to Uncle Silas, the Reverend.

'What street does he live in?'

'Muttich Street. That's stingray, our language. If you can't find him come and get me. Pikkuw Street. That's crocodile street. Where all the fighting is.

'In my first term as mayor, when the bitumen was going down, the kids at the school came to me and said they'd named all the streets and said they named it Pikkuw Street because that's where all the fighting is. Crocs always fighting – territorial fighting. Now, when the people are fighting, kids can ring the police and say come to the corner of Pikkuw and whatever street.'

We say our goodbyes and drive to the cemetery, past the Clear River Tavern, which looks like a modern resort done out in fashionably muted tones. Easily the flashest Aboriginal drinking establishment we've seen. Its large, covered outdoor area with tables and pool tables is filling up now at 3 pm.

At the cemetery, lines and lines of plain white crosses are covered in thick blankets of plastic flowers. Each row back, the flowers get thinner and dirtier, back through the years. Two at the front with the brightest and thickest wreaths are for two Yunkaporta women buried on the same day two weeks ago.

False Pera Head, Queensland

MARK 'I'm going to shave my legs now,' says Amy, 'but the only way to make it a pleasurable experience is to have a cigarette and a red wine. Do you want one?'

'No thanks,' I grunt. 'I'm growing a beard, remember.' She insists the occasion warrants such spoils since her legs have been free range for more than five months.

She is now leaning over the green washing-up bowl, shaver in her right hand, ciggie in the left. The sun is setting over the Gulf, lighting the red bauxite shelf of rocks behind the beach at False Pera Head – named for the boat that followed the *Duyfken* in 1623.

Our tent is just above the beach on the low bauxite. Even though the sea is only thirty metres away, we are shaded by some sort of pine tree. At low tide, water leaches from the beach, forming a little stream that runs into the sea. I taste the water and it is quite fresh.

When Jansz left this coast behind as worthless, he was not thinking of tourist potential. The Aurukun Council is. There are trucks and tractors seeming to do their best to ruin the place's natural charm. Maybe it'll be nice when it's finished. It costs thirty dollars for a car for a week, plus five dollars per person per night, plus GST. Even without toilets, fifty-five dollars for two nights is worth it.

But after two days in paradise, we return to Aurukun where the Saturday-morning stares of the people in their yards and on the street seem somehow more intense than the ones we'd received on Thursday. We dodge slow dogs in second gear on the way to Muttich Street where Reverend Silas's home stands out like lime green houses do.

We feel the neighbours' eyes on the back of our necks as we approach the door, walking past a cattle dog with its tail between its legs. The house is dark, a bomb shelter. No-one answers our call from the open door and we are leaving when a fine-boned woman in a brilliant lemon-coloured dress approaches from the street.

'Excuse me, are you looking for someone?'

'Reverend Silas Wolmby.'

'I'll get him for you.'

'We called out. There's no-one there.'

'He's a little bit deaf.'

Sure enough, she brings out an old man in a neat straw hat, checked shirt, black trousers and bare feet. His skin is very dark, his hair and trimmed beard very white. He'd been expecting us. He doesn't want to talk here, though. There's good shade in the vacant block behind, so we start to walk around the back with him.

'Don't leave your car here,' warns Silas. 'Thieves.'

'They'll smash the window,' adds the fine-boned woman who has introduced herself as his wife, Rebecca.

We crawl in first gear behind Silas to some tall, spare eucalypts.

'Have you been keeping well?' I ask by way of small talk.

'Good. I haven't drunk for twenty years,' he answers – a man in whose mind drinking and bad health seem entwined.

Silas sits us on the ground. He is straight-backed and square-shouldered. Seventy-two years old. He crosses his legs, formally. Now we are getting the official story. He asks my permission to 'speak in front of the lady'. He won't look at Amy, even when she speaks. She feels invisible. We feel obliged to tell him that Jacob and Peggy haven't told us much at all, in order to protect them from charges of talking out of school.

He begins the story, explaining that this is before Captain Cook, staring off into the far distance, giving the feeling that the story is coming from elsewhere.

'The *Duyfken* anchored halfway down at Cape Keerweer. They really wanted to go past but my people they seen this boat. "What that thing there goin' along the gulf? But, anyway, we got to make a smoke, a signal to find out what that white thing there."

'So the boat turn back and anchored at Cape Keerweer. They had this dinghy with a lot of paddles rowing up. When they got to the beach they had about nine barrels.

'They said to the people, a big mob of my people, they said to them, "Is there any water? Water. Water." They made a sign.

1 6 7

They couldn't speak English so they bin keep making the sign with their hands. Water. water.

'One of the Dutch has grabbed a girl . . . and my grandfather Peter Pumpkin said, "Kill 'im." So my grandfather hit one of them. They killed nine of them. They wanted to go to the boat. They had some sort of machine, I don't know what sort of gun but it had thick behind and it blowed.

'A big mob of them wanted to go to the boat now to kill them, I think, and they had to fire that gun . . . a shotgun or .22 or something like that . . . bang! And knocked them along the beach there, so the *Duyfken* went away from there then. They stayed in peace, my people, but again others came back.'

Silas's story corresponds roughly with a version given to Dr Peter Sutton in 1976 when he lived at Aurukun and learnt the language in order to record a much more detailed version of it for his PhD thesis. He noted that Pumpkin and other people named by his informants were young men in the late 1800s, during the period of lugger contact. This raised the likelihood that if there were elements of the actual *Duyfken* story still circulating, that they had been mingled with elements of more recent history. Certainly he noted that the figure nine probably came from the English merchant, Captain Saris, via the missionaries.

Silas's version holds that the Dutch grabbed only one girl and that was as far as they got, while the Yunkaportas' version as given to James Henderson, is that several girls were taken on board the boat and the Dutch were attacked when next they came ashore.

Silas naturally says his version is the right one. 'The Dutch never take them girl down to the boat, that's another story, that's a lie.'

Silas never tries to hide the 'man-eating' business, though, as alluded to by the Dutch accounts. 'My grandfather, he was a real cannibal you know, he was a leader of the place . . . Very cruel old man that fella, my grandfather . . . It's not only European fella . . . my grandfather used to pick maybe a young lad, like them up there playing, something like that, he go away and take him, he cut him up and he eat him. He's a man-eating old fella. Even big people's flesh he used to eat. He didn't like other tribes too. Very angry, very bad-tempered old grand-father.'

'How long ago did he die?'

'I was only a little boy then. Maybe, them a bit too small,' he motions toward the group of boys who might be nine.

Silas was born at Keerweer. 'I bin little boy when my father brought me here. I'm saying today, now, mate, I want to go down there and die down there. On my own land.'

We ask if Father MacKenzie, a somewhat legendary mission-ary, made him come to Aurukun.

'No, my parents brought me. When I was a little boy. My uncle said, "No, I want the boy here where he can hunt the game for me", but my father, oh look he a tough man too . . . they had a fight and threw spears at each other.'

'Over you coming to school?'

'Yeah, my father said, "I want my son to go to school to learn the English schooling". Because my father bin up working New Guinea way long time. Pearl diving. My father speak pidgin. Them old people they used to speak pidgin.'

'He knew it was important to learn the whitefella ways?'

'Yeah. It's good. I learnt a little bit somewhere and I'm glad that I can speak a little bit of English, but most of the time I speak my mother's language. I speak Wik Ngatharra.'

'When did you become a reverend?'

'I used to drink a lot and I used to fight a lot and I used to chase a lot of woman when I was a young fella. Too much for me. And then one day I got lost. I got lost and I didn't know where. I was that way'. He points south. He was out of his own country, about 130 kilometres south of Keerweer, chasing a bull. His horse was bad. He was gone for about six days with hardly anything to eat or drink, just a bit of bush tucker.

'I said "Lord, look. I'm just about dying. I'm here now nearly for a week. I want you to send me someone

169

tomorrow." ' He stretches the words. 'I was really . . . really . . . tired. I lay down. I can hear this crow. Very close. I said, "Are you going to poke my eyes or what? . . . Ahh," I said, "My Lord you send me a crow instead of a human being." '

Then another two crows flew down, but the first one chased them away. Silas followed that one. When he stopped, the crow flew back to him. He followed the bird right through to the coast. They came to a river. He doesn't know where.

'Lotta crocodile there. But that crow he be crowing other side of the river.' So Silas swam it and still the bird crowed at him.

'What do you want now?' Silas implored.

Then he looked down and there was water at his feet, right on the beach. Fresh water. The bird just flew away.

'I say "Thank you. Goodbye . . . Lord, you sent someone for me. From now on you're going to be my God. You have made everything. You are the Great Creator of the Universe." '

Silas never drank again.

'I bin studying Bible for nearly seven or eight years. In 1983, I was ordained.'

He doesn't remember what year grog came to town, but things have gone downhill since.

'The old folks try to tell them. (But they say:) "We don't want to listen to youse no more." I said, "Okay, keep going, keep making trouble. You'll be goin' to jail again." '

He remembers trying to rebel like that when he was a young fella but his father belted him around and kept him in check.

'Them old people they could tell us. But today – the place is like a Garden of Eden, but it's the people, my people, they're actin' no good . . . The little fellas are alright. The young fellas coming up.'

He is taking a mob of boys back to Keerweer next month. He'll stay as long as they want.

'But the boys say, "No, old fella we want to stay with you. We want you to tell us stories. Long time stories. Dreamtime. Like your father bin tellin." '

The story of Keerweer will no doubt be told, and it will be a proud story of defiance. Whether or not it really does relate to the Dutch or a later invader doesn't matter, because Silas believes that when he's got those boys around him, listening, it is his only chance to turn things around.

CHAPTER 20

THE VERY JAWS *of* DISTRUCTION

Thursday Island, Queensland

AMY ▶ Overlooking the wharf from Aunt Mary's Bakery where we are having coffee and donuts for breakfast, we notice a Cairns barge, the *Malu Warrior*, backed up on the sand. There are men hurrying in all directions. The old guy unpacking soft drinks in front of us points out her missing right propeller. 'Hit a reef a couple of days ago.'

At first glance, Thursday Island, crowning the tip of Cape York Peninsula, looks very much like any other small country town but for the women fishing off the end of the wharf with fuzzy hair and colourful tent dresses.

This is where James Cook's Barrier Reef adventures came to an end.

The passage north from Cooktown was, as Cook had suspected, rough going. In an effort to avoid a repeat of his Endeavour Reef tribulations, he tried hugging the coast. Threading the *Endeavour* through the intricate web of shoals, Cook judged himself 'to be clear of all danger, having as we thought a clear open sea before us'. His relief, however, was premature. Looking back he would christen the lofty promontory on the mainland, past which they were then sailing, Cape Flattery; for he had flattered himself that all was well.

Cook wanted to stick to his orders and keep mapping the coast, but reefs blocked his path north and he was running out of time; the ship now carried just three months' provisions. He decided to leave the coast, and eventually found a narrow channel out of the reef to a deep sea rolling in from the south-east.

'Satisfaction was clearly painted in every man's face,' wrote Banks.

But Cook only stayed outside the reef two days. Fearful of overshooting the passage he thought existed between Australia and New Guinea, he sailed west and re-entered the labyrinth.

Seeing breakers both north and south, and with fickle winds, he knew they were in trouble. He had few options now, though, and pushed anxiously through the night towards the reef. At 4 am surf was roaring, fear engulfing.

By the dead calm of dawn, they could see the breaking waves just ahead, but where they were was still too deep to anchor. Cook had 'nothing but Providence and the small Assistance of our boats' to rely on. The boats had been sent out in an attempt to tow the ship around the breakers. 'The same Sea that washed the sides of the Ship rose in a breaker prodigiously high the very next time it did rise so that between us and distruction was only a dismal Vally the breadth of one wave.'

Just when all hope was gone, a gentle breeze sprung up. Only a puff. But combined with the boats' towing, it was enough to move the *Endeavour* away from the reef, and in less than ten minutes they were in calm water. However, Cook still needed to find a way through the reef.

A small opening, narrow and dangerous, was his only escape from 'the very jaws of distruction'. It was do or die. The *Endeavour* churned through the gap. Cook had triumphed over the reef, and named the opening Providential Channel.

The *Endeavour* continued her course north along the shore, and Cook took great pleasure in reaching Torres Strait. He had been right. It did exist. On his chart, stretching over all those reefs north of Cape Tribulation, Cook wrote 'LABYRINTH'.

Thursday Island, Queensland

AMY Captain John Foley, meticulous with his dark, thinning hair slicked back and his formal brown-shorts-and-long-socks ensemble, boards the pilot boat from the Thursday Island wharf, and we follow. Also on board is Matt, at the wheel, and Marsing, who is crewing. Inside, four seats are perched high atop a con-certina suspension base like the oversized front forks of a trail bike. They rise and fall slightly as we head out onto the choppy sea.

Captain Foley would have been a handy man for Cook to have had on the *Endeavour*. He is a reef pilot based on Thursday Island and has been running boats through the labyrinthine area since the early 1960s. This afternoon, the pilot boat is dropping him out near Goods Island to board a Chinese container ship making its maiden voyage. Once on board, he won't physically take control of the ship, but the container ship's captain will hand over navigation. Foley will direct the helmsman through the intricate Inner Route of the Great Barrier Reef as far south as Cairns. We have been invited to watch him board the ship – an adventure in itself – before it enters the Reef.

Cook certainly isn't the only one to have taken a battering from the Great Barrier Reef. It is literally littered with wrecks, Wreck Bay, Wreck Island, Wreck Reef. The outer reef alone has notched up over 500 shipwrecks.

New South Wales Governor King first suggested the use of pilots to assist ships through the maze in 1805. However it wasn't until October 1991 that compulsory pilotage was proclaimed for the Inner Route between Cape York and Cairns for all vessels over seventy metres.

Sensitive environmental issues also affect the Great Barrier Reef's Inner Route between the coast and the outer reef. Ships bring the threat of oil spills and pollution to the national treasure. But Foley argues there is no practical alternative: 'If a tanker breaks down outside the reef it's too deep to put an anchor down, you just drift. The nearest salvage tanker's Brisbane.' If a ship breaks down or runs aground inside the reef, however, it is accessible. Even were a ship to run aground on the mainland, Foley says, it would be possible to protect the area. The wind and current would drive anything onto shore, rather than back up onto the Reef. Still, 'you've got to be very careful – they're treacherous waters'.

Churning along towards Goods Island we pass Waiwea Island on our right, a low mound rising out of the water known locally as Honeymoon Island. During World War II, newly married soldiers and nurses on Thursday Island went there for privacy.

Foley is now wearing coarse cotton gloves and a life vest with a light attached. Mark asks if he has ever needed the life vest.

'No, not me. It's usually worst boarding a vessel because you don't know the state the ladder's in. Some of them are shocking. You get to the top to find it's only held on by a sailor with his foot on it.' With the talk of all the Reef's dangers, the difficulties of simply boarding the enormous ship from the dwarfed speck of a pilot boat hadn't even occurred to me.

'This boat today should be all right because it is its maiden voyage. Only one pilot has been killed in all the time I've been with the service. And, strangely, that was disembarking. The ladder broke and came down on top of him. He was dead before he hit the water.'

The new Chinese ship appears in the distance with its brightly coloured containers stacked high like building blocks.

But also looming on our right, and heading towards the Chinese boat, is a bauxite ship, the *Endeavour River*, doing the run to Weipa. It seems to be worrying Matt and Foley, but the reasons aren't immediately clear to us. Matt steers the pilot boat around the stern of the container ship, which has been instructed to sit on six knots.

Marsing moves to the deck of the tiny pilot boat. Way above, smiling dark Chinese faces hang over the rail of the container ship. They lower a rope ladder with thick wooden rungs for Foley to climb. But we are being tossed about, and the ladder is flinging wildly. White water boiling up from the side of the ship is soaking Marsing who is attached to the pilot boat by a safety harness. Just one slip would see him crushed between the two vessels.

It takes ages for him to give Foley the all clear to go out on deck to board the ship. We wonder what it must be like on a dark rough night.

'This is a bad one,' yells Matt, who is steering the launch right in order to nestle its padded gunwales into the towering grey hull beside us. Normally, Matt explains, the ship would steer gently left in front of the pilot boat, providing perfectly flat water. With the bauxite ship approaching from the left, though, that isn't an option.

Foley eventually scuttles up the rope to board the container ship, his mild-mannered appearance incongruous with this feat of derring-do. Marsing then has to battle for another five minutes to attach Foley's two suitcases to a thin line the crew has lowered.

As we pull away, we see Foley, his long white socks flashing in the distance, striding urgently towards the bridge, escorted by a seaman. And as our suspension seats cop a full workout heading into the easterly trade wind, Matt radios base to tell them Foley is on board and due in Cairns in twenty-eight hours.

Mark and I won't be far behind.

Seisia, Queensland

MARK Poor old Frank, who complained loudly all the way up Cape York Peninsula, is hoisted onto the deck of the MV *Trinity Bay* for the easy way back to Cairns. We check into our small cabin for a forty-eight-hour cruise. It certainly isn't the *Oriana*, but after bouncing around the Gulf and up the Cape it feels like the *QEII*.

We are standing next to the bridge watching the last minutes of sunlight bathing what we think is Possession Island, where

Cook claimed 'New South Wales' for Britain. There is a Japanese guy, silver mane and dark tan, beside us. His name is Zen. Drew, the youngish captain of the *Trinity Bay*, comes out and says something to Zen about the red yacht sitting high and dry on the deck forward of Frank. We realise the yacht is Zen's and that he's come a gutser in it.

I ask Zen where his yacht came to grief.

'Escape River,' he says. We don't quite believe him.

Captain Drew runs into the bridge to grab a chart. He seems keen to know the grisly nautical details.

'Was it there, at Sharp Point?'

'No, there,' says Zen, pointing deeper into the river mouth with a long, neat pinkie nail. 'It was the spring tide, very fast. Eight metre, eight metre, five metre, eight metre, one metre, bung.'

Drew laughs. 'Beautiful in there, isn't it.'

Drew goes back to the bridge to steer the ship and I comment on the name of the yacht, *Zen*, scrawled in cursive down its side.

'I am a Zen Buddhist. I am practically a monk. I spent seventeen years studying Zen meditation techniques.'

He says he has been at sea five years. His boat is so small, he can't take much water. When he arrived in Canada after crossing the Pacific, the people at the marina asked him how long since he showered. 'Fifty-two days.' They scattered.

He went down the west coast slowly over the next year or two. Then tramped his way across the Pacific, arriving in Bundaberg, I think he said three years ago, and has just been hanging around ever since.

Zen seems conversant with Phillip Parker King's original escape at Escape River. King (of Disaster Bay fame and also the son of Governor King) ran aground in the *Mermaid* while investigating the inlet behind Bligh's Turtle Head Island. The circumstances of his grounding were almost identical to Zen's.

Zen was doing six knots when he got there. As he said, the bottom went quickly from eight metres to one metre. He hit it hard. Was thrown from the cockpit into the back of the cabin, hurting his knee and ribs. The boat cracked all the way around the keel, but stayed afloat. He had to wrestle the limping, leaking boat forty-five nautical miles back to Thursday Island.

We had tried to get to Escape River just before we reached Cape York. (It was also the spot where the explorer Kennedy was fatally speared and his guide Jackey Jackey began a long escape to rescue.) But after thrashing our way fifty-six kilometres in four hours, we came out on the coast and realised we'd read the map wrong and it was a few kilometres north of us. The bush was so thick we had to accept we weren't going to get there.

When we first boarded the *Trinity Bay*, all the oldies on board lined their plastic seats up along the right-hand side of the deck to watch the jagged mountains drift by. Shortly after Restoration Island and Cape Direction – where Bligh lined up his approach to the reef – the hills disappear over the horizon. The oldies move their chairs to the left, as the white breakers of the Outer Reef take the spotlight.

The ship passes Cape Flattery during the night and glides by Cape Tribulation at the crack of dawn. A couple of whales swim alongside, giving a grand show to the few passengers up early enough. Up on the bridge, Drew sits watching. He still gets a kick out of seeing that stuff. It's just good to know they're out there.

The reefs scroll by on a computer screen as the boat moves southwards. Two black radar screens blip away on the opposite bench. Despite the high-tech gear, there still needs to be a human on watch at all times.

'Do you have any sort of warning system if you're about to hit a reef?'

'Nah,' he says, dismissively. 'Sonar only goes out directly beneath the boat, usually under the wheelhouse. See that?' he says, pointing to the paper chart. 'The depth goes from thirty-six metres to one metre. By the time you had the warning, the bow would already be on the rocks.'

Cairns, Queensland

AMY We roll out the Map of Misery, a little grubby and tattered, on our friend Anna's dining table. We have been on the road six months, the first half of our journey now a raggedy, satisfying line, 24,300 kilometres long, marked in blue highlighter across the centre of the continent and back again along the top.

After twenty-six weeks we, too, are a bit raggedy. Mark's grown a bushy red tangle of a beard and looks like a bush-ranger.

I haven't washed my hair since the first weeks of the trip. I've come close a few times, but Mark has always talked me out of it, in the name of science. I had a theory that if I deprived my hair of shampoo it would eventually learn to look after itself. It was based on the fact that shampoo doesn't exist in the natural order, no matter how much lavender and passionflower extract they might put in the stuff for natural body and bounce. What better time to test the theory?

I've rinsed and combed, just tossed away the shampoo.

We've watched my hair go through some bizarre changes: the inevitable but thankfully brief limp phase, followed by the heartening soft-and-curly phase. ('See, I was right!' I claimed. 'Mmmm. Feels like lanolin,' Mark agreed.) But then came water-resistance, the bird's nest and now something that could be a forerunner to the dreadlock. It reminds me of the low-rent wigs we used to have in our dress-up box when we were kids. Recalcitrant, clumpy and itchy.

Having observed other women in the loos of caravan parks, I've concluded that I am completely alone – and maybe a bit weird – in this hypothesis. Indeed, hairdryers and bulging vanity cases seem to be de rigueur. And although I haven't spied any yet, I'm suspicious that there is some heavy hot-roller action going on inside some of those campervans. It's all a bit intimidating when I creep in with just my matted hair and a bar of soap.

I've now accepted that either my theory was misguided, or

you need a lot longer than six months to see it through. I don't have the stamina, although Mark is still in favour of science. Fine for him, he doesn't have to wear this horrible mop.

This all becomes relevant now, because the Map of Misery is rather barren south of Cairns. The second half of our trip will take us through the southern states, but for the next two weeks, we have the Sydney Olympics in our sights. ABC radio is gripped with Olympic fever and we want to be too. So we charge down the highway to Sydney, still debating the hair-washing, and are pleasantly surprised to see people lining the streets to wave us home with little Olympic flags.

We crash at my brother Michael's house for the fortnight and fling ourselves into the patriotic festivities. The city looks pretty and clean. So many glamorous people. I throw in the towel and crack open the shampoo. Nevertheless, with all our clothes in storage, we feel a tad provincial.

I'm nearly laughed out of town when I say 'city folk'. An appalled friend orders me to the beautician ('I can't believe you haven't plucked your eyebrows!'), and we are rejected by a trendy new city bar. 'Too casual,' according to the bouncer.

I translate that as, 'You must be joking if you think we'd let those skuzzy old jeans and sandals in.' But Mark thinks it means: 'No bearded yokels in here, mate.' Either way, it's time to get back to the Map. Our plan is to zoom straight out of New South Wales, along the Murray River into South Australia and to a place called New Era.

CHAPTER 21

OBEDIENT *and* RESPECTFUL *at* ALL TIMES

Adelaide, in the winter of 1893, was trudging through a drawn-out depression. The colony's rural economy had been torn apart by drought. Banks were collapsing. Unemployment was high and strike action rife. Men camped out in the old exhibition grounds and Botanic Park. They queued on the bank of the Torrens for rations of bread and meat.

On 8 August that year, a peculiar Bill was introduced to the South Australian parliament which set out to address the problem. It proposed unprecedented government support for communal living. Under the Bill, the state would set aside land and loan money to groups of twenty or more people wishing to set up a communal Association.

The idea wasn't entirely out of left field. Bristol-born journalist William Lane, who had moved to Australia and become influential in the labour movement, had been trying for years to convince Australians they could find earthly paradise in communal living. His Utopian plans had met with such resistance that in July 1893 he sailed for Paraguay with his followers to establish the New Australia commune.

When the South Australian Bill was introduced to parliament the following month, it too met with great resistance. 'Hideous!' the critics cried. It was communistic control over people, completely antagonistic to human nature. It would never work. It opened the door to slavery and corruption and deadbeats; failures who would evermore rely on state aid.

In delivering the second reading of the Bill in the Legislative Council, though, the Chief Secretary quelled the opposition by pointing out that the Bill could always be repealed. And so, daringly, it was passed.

The jobless loved the idea. In January 1894, just days after the second boat of Utopians had sailed out of Port Adelaide bound for Paraguay, a large crowd of unemployed gathered in Adelaide to get the local plan moving. They elected seven men to lay the groundwork for the new settlements. The idea was share and share alike. Mateship. No-one need buy land, no-one owned produce, nor would they want an income. Each settlement would be locally governed by an elected Board that controlled almost everything.

Villagers, as the residents were called, could still own personal effects provided that they could not be used for production or trade. Setting the tone, the Rules expressly forbade Asians, or for that matter anyone who didn't speak English. Alcohol was contraband and 'no man or woman shall live together except in lawful marriage'. Holidays would be allowed – two weeks a year – but the Board would decide when they could be taken. As for authority: 'Every member shall be obedient and respectful to the Trustees at all times'.

Despite some of the more tyrannical rules, within a month of the Bill becoming law, the first Village Settlements at Lyrup and Mount Remarkable (a lofty peak named by Edward Eyre) had been formed. Over the next eleven months, thirteen more were established, all but two along the Murray.

The optimism with which Villagers arrived by paddle

steamer, armed with little more than a few chooks and sheets of iron, to carve a life out of the mallee, was summed up in the naming of one of the new settlements. On 25 April 1894, twenty-two families set up camp on 2095 acres (about 850 hectares) in a narrow valley and called it New Era.

Cadell, South Australia

AMY ▶ We can't find New Era in our atlas, but we do know it's in the vicinity of a little town called Cadell. So we've taken a punt, hoping we'll stumble upon it.

On the car ferry crossing the Murray River to Cadell, Kevin, the ferry operator, knows something of New Era. He says the name is only vague now, and points us towards a rise on the other side of town.

We have traced the wide brown river out of New South Wales – after a four-day stop in Wagga Wagga waiting for parts for Frank – briefly through Victoria and into South Australia. Through vineyards and grey-green scrub to Cadell, north-east of Adelaide, just before the Murray turns south to the sea.

Cadell is small and neat. Brick and limestone cottages. Perfect rows of fruit trees and tidy lines of grapevines. We drive through it, past the Corrective Services Training Centre and top the rise we suppose from Kevin's directions must herald New Era. Pulling up by a terracotta-coloured ruin, a plaque reveals it: 'NEW ERA 1894–1994. This is the site of the first irrigated fruit growing area settled in the Hundred of Cadell.' The floor inside is overgrown with dry weeds.

Across the road, another sign: 'New Era. No Fresh Fruit'.

We wander down a driveway into a yard filled with vines, fruit trees and chickens. A door adorned with hand-painted fruit encourages: 'Please enter New Era fruit'. We're half hoping the current residents have inherited something of the communal philosophy. At the very least some ageing hippies to link with the past and counter New Era's gurgle towards oblivion. But there's no-one about, just a homegrown fruit and veg shop based on an honour system. We grab a butternut pumpkin and a bag of dried pears and put $2.60 down the slot.

At the main house, a softly spoken young woman answers the door and tells us that her husband knows a bit about the old New Era, but he won't be back until late this afternoon. In the meantime, we go in search of a campsite. We find a nature reserve full of birds and pitch the tent by a billabong. My sister Jo has joined us on the road for a few weeks' holiday, and with a storm brewing, we leave her to defend the tent and cook the dinner while we return to New Era.

We find Andrew Barty, Robyn Martin and their six-month-old son Matthew in the garden with the dogs, chooks and geese.

Inside, Andrew has laid out all his books and photos of New Era on the dining table. Andrew and Robyn moved here a couple of years ago. Previously, they were on about four hectares at Loxton. It wasn't enough to be viable. Andrew drove trucks and Robyn packed oranges to pay the bills.

'We seen the For Sale sign in the local newspaper, and one rainy day we thought we'd go for a drive and have a look, nothing else to do. Found the place and thought, this'd be nice.' At about forty-five hectares, their mixed fruit farm is only a fraction of the original New Era, but they inherited the historic ruins and the name.

Since moving here, Andrew has collected whatever he could find relating to New Era: books, documents, old photographs from the local museum. The black and white photos show the original pump, the paddle steamers, irrigation channels, tin and canvas shacks, and the dugouts used to cope with the searing summer heat. It gets damn hot here, he says, but the heat was the least of the commune's worries.

The Villagers' most daunting task was to clear the land, made especially difficult by the size of the box trees covering it. Most of the people were tradesmen or labourers and had little or no knowledge of agriculture. They did, however, have the will, and they worked hard. By mid August they had cleared about fifty-six

Amy atop Mount Hopeless, South Australia. Explorer Edward John Eyre thought the view 'would have damped the ardour of the most enthusiastic'.

Amy in the shallows of Lake Eyre, South Australia.

Paradise found in a paddock, South Australia.

Miner Jack Stanley's grave on the outskirts of Coober Pedy, South Australia. His home became known as Deadman's Dugout.

Peak hour on the Gunbarrel Highway, Western Australia.

The Purnululu mob pile into a ute to visit their abandoned outstation, Kawarre, in the Bungle Bungles, Western Australia.

Shirley Drill (left), head of the
Purnululu mob, and Tanba Banks
(below), with her son Peter at
their camp near Blue Hole, have
overlapping Native Title claims
in the Bungle Bungles, Western
Australia.

hectares and planted twelve hectares with crops, one hectare with vegetables and 400 fruit trees. Two kilometres of posts, for which nearly every hole had to be blasted in solid rock, was ready for wire netting, and they had built a twelve-metre wharf and a store.

It was a good season. Their first crops were a success. New Era was well positioned to take advantage of the fertile soil silted up over thousands of years in the lower part of the valley. There was plenty of rain that year and they ate well. There were fish and rabbits. Whatever else they needed they bought in Morgan with the government money.

A year later, it had all gone pear-shaped. Rain didn't come, and their crops were virtually worthless. What they did grow, the rabbits got first. Their sheep, struggling to find feed, wandered off and got lost in the mallee scrub or were taken by dingoes.

More fundamental problems were also emerging. Apart from erratic leadership, the Rules weren't turning out to be as con-ducive to earthly paradise as had been hoped. Insubordination, disobedience, even leaving the Village for more than two days without permission, were all grounds for expulsion.

Sitting at Andrew and Robyn's dining table, we read in David Mack's history of the Village Settlements a swag of outlandish excuses for expulsion. One Villager was all set to go on his approved holiday when, out of the blue, the Board postponed it for a few days. The Villager headed off anyway. Upon his return, he was charged with malingering and expelled. Another man was fined for killing a sheep given to him by a relative. He had brought it to the village as meat for his family but was told it therefore belonged to the Association. You certainly couldn't catch fish or grow vegies in your spare time and expect to eat them. It all belonged to the Association. Perhaps most unfair, though, was the situation in which the teachers found them-selves. They weren't even Village members, yet were forced to hand over their Government pay to the communal fund.

The settlement had grown to twenty-seven families, but by September 1895 the numbers started to fall. Some moved back to Adelaide, some on to other settlements.

'There was a lot of dissidence toward the end,' Andrew says. 'The single men got enough for themselves but the married men took enough for their families. It only lasted two years.'

The biggest problem at New Era, though, was the water pump. The huge old steam pumps were too heavy to adjust to varying water levels.

'They came here on a high-river year and set all their pumps up,' Andrew explains. 'The following year was a low river, and of course the pump couldn't suck that far up the hill, so that's the end of it.

'All the money came from the Government to set the place up, and they had to pay that back. Because they couldn't grow the crops, they couldn't pay back the Government. So the Government foreclosed on them.'

New Era was abandoned in March 1896, one of the first settlements to fold. After that, the property was leased to various people who tried to make it pay. All failed. Only the New Era Fruit Growing Company had a minor success from 1900 to 1921.

Andrew and Robyn, with baby Matthew perched on her hip, lead us outside for a wander. Just out the back are a couple of lovely old buildings. The couple isn't sure if they date right back to the first settlement, but they were certainly built in the early days. The grander of the two is made of mud brick. Inside, it has fantastic high pressed-tin ceilings. You can't help thinking that if they'd been within earshot of Sydney or Melbourne, they'd be tea houses or craft shops. But here in South Australia they're just another ruin. The walls are starting to crumble away and it's up to Andrew and Robyn to do their best to preserve them.

'It'd take a bit of money,' Mark says.

'A lot of time,' says Andrew, 'and we haven't got much of that.'

As we're saying our goodbyes back at the house, Andrew says, 'New Era may have been a complete failure at the time, but it proved that fruit could be grown in the area. They were the fore-bears to the Riverland.'

We return to our camp to find poor Jo battling with dinner in a gale that has sprung up. She lost a bout with the sail of tarp we had erected, after the pegs were wrenched from the ground creating a violent, flapping mess.

In the end she had no choice but to pull the whole lot down, leaving us to spend a blowy old night in the wind as we decide where tomorrow will take us.

The name that catches our eye is an antidote to the spirit of New Era. Next morning we find ourselves searching for World's End.

An hour's drive from New Era, near the town of Burra, we turn off onto a quiet country road and come to a couple of ruins in a paddock. We presume one of them must have been the World's End Creek Post Office.

The name was taken from the World's End Run, a station held by a D. McDonald. And it's unlikely he was joking when he named it. In 1865, South Australian surveyor G.W. Goyder had drawn a line through the colony, separating agricultural land from the more marginal country – Goyder's Line. McDonald's run lay outside Goyder's Line. As far as he was concerned, it seems, it was the end of the line.

Hard to imagine now, though. With all the rain this year, the paddocks are lush and green, rolling up to a series of velvety hills. The broken-down building is riddled with bullet holes and reeks of sheep poo, but it's hardly the end of the world. There's mobile phone coverage.

CHAPTER 22

A VIRGIN SACRIFICE

Elliston, South Australia

MARK It is with some trepidation that we drive into Elliston on the west coast of Eyre Peninsula. During the Olympics a board-rider was taken by a white pointer while surfing at nearby Blacks Beach in Anxious Bay, and we imagine people might still be upset about it.

We ask at the shop for directions to Blacks Beach. A friendly woman having an unusually large supply of Coca-Cola checked through with her groceries points the way.

'How will I know when I get there?' I ask her.

'You'll see the cross.'

We follow Anxious Bay Clifftop Drive. It's desolate and rugged. The top of the cliff drops sheer to the Southern Ocean. It's blowing a chilling wind, and with dark grey clouds spitting on us, the place feels ominous, especially with the newly erected cross perched on the edge.

Someone has bound two sticks together and planted this crucifix with a view over the surfing reef below. The shells and flowers decorating the cross have stood their ground against the elements. There's also all one needs for the afterlife: a miniature surfboard, some surfboard wax and a couple of full stubbies of beer.

There's no-one surfing today. Right below us, the white water crashes on the rocks. We can't work out how you get down the cliff to the water. There's just the ghost of a walking track that disappears to the right.

Seventeen-year-old Jevan Wright from Port Lincoln had been surfing with his girlfriend's forty-year-old father, Graham Chapman, when he packed it in for the day. Wright was almost at the bottom of the cliff, in three metres of water, when Chapman saw fins and thrashing. A piece of board bobbed up, but no sign of Wright was ever seen again. Not even blood.

Further along the clifftop drive, there is a calm beach with a boat ramp. A sign notes that you aren't allowed to use blood, bone, meat, offal or the skin of an animal for berley within five kilometres of the mainland. 'If you are fishing for shark, please note the great white shark is now totally protected in all South Australian waters.'

Maude Agars had been pointed out to us as the oldest lady in Elliston. Her little house is hidden behind a large cactus garden. She is wearing a lot of red lipstick and her hands are blackened with age. We tell her about our placenames search, and her voice is strong.

'You know about Flinders and Anxious Bay, of course.'

'We do.' Matthew Flinders named it for a nervous time he spent there in 1801, but we're going to come back to that.

'Blacks Beach,' she continues, 'was always known as Black-fellows, but I don't know where that name came from. It's all lost, see. No-one remembers.

'My grandfather was on a boat, though, that was sunk in Anxious Bay. The *Firefly*. It was only small, you know, about eighty ton. There was a captain, his brother and a couple of crew. We don't know how it happened or how they survived. It's all lost, see. But that's how he came to settle here on the west coast.

'The captain eventually got to Port Lincoln, but how I don't know. It was a long time before me. I was born in 1914.'

Maude suspects Blackfellows was probably an Aboriginal camp, but that preceded her time. No-one made any fuss when its name was changed to Blacks in line with more current thinking a few years ago.

'Why would they?' she asks.

When Jevan Wright's parents received the phone call that their son had been taken, they were sitting in their kitchen reading newspaper reports of another surfer, Cameron Bayes, who'd been attacked and killed by a white pointer the day before at Cactus Beach, 240 kilometres west of Blacks.

We drive west to the Nullarbor Plain.

Penong is a lonely little place on the edge of the vast plain, where you can't get groceries on a Saturday or Sunday afternoon. It has four bowsers of diesel at city prices for the huge trucks rumbling across the country. The beer garden at the pub goes by the name of Surfers Paradise, which could seem really weird. But then on the side of the road we see an orange juice bottle that has been styled into a bong and the place starts to look more like a surfie town.

The sign to the remote and legendary surfbreak at Cactus has been painted over with green paint. Surfers, like fishermen, keep their secrets close. A few kilometres down the gravel turn-off, through scrubby desert country, we catch the word 'INBRED' on a road sign. (Jo thinks it says 'naked' but she's driving so she can be excused.) We chuck a U-ey and go back for another look. Someone has gone to great pains to stick masking tape on the sign and write in various colours, 'Campsite owner is a fucking INBRED'.

This causes some nervousness among us but, combined with the lack of signage and the shark attack still not three weeks old, we wonder if it's another ploy to keep the numbers down.

Further on, amongst the yellow dunes and waxy shrubs, we see a rusty old caravan and know we must nearly be there. There are surfboards scattered around camps and campfires with huge windbreaks. It's still blowing hard. Apparently October is known as Blow-tober around these parts. With beanies pulled well down, we stroll to the beach. Picking our way across the rock ledge, we see a sea lion lolling on the sand. We tiptoe down and he/she keeps a lazy eye on us. We keep a respectable distance, but the animal's not too fussed. Well, it's not moving.

Later, we meet Ron, the ageing surfie campsite owner, and he doesn't seem like an inbred at all. Ron has 1970s hair, still wavy down to the shoulders, but thin on top and perfectly silver. We'd been warned that he might not want to talk and, indeed, he is prickly about Cactus, but eventually agrees to have a yarn later.

Next morning, Amy and Jo are sitting outside the tent when Ron and three twenty-something surfies walk by carrying a table to the beach.

'We're going to make a sacrifice to the surf,' Ron calls out. 'We need a virgin.'

They laugh, but it's not as funny as it might have been. The shark attack still hangs heavily over the place. The table is to be used for a memorial service in a couple of days.

Ron is prickly about the whole shark business, too. When we eventually pin him down for a chat he launches straight into a story about a mate of his in 1977.

'A 14-foot shark attacked him and he survives. Then he doesn't put his seatbelt on driving back from Penong. He went off the road – he was always going off the road, a terrible driver – and was thrown out the window when the car rolled. It landed on him and he was killed.

'He can die like that and no-one gives a damn. A hundred people can die like that and no-one gives a damn, but one poor bloke gets killed by a shark and the whole world wants to know. It goes back to the human's basic fear of being eaten. It's in our genes. We're fascinated by it.'

Ron's description of when he first came here in 1974, just passing through, evokes something of *Mad Max*. Back then it was a collection of tin shanties dug into depressions behind dunes. There was garbage everywhere. One of the dunes was known as Shit Hill because that was where everyone crapped. An old surfer once told Ron he was in the first group to ever surf here, and that it used to be called Rosella Point because of all the Rosella soup tins thrown about by the fishermen who came before the surfers.

During Christmases in the 1970s there were hundreds here. The original owner of the campsite, Paul Wirtzig, started to cart wood in so that the surfers would stop ripping up the scrub for fires. The Government gave 10,000 dollars to help build fences around the dunes and make fire pits.

There was resistance bordering on violence. Surfers don't like being dictated to. Water tanks and other structures were vandalised. Within hours of a windmill being put in, it had 'Fuck off Wirtzig' fingered into the cement base.

Ron lived here for a few years, just surfing, but was then banned from the camp by Wirtzig. He'll only say it happened because of a complaint.

'They were paranoid campers, that's all they were. Just dickheads, if you know what I mean.'

He moved into Penong and, after making three offers to buy the place between 1979 and 1986, he eventually got it.

'Why don't you have a sign at the road?' I ask.

'Some of the boys painted over the sign with green paint. Before they did that, I was about to go out with an oxy torch and cut the whole fucking thing down. I never advertise. Word of mouth is the best form of advertising. It's no secret spot but the people who want to come here will find the place. Quiet people associate with quiet people and dickheads associate with dickheads, so if a dickhead goes home and tells all his mates not to come because the campground owner is a dickhead, well, that's good.'

The day Cameron Bayes was attacked here, a group of locals was out surfing, but Ron couldn't make it. He had a fiftieth birthday to go to, so he'd emptied the bins and the stinking plastic liners from the toilets early. Those that were out there noticed something strange with the dolphins, the way they all clumped close together.

'It's the same when whales are about, the dolphins go off,' says Ron.

'They're scared?'

'Nah, they just dig having their cousins around. Sometimes there's fifty in a pack and sometimes it's kindy time, all mothers with their babies. They're just like us. They ride the waves with us. You always know there's a set coming because the dollies turn up. They won't let you touch them, they're too smart for that, but sometimes they'll ride the wave with you then paddle back out just under the nose of your board and catch wave after wave.'

Two or three years ago, a southern right whale drifted underneath Ron. One bloke he was surfing with could've touched it. 'It only had to move one of its flippers and we were history.'

He's got no idea how big it was. Just bloody huge. The size of a house. 'It's the greatest experience of my surfing life. He drifted away and then the sets started coming in, and fifty metres away he came completely out of the water and did a roll.'

The point he makes often is that those who live here, live with nature and deal with its awesome powers daily; such that locals talk of having an ability to sense sharks in the water, and that Cameron Bayes, being a new boy, didn't have it.

He was twenty-five, on honeymoon from New Zealand with his wife, Tina. He'd been surfing for an hour when the shark appeared at seven-thirty on the Sunday morning. He was just fifty metres offshore. Witnesses saw the shark circle around him with such speed it looked like several sharks. Then it hit and took him down.

'I saw him come to the surface, get his board and start paddling towards the shore,' a witness standing on the sandhill was reported as saying. 'I saw his face . . . he looked quite calm. But he only made about three metres before it atttacked again . . . then, suddenly, he was gone. There were a few bits of board floating, and a pool of blood.'

The shark surfaced about 500 metres away and spat out pieces of board.

Ron and a mate went out four days later. Plenty of guys wouldn't go back in the water for weeks.

This was the first day since the attack that the surf was any good. 'I don't know the exact word, but it was fairly peaking. We didn't know if the thing was still around, but I had to be back in the water to be back on top of my life, you know,' says Ron. 'You don't want to be dictated to, and if you aren't surfing there's no point living all the way out here.'

They'd been out twenty minutes when his mate caught a wave. Looking back to shore into the morning sun you get a glassy ripple on the water and can't see a thing. Ron saw his mate pull off the wave, and in between them was a black figure.

'Here we go.' When it came out of the glassy light they could see it was a dolphin and her calf. They relaxed, because they knew she wouldn't be there if there was a pointer around.

We say our farewells to Ron and drive the twenty-one kilometres back to Highway 1, noting on the way that the 'inbred' sign has been removed.

There are no more red dots on the Map until the West Australian coast at Shark Bay. More pressing is the radio news, full of reports that police are waiting at the West Australian border for 400 bikies heading to Perth for their annual conference. They must be just in front of us.

CHAPTER 23

CARNAGE

The Nullarbor, South Australia–Western Australia

MARK ▶ The radio tells us that the 400 Rebels are being searched at the border for weapons and drugs. When we get there, however, there is no sign of them. Upon the threat of being searched ourselves, we hand over two tomatoes, a lemon and some Home Brand honey – the third bunch of groceries we've sacrificed to quarantine stations in a week.

At Eucla we see the first stragglers, then a few smokers by the side of the road, then ever-building numbers of 'outlaws' drinking and loitering at each roadhouse. When they overtake, they seem to make it a point of honour not to go into the oncoming lane, but to squeeze through the couple of centimetres between us and the dotted white line.

It's certainly a good way to stay entertained while crossing the Nullarbor. The vast plain, however, is not all it's cracked up to be. Firstly: 'null arbor' means no trees. Apart from a quick twenty-kilometre stretch at the very beginning of the South Australian end, there are trees everywhere.

Secondly: too many bends. There is even a section you could almost call winding. It's not until you get to the very western end that a sign announces the '90 mile straight' which at least sounds snappier than the '146 kilometre straight'.

At a roadhouse, the woman serving our pies doesn't know

what all the bikie fuss is about: 'We had 'em all in here. They were a hell of a lot better mannered than the police.'

Arriving at Cocklebiddy Roadhouse late in the afternoon, we find a largish contingent of bikies hitting the beers and oozing menace. Amy gets ogled, and both she and Jo are not sure they like these guys. We head off a little down the road to find a campsite in the scrub.

A bit after seven the next morning we hear them long before we see them, like they had their mufflers confiscated at the border. We are a kilometre from the road but their almighty roar cracks the morning. They flash by with three police cars at the head of a convoy, which, upon counting, contains only twenty-six bikes.

The radio news is full of them. By the time we get to Balladonia Roadhouse, there are hundreds of them waiting around, along with a large contingent of police in variously coloured coveralls and uniforms. You half expect Clint Eastwood and his orang-outang to drive in.

We squeeze our way to the bowser, praying we don't hit any of the bikes parked randomly around. We act cool, like this sort of thing happens to us every second day. I think they buy it.

At the diesel bowser, we have to vie for space with the police van carrying all their machine guns and stuff. Our rear window needs a clean, but it all feels so intimidating I don't want Amy or Jo to get out of the car. As much as the whole thing gets our adrenaline pumping, the scientific copper videotaping every-thing, presumably for potential evidence, is somehow the scariest, turning our thoughts to the Milperra bikie massacre, and the assorted bombings, housefires and shootings that make news.

As we near the goldmining town of Kalgoorlie, we see about twenty-five Aborigines standing at the turn-off to their com-munity looking like they are waiting for something. As we get closer to town, we see others doing the same. It is like the day we arrived in Sydney and went down the Olympic torch route.

The bikies have taken up a large place in the consciousness of the town and we know how the town must feel. Something like the Mexican villagers in the *Magnificent Seven*.

About two dozen Rebels are staying at our caravan park, supported by a slick white truck full of gear, much like the trucks you see at film shoots. They certainly aren't the noisiest campers we've encountered, but there's still something about their presence.

I check that the TV room is empty before we go over to watch a show that Jo had worked on. But a shaven-headed biker in early middle age has taken up a position on the floor, talking loudly on his mobile. He is terribly polite and orders us to change the channel because he isn't watching it. He seems keen to distance himself from it – *Open for Inspection*, a reality show on home auctions.

He leaves but returns about twenty minutes later with his mate, a big fella with a sizeable gut. Both are carrying their bedding. This is of some concern, but they are again terribly polite as they lay out their gear on the floor and set up camp.

'Don't be intimidated or nothing. People think we're bad but we're just normal people. Watch whatever you want. Don't worry about us.'

Lying in their beds, they weigh straight into a routine for Amy and Jo's benefit. 'What do you call a bunch of Lebanese women in a sauna? – None of youse are racially prejudiced are ya? Your mate's not Lebanese is he?'

When we give them a no on both counts they continue.

'Gorillas in the mist.'

'What do you call a pretty girl in Lebanon? Asif.'

'What do you call a guy standing between two buildings in Lebanon? Ali.'

They are cacking themselves and so are we, but it's hard to know if it's because they are funny or we are feeling the need to be polite.

The big guy with the gut complains of a sore bum. They have ridden all the way from Penrith in western Sydney in four days. But does anybody consider the feelings of a bikie's bottom?

'Where'd you come from today?' I ask.

'Balladonia.'

'Oh, yeah, we saw a big mob of you there.'

'Were you intimidated? Did any of us pass you?'

'Oh, yeah. We were listening to all the reports on the radio.'

'Radio?' he says. Big deal. 'We were on the *tele*.'

The bald one, who we establish is called Johnny, tells us there have been ten or twelve prangs on the way, plus a heart attack. 'Just guys skidding out. Going too hard. Being idiots.'

'How many of you guys are there?'

'About 350. It's a world record for the biggest meeting of outlaw bikers in the world and it's the longest run by outlaw bikers in the world,' he says, proudly. 'It's compulsory to come.'

'Can you bring a note from your mum or something?'

'The only excuse is if you're in jail.'

'Or in hospital,' adds Beer Gut.

'Or on parole and can't leave the state,' says Johnny.

We later read that seventy have been thus affected.

Reminiscing about the AGM in Townsville a couple of years back, Beer Gut sniggers, 'I didn't go to that one,' leaving us wondering where he was detained.

Beer Gut rings his girlfriend, Trace, on his mobile, but she says she'll ring back because she found a phone and it is still working fine. Mid-conversation, he raises his voice: 'Ah, ya fuckin' dickhead. Why didn't you tell me?'

Shortly after: 'I love you too, baby,' soft and gentle.

He hangs up and rolls over to Johnny in his sleeping bag and whispers: 'Mate, I should be home. She had an abortion today.'

'Oh, fuck. She alright?'

'Yeah.'

We make our excuses and leave them watching the opening ceremony of the Paralympics.

Our intention had been to take a leisurely drive north and west out of Kalgoorlie until we hit the coast about 900 kilometres north of Perth. However, we have bikies firmly on the mind when we look at a map and find there is a Mount Carnage about seventy kilometres north of town. To our surprise it is right next to Ora Banda, another town we've been hearing about on the radio. It, too, has bikies on the mind. Or it would if there was anybody left there.

Seventeen days ago there was a bit of trouble at the Ora Banda pub in the late afternoon. Nothing serious, but three drunk Gypsy Jokers were ordered out by the publican, Don Hancock, the retired chief of the West Australian CIB (Criminal Investigation Branch). Hancock grew up in the two-horse town and returned to it upon his retirement from the elite detective bureau. The pub, built in 1911, had been abandoned in the 1950s, but was restored in the early 1980s before Hancock bought it in 1994.

The Gypsy Jokers left the pub and retired to their camp, about 300 metres across a dirt camping area-cum-picnic ground that is described, somewhat hopefully, as the Ora Banda race-track. About seven-thirty that night, when most of Australia was watching the Olympic closing ceremony, there were about seven Gypsy Jokers sitting on a long, backless bench staring at a campfire, under the light of a globe powered by a generator humming in the back of a ute.

Suddenly the campfire exploded. One of them jumped up and shouted at his mates to hit the deck, they were under fire. He grabbed his binoculars and scanned the darkness.

They told him to sit down and shut up.

Minutes later, Bill Grierson, a bikie with a shaved head and long, bushy beard, slumped forward, and then his mates knew they were being shot at. A high velocity bullet had gone through him from behind, fatally wounding him. He was thirty-nine. The youngest of fourteen children and the father of two. He had apparently drifted into the bikie world after a bad marriage break-up. In his wallet, he carried the ultrasound picture of a baby expected by his new partner.

That was Sunday. By Wednesday, most of the town had cleared out, including Hancock and his family. When television news crews from Channel Seven and GWN were leaving town with their footage, they found themselves being chased by several carloads of bikies. The GWN car escaped cross-country and called police on a mobile. But the Seven crew was stopped and surrounded. Bikies kicked the doors and threatened them until they handed over their tapes.

Meanwhile, it emerged that Hancock was one of several people interviewed by police on the night of the murder and that someone had made threats to burn down his pub. He felt the need to publicly state that he was not the murderer. (The crime remained unsolved at the time of publication.)

Grierson's funeral passed with little incident as about a hundred bikers came to Kalgoorlie from all over Australia and left peacefully. Life stuttered back to normal in Ora Banda.

Twelve days after the murder, staff had closed the bar and ten patrons had just left when an explosion ripped through the front of the old stone building. Then another. A fire was lit with petrol from a jerry can later found on the road from Coolgardie – the back way into town.

Ora Banda, Western Australia

MARK▶ The first thing you notice driving into Ora Banda, sixty-six kilometres north-west of Kalgoorlie, is the caravans, sad and old and lived in, behind a row of prefab houses. There are about twenty-five vans and none look like they've been on the road for a long time. There are three ancient bowsers on the street in the few metres before the Ora Banda Inn. It is a lovely old stone building with a verandah around the front, decorated in blue-and-white-checked police tape.

It is one week since the bombing. At the corner, the stone walls have been blackened by the blast and the windows and doors are blocked by black boards. 'Danger Live Wires Keep Out.'

Painted on the stonework in faded white paint: 'This pub is haunted'.

I had rung the Kalgoorlie police to find if it was safe to come here.

'There's nothing to go there for,' said the female voice at the station.

'Well, that's my business. Is it safe?'

'The hotel got blown up last Friday night and nobody has been apprehended for that. We are not saying it's unsafe to go there, but we're not saying it's safe, either.'

'Thanks.'

Grant Taylor, a journo on the *Kalgoorlie Miner*, told us that the Gypsy Jokers had all gone to Adelaide a couple of days before the bombing. So we weren't nearly as scared as we might otherwise have been as we drove in. The country might be beautiful in a desolate sort of way, but the tracks and tailings scarring the red earth leave it ugly.

We see some movement by a caravan with flat tyres. There are two suitcases and a baby stroller outside near two small cars. A man in a blue singlet retreats into the caravan as we walk up. A woman approaching fifty with a young girl's long, jet black hair comes out in his place. She is wearing stretch jeans and a tight black top.

'The police told us not to say anything about the case,' says the woman.

'Are you leaving for good now?'

'Yeah. We're leaving this lifestyle behind. Gone, just like that. The police told us to get out for our own safety. We don't want to end up like them over there, do we,' she says glancing towards the pub, thirty metres away.

She went to Perth after the shooting and has returned to pack up and leave. Her pot plants have all died, except for two bright white flowers that must have thrived on two weeks without water.

'That's me job gone now. Up the spout. I was the cook at the pub. We'll be going to Perth and be dole bludgers, I suppose.' She laughs, but it looks like she might cry at any moment as she pulls her hair back to compose herself.

A male voice comes from within: 'That's enough, Vic.'

'Anyway, I've got to go now. Why don't you talk to Steve. He knows everything about it.'

We've got lucky because the publican's son, Steve Hancock, is over near a Grace Removal van. He is flanked by two men, the big one of whom we later hear is a bodyguard.

He doesn't know where Mount Carnage got its name, but tells us that Ora Banda was a rough translation from the Spanish, band of gold.

'Will you be coming back?' I ask him.

'It's really up in the air. We don't know how much it will cost to repair the pub. It's up to the insurance company. It's really sad.'

The pub and the caravan park support a community of thirty, but when there's a lot of mining activity, the numbers have swelled to 120.

We walk back to the car and Grant Taylor and a photographer from the *Miner* are pulling up. Grant points to a tree off in the distance with some 44-gallon drums around it: 'That's where it happened. See how far away the bush is. From there it's at least a hundred metres to the nearest cover, but I suppose you can shoot something at half a kilometre with a high-powered rifle.'

Grant turns to the pub: 'You can just imagine people sitting at tables out here on a Sunday afternoon, having a beer. And look at it now – it looks like a war zone.'

As we're pulling out, two neatly dressed men get out of a tiny town car. We guess they are the assessors come to pick over the bones.

We can see Mount Carnage, a low pimple off to the west. A stint in the local library, and later at the Battye Library in Perth, reveals little of the origins of the name. The records show a surveyor from the Department of Mines, Godfrey William Ellis, came through in 1900 and gave the name to the hill and a lake. But it appears he might have taken that name from Carnage mine, which was opened by the Berry Bros some time before 1894. It had 'wonderful gold' at eighteen metres. Information about what carnage took place there, however, seems well and truly lost.

Just a few hundred metres out of town is the old Mount Carnage homestead. It's an ordinary-looking fibro and tin place with a broken green lattice out the front. A large sign on the gate screams: 'Shut the bloody gate.'

And a smaller one: 'Drive slowly. Housemaid getting silicosis.'

We drive north and then west through the big, lonely heart of Western Australia. The Map is largely devoid of interesting names until we hit the coast, where they return with a flourish. Until then there's just a Hope River, north-west of Meekatharra, whose origin eludes us. Judging from other 'hope' placenames, though, they certainly weren't indicative that all was well with the world.

Explorers could be a miserable lot; there are two Mount Miserys for every Mount Hope. Even then, 'hope' was often a final straw grasped from the depths of despair. Anyway, there's no-one around to ask about this one, so we give it a miss and head for the coast.

After 974 kilometres of gravel road, not counting a diversion into the spectacular gorges of Kennedy Range National Park, we hit the Indian Ocean at Carnarvon. Banana country. A wicked wind howls all day from the south-west.

Jo leaves us, taking the 3 am bus to Perth, then a flight home. I'm alone with Amy, who has given up cigarettes. Tensions have been rising since the first nicotineless days in Wagga Wagga. It's like she's a different person, but Jo has at least had a calming influence. So when she was going to leave us in Kalgoorlie, I was very keen on her staying.

'You've got to see some real outback,' I had said.

Now it's just me and a girl who's really hanging for a smoke, heading to Shark Bay on the trail of a couple of bitchy Frenchmen.

CHAPTER 24

CAMP *des* MECONTENTS

Denham, Western Australia

AMY ▶ I hear Mark slip out of the tent, trying his best to be quiet in the pre-dawn light. I need to go to the loo but it's my birthday and I don't want to ruin any breakfast-in-bed surprises he might be putting together out there.

As I wait, though, my birthday spirit drains away. We've had a lovely few days playing in the Shark Bay World Heritage Area, but it's now three weeks since I gave up smoking and it hasn't been quite as smooth as we'd hoped. Indeed, the word disastrous could be applied to the situation. Certainly by Mark, anyway. Even the dolphins at Monkey Mia and the dazzling blue lagoons failed to lift my spirits. And since Jo left, Mark has had to cop all this irrational, weepy behaviour alone.

What's taking him so long? I can't wait any longer. I need to pee and now I'm crabby. By the time I step out of the tent, my evil twin has unleashed herself on the morning. She is on the loose, wild-eyed. She spots Mark still writing a birthday card.

'You could have written it yesterday!'

'Oh, yeah, when? We're always together.'

'When I was in the shower.'

It's been three weeks coming, and now we're heading into one almighty domestic. Mark has had it – he cancels my birthday. No discussion. Even when I explain it's not me but my nicotine-deprived evil twin. Then the mobile rings. My mum and sisters launch into a raucous rendition of 'Happy Birthday' down the line and I promptly burst into tears.

'Are you crying?' they laugh, thinking it's their singing.

But their singing isn't that bad. The line goes quiet as my sisters slink away, leaving Mum to deal with me.

'What's happened?'

'Mark hates me.'

'Mark doesn't hate you.' She makes all the soothing maternal noises, blindly taking my side, but I only half listen. I know I'm guilty.

'Anyway, I have to pull myself together,' I eventually say. 'We're meeting someone out at Useless Loop this morning.'

Useless Loop is directly across the water from our caravan park in Denham – fishing village and tourist centre for the Peron Peninsula. Denham's claim to fame is as the westernmost town on the Australian mainland. Officially, anyway. Useless Loop actually juts out a tiny bit further, but being a closed mining town it somehow gets overlooked for the title.

Going by car from Denham, the journey takes three hours on a mostly bumpy road. They don't exactly encourage visitors here. We drive in silence through coastal scrub, past Disappointment Loop, another one of the frustrations scattered around Shark Bay. There's also Useless Inlet, Hopeless Reach and Disappointment Reach. This place was a serious letdown for someone.

Maybe, like us, they thought they'd be allowed to pat the dolphins at Monkey Mia.

Seaman Nicolas Baudin hit the big time in France in 1798 when he returned from Puerto Rico laden with exotic plants. He struck it lucky by arriving back in time for a procession to the Champ de Mars, part of the Fêtes de la Liberté. Baudin's timing meant his banana tree, coconut palm and pawpaw tree were displayed to the throng alongside the spoils of Napoleon Bonaparte's Italian campaign.

With his newfound fame, Baudin was appointed to lead an expedition to New Holland. The French had commercial and political motivations for the trip, but it was primarily a scientific excursion for which no expense was spared. Twenty-three scientists set sail for Australia in the most comprehensive scientific voyage to the huge island. Bonaparte gave the order to expedite the mission even as his Army of the Reserve was crossing the Alps.

Scientifically, the voyage was a success, but it was awash with bad blood between the scientists and the seamen, epitomised by the feud between Baudin and the naturalist François Peron, who became scientific leader following the death and desertion of many more senior colleagues. Baudin and Peron couldn't stand one another.

As expedition leader, Baudin had the upper hand, but his untimely death towards the end of the journey saw Peron seize a priceless opportunity. Peron was left to write up the official narrative with cartographer Louis de Freycinet. He exacted his revenge by never once mentioning his commander's name in the entire voluminous account of the journey, but still painting the unnamed leader as an irrational, incompetent tyrant.

Then Peron and Freycinet really stuck the boot in by wiping Baudin off the Australian map, and at the same time writing themselves all over it. They renamed most of the places Baudin had christened here.

Almost certainly, Baudin was neither as horrible nor insignificant as Peron would have us believe. Mind you, like Peron, Baudin was prone to taking his own swipes via the map.

After hitting the West Australian coast at Cape Leeuwin on 27 May 1801, Baudin traced the coast northwards and soon came upon Geographe Bay, named for his ship. Infuriated by what he perceived to be gross disobedience by a sub-lieutenant there (Sub-Lieutenant Picquet had failed to make it ashore in the longboat due to dangerous conditions), he named what is now Cape Naturaliste, Cap des Mecontents. Cape of Discontent. Not only did Peron later change that name, he named a nearby promontory Point Picquet after the same sub-lieutenant.

A little further up the coast a group of scientists, including Peron, went ashore near present day Wonnerup and got lost. Meanwhile, two drunken sailors wrecked the longboat. Baudin, back on the ship, had heard no word back from shore in two and a half days. He started to cry, fearing the whole expedition was ruined. He went to his cabin to be alone.

That night, having given up all hope, Baudin was astonished when a rescue boat returned with Peron, albeit 'more dead than alive'. The rest of the party were alive and still ashore. It turned out they had been sheltering behind sand dunes in a makeshift tent. Battered by howling wind and scared by howling natives, they were miserable, thirsty and exhausted. They'd had little to eat, had been drinking salt water, and were terrified the ships would be forced to leave without them. But Baudin's relief turned to fury that his men had disobeyed orders and remained onshore. He expressed his displeasure by naming the place Anse des Maladroits. Incompetents Cove.

Peron cleaned that one off his map, too.

The story of how Useless Loop came to be, then, is comparatively tame. By August, the French had reached Shark Bay and were pottering in and out of all its little bays and inlets.

Peron wrote in *A Voyage of Discovery to the Southern Hemisphere*, that 'we soon came into a very pretty small harbour, but which unfortunately being closed in by a sand-bank on which there is not more than three feet of water, it can never admit a vessel of any size. For this reason I named it Havre Inutile (Useless Harbour).'

The name was anglicised in 1858, when Commander Henry Mangles Denham charted the area as part of his nine-year survey for the British Admiralty, calling it a loop rather than a harbour. Finding the country rather bland and certainly not fit for settlement, Denham followed the French lead, adding Hopeless Reach and Disappointment Reach to the chart.

Useless Loop, Western Australia

AMY The salty shallows of Useless Loop turned out, in fact, to be very useful; its conditions were ideal for producing salt. The brilliant green evaporation ponds of Shark Bay Salt are the first thing you notice driving into Useless Loop. The colour is dazzling.

'Why do you reckon it's so green?' Mark asks.

I don't know. I'm just relieved we're back to sane conversation.

We follow the signs directing visitors to the Town Office. I phoned the site manager a couple of days ago for permission to come out, and he promised to arrange for someone to meet us here today. Only now the Town Office is locked up and it seems our appointment has been forgotten.

Sue Stokes, the new Town Officer, is very good about it when we interrupt her day off. Without hesitation she offers to take us on a tour. Anyway, it's a good excuse for her to avoid the housework.

Heading back towards the salt ponds, we ask Sue why some of them are so green.

'Actually, it's food dye,' she says, a hint of guilt anticipating our disappointment. The darker colour speeds up the evaporation process.

The colour variations from pond to pond document the various stages of salt-growing. First, there is the murky water straight from the sea, then the emerald food-dye stage, followed by a spectrum of fading green until, two years after first being sucked from the ocean, it becomes a blinding white bed of crystal. So pure, Sue tells us, you could eat it.

We thought that was what it was for, but apparently the huge mound of clean salt awaiting shipment to Asia is for use in ion exchange membrane claw alkali plants. Whatever the hell that means.

We drive out to the dirt airstrip, with its little wooden shack announcing, 'Useless Loop International Airport'. This is the main contact with the rest of the world for the one hundred adults and thirty kids living here. The plane brings mail three times a week, the flying doctor once a fortnight, the police and the dentist once a month and the vet twice a year.

When salt mining began here in 1965, Useless Loop was a rough place. Everyone living in caravans and annexes. The company started building houses until it grew into this orderly, groomed town we're driving through now.

We pull up at the pub, which has sensational views of the water and the salt pile. Fishing awards cover the walls. Behind the bar is Timmo Wedding, rugged and jovial. He came here seventeen years ago after he shot through from the army.

'It's not a bad place to stay. You need to like water sports and fishing, 'cause there's nothing else to do,' says Timmo.

'Everyone usually gets together on Sunday to weigh in for the fishing competition. We've got the Useless Angling Club. Actually we're not that useless. I've got a few state records up on the wall. So do quite a few people in town.'

There are only two single women living here at the moment, which makes the social whirl a bit sedate. But it's safe and quiet.

'It never used to be closed, but the story I heard was, these tourists decided to drive onto one of the salt ponds and do some circle work. Now, motor vehicles and salt ponds don't mix. They broke down and leaked oil everywhere – ruined the whole harvest. We do still get some tourists come in, but the Denham police aren't far.' (A mere 170 kilometres away.)

We finish our drinks and it's time to head off. We take the roller coaster track west through the dunes to Australia's westernmost point, Steep Point, and around to Zuytdorp Cliffs, a majestic 150 kilometre stretch of rock with its own mysterious past. The ice between Mark and I has thawed a little, and after a photographic frenzy out there and some restored rationality we agree that this relationship needs either one whopping injection of nicotine or a continent between us. And so I decide to take my evil twin to Sydney for time-out.

CHAPTER 25

DESPERATE
MEASURES

Nambung National Park, Western Australia

MARK So I drove Amy to Perth airport. It all became increasingly amicable. We decided she would start writing the book in the five weeks she would be away. She was looking forward to the challenge and to the opportunity of doing it without me looking over her shoulder.

We went out to a suburban Chinese and discussed elements of style before she got the Red Eye to Sydney at 11.40 pm.

The closer the moment got, the harder it was to remember why she was leaving in the first place. Even harder to believe she was actually going.

She went.

I had been thinking through all this that the thing for a bloke to do now was to go out and get horribly drunk. I could easily justify this, since the next name heralded by the Map of Misery was Hangover Bay, 200 kilometres north of Perth. I had no idea how it got its name, but I was going to give the place a good workout in 'method' journalism.

At Lancelin, a dull little town cut into the sand, I bought a bottle of the cheapest Scotch they had, 100 Pipers. North of town looked like a ski field with its huge, white, treeless dunes. The track north was marked by high orange posts that would be visible in the harshest blizzard. Off to the right was a designated 'off-road' zone where you could go for a genuine hoon in the dunes. I felt the urge, but a side of me, all alone, took on Amy's role as the sensible one. The dunes looked steep and the sand deep.

I drove on, up a hard little white track for some sixty or seventy kilometres with Saharan dunes popping up periodically and the West Australian scrub doing its usual wild flower thing, with huge banksias and pretty little petals bursting out every-where. But the banksias grew closer and closer to the track until there wasn't much track left and horrendous scraping noises started squealing along the duco.

Late in the day, with Frank worth about a thousand dollars less than he had been in the morning, I came to a sign pointing to a 'Grey Shack Area'. Curious, I followed the track and found a strange little village of – you guessed it – grey shacks. They were all corrugated iron, and temporary looking. Crowded close together. There were no cars and no boats. No people, either. Yet none of the places seemed dilapidated. It was eerie. I drove on, and around every bend there were more shacks. There must have been close to a hundred. I concluded that it was a temporary crayfishermen's base.

Towards dusk, I made it to the Nambung National Park, where the sign showing a red line cutting diagonally through a tent clearly meant that one could not erect a tent. So I found a little spot overlooking the white sandy beach and laid out the tarp. I pulled out a chair, binoculars, notebook and sunglasses, and settled down to stare at the setting sun with 100 Pipers playing loud. To wallow in my bitter loneliness.

Which is what I'm doing now.

It doesn't seem to work, though. I have a few good swigs but just can't kick on. I don't feel particularly bitter, just mellow. The sunset is one of those dull West Australian shows people seem to love watching. There is no cloud and no pollution, so the sun just drops into the ocean out of a sky that turns orange, then dark orange.

I wonder what the next month holds in store, with me all alone. Whether Amy will even come back. Another swig. It's 7.47 pm. Time for bed.

Hangover Bay turns out to be a well sign-posted tourist destination, complete with national parks interpretive material on how the dune system is a remnant of ancient coastlines going back two million years. The beach has brilliant white sand and clear, flat water, though for my money the best hangover cure in the world is a body surf.

There's been another white pointer scare reported on the radio this morning, with a shark harassing some fishermen in a boat. There is no-one about here, and so with my pathetic excuse for a hangover, I go in nude – a most liberating feeling. But I don't go in much past my knees. Nothing to do with sharks at all.

In nearby Cervantes, named for the wreck of an American whaler, not the author, I see the Thirsty Point Liquor Store, so decide I'd better buy some red wine to give Hangover Bay another shake.

Handing over my $12.99 for the two-litre cask of shiraz cabernet, I ask the cashier where the name Thirsty Point came from, but she has no idea.

The woman at the general store is more on the ball. 'I'm pretty sure it's to do with the old crayfishermen. They used to have a camp down there and they were very big drinkers. *Very* big drinkers. I used to know one or two of them. They would get in from fishing and there wasn't much else to do, so they drank.'

The Geographic Names Committee of Western Australia notes merely that Thirsty Point used to be called Wreck Point, from the wreck of the *Cervantes* – not fishermen's livers – but the name Thirsty Point took over because of common usage. So Thirsty Point it is.

Similarly, Hangover Bay was a fishermen's shantytown. The fishermen tried to make the name official in the 1980s, but the council was evicting them off the Crown land at the same time, so they wouldn't give them the name. Then the name started appearing on a few signs, so the name stuck – but the village didn't. All the shacks have been obliterated.

My map also shows something called Desperate Bay just up the coast a bit, north of the town of Leeman, so I head that way. Approaching it, signs proclaim that no new squatters' dwellings are to be erected after May 1992 and all existing ones can only stay until 1998, but a few shacks have defied the deadline. I can't find Desperate Bay, though.

Asking at the Shire office at nearby Dongara, the terribly helpful woman there says I should go back to the place marked on the map as Coolimba.

'That's Desperate Bay's proper name, but none of the locals call it that. Speak to Mr Akerstrom. I can't remember his first name, but his son's name is Sean.'

There are four shacks in 'Coolimba'. Two placid Staffordshire terriers walk me to the gate of the first. I call out hello. It seems deserted but for the washing on the line, including a lot of baby stuff. Eventually a guy aged about thirty comes to the gate. His baby beer gut protrudes from a ripped singlet. It's Sean Akerstrom.

He takes me over to his dad's shack, a more basic tin construction about thirty metres away. He leaves me at the door while he goes in to explain who I am before returning with the info: 'It's like I said, a guy named Andy Robson, a crayfisherman, drove in and said "geez, you'd have to be desperate to live here". And ever since that, they've called it Desperate Bay.'

He yells back inside: 'What year was it?'

'The '60s, early '60s,' comes a female voice, his mother, Christina.

'It took eight hours to get here from Perth then (compared to three now). You had to have a four-wheel drive or Volkswagen.'

An older man's voice comes from inside: 'We did it in a modified ute, but we were out pushing it a lot of the way.'

Old Mick's gut reaches the door before he does. 'It was a terrible place to get to, even to get from the road to here took hours. Them days, the main highway north was 100 kilometres inland until the Brand Highway was put through in 1966. That was still thirty kilometres inland.'

'So where did this name Coolimba come from?'

'Coolimba Bay is something to do with Aborigines. It's only been used for the last twenty years or so. It's like Leeman, it used to be Snag Island. And Dumper Bay round the corner, that comes from the Finlays who lived there, used to dump everything there.'

'This shack scene's amazing. I've never seen anything like it anywhere else in Australia,' I say.

'Well, you'll never see it again, because they are slowly getting rid of us all. There used to be forty places along this stretch.'

'Forty-one,' adds Christina.

Which explains why Coolimba warrants a dot on the map as if it were a small town, when all there is now are the Akerstrom shacks and two others.

'There were fifteen up there towards that sandhill, ten down there,' Mick says, pointing at the beach, 'and more back behind us.'

'Who were they?'

'Fishermen or jokers on the dole, but mostly holidaymakers from Perth.'

'So anybody could just come up here and build a holiday shack on Crown land?'

'Yep.'

This seems too good to be true to me, but in fact it was just too good to last.

I later ring the Chief Executive of Carnamah Shire – the Town Clerk in the old speak – Lance Croft, to ask why the squatters had to be removed. He says that the good roads now make it too easy to squat. That squatter numbers in the Shire increased 200 per cent in the four years to 1992.

'It was felt that something needed to be done then, or get a larger problem. A few squatters would have a minimum impact, depending on their attitude to the environment, a lot of squatters would have a much larger impact, depending on their attitude to the environment.'

Still at Desperate Bay, Mick explains that they've been allowed to stay because they are professional fishermen. 'We might get eighteen months more, but that's it . . . we'll be packing up and going to Leeman or somewhere.'

'It used to be unreal here,' says Sean, reminiscing. 'A tight little community. People used to come to the old man: "Can we do this? Can we do that?" Oh, yeah. He was sort of the elder man.'

'How was the crayfishing then?' I ask, expecting tales of wonder about how free and easy it was.

'The crays are better now than they used to be,' says Mick. 'Everybody used to do what they want, take cackers (undersized crays), and it was a mess. There was no money in 'em anyway then, and most of us were more fishermen than crayfishermen. Up to about 1977 almost the entire catch was shipped frozen to the US, but then the Japanese came into the market. Then Asia and Europe wanted them alive, and suddenly a lot of us desperates were making real money.'

Sean is a fourth generation fisherman in these waters. His great-grandfather, a Swede, drowned off Geraldton maybe a hundred years ago. An uncle has the record catch for 'wet-lining' – using lines rather than nets – 36,000 pounds (over 16,000 kilograms) of mainly pink snapper in three days. He died young, too, of septicaemia from a fish bone caught in his throat.

Sean takes me for a drive around the sandy tracks, pointing at the little clearings where shacks used to be. We stop at an intact stone hut. 'The guy who built this had an interesting story. They called him "Bank Robber" because he robbed a bank once, and a few hours later the police came and knocked on the door. When he passed over the slip with the demand, you know, "Give me all your money or I'll blow your brains out" sort of thing, he'd written his name on the back of it.'

He goes on pointing at bare patches of ground, some with concrete slabs, most just piles of sand and dried seaweed. 'It used to be good here. All the blokes had bikes and buggies, and we'd all get around. We got on well with everyone. There were a few arseholes, but they got weeded out. Yeah, some real characters.'

Christina took Sean and his brother to Perth to be educated, but they came back every weekend. When Sean brought mates up, they could hardly believe the lifestyle. 'I had a motor bike before I had a pushy.'

There wasn't much in the way of sewerage. 'Bog drill' was the procedure for emptying the 44-gallon drum that lived under the thunderbox toilet. Dad would reverse the ute up to the water's edge fast, then brake and let the thing go flying in. Leave it there for a day so the sea could wash it. Sean remembers the time a car full of sightseers turned up and saw the purple patch of water. 'Oh, look at all the fish!'

'And in they went. We all sort of made ourselves scarce.'

He invites me to join them tomorrow, the first day of the cray season, when they bait their pots and drop them in.

There is little desperation about the Akerstroms' boat, *Desperate Measures*. She's a brand-spanking-new white aluminium thing with shiny stainless steel controls and plenty of screens, only distinguishable from a flash pleasure craft by the long, flat space out the back for working the pots. And the smell of rotten flesh swinging sourly with the breeze.

Sean's making most of the calls, but Mick's still doing his bit, and Johnno the deckie works hard, killer hangover and all. He chops rotten fish and pristine New Zealand blue mackerel and puts them in a red plastic box. He jams another box with a section of salted cowhide. The fish brings the crays into the pot, but the cowhide keeps 'em in there, gnawing at the hard, salted skin.

I try to help here and there, but just get in the way, so confine myself to pulling a few bits of weed off ropes and buoys as they are hauled on board.

Mick is steering, high up on the fly bridge.

'She's a pretty nice boat,' I comment.

'It'd wanna be for half a million dollars,' he says.

There's big money about these days. The Akerstroms got 16,000 kilos last year with their sixty-nine pots. Crays fetch around twenty-five dollars a kilo, so the sums start to add up. Still, Mick says he's always been a step behind the big players. Just when he got the money together to buy twenty new pots, they took eighteen per cent off him, so he was back where he started, but still had to pay 'em off. The big blokes now have 120 pots working, but even a battler can do alright. If the Akerstroms sold their sixty-nine pots, they'd never have to work again.

The rules that Fisheries put in place, giving quota only to existing fishermen, have made them rich men. Millionaire shack dwellers. But the shacks are going and the Akerstroms will move into Leeman, an unattractive town like all the others along this strip. Modern brick veneers and fake weatherboard. Someone will probably turn the last couple of shacks into tourist attractions once they realise they've destroyed something unique and appealing to those of us destined to live our lives in rate-paying monotony, dreaming of an era when all you needed for your own beachside holiday house was a cement mixer and a Volkswagen.

CHAPTER 26

OPEN YOUR EYES

Abrolhos Islands, off Western Australia

MARK ▶ The next name on my itinerary, the Abrolhos Islands, is a Dutch bastardisation of a Spanish bastardisation of a Portuguese expression, whose warning to mariners was essentially: be very afraid. Not enough of them paid attention.

I've teed it up so that part of my conditions of travel to the islands, 60 kilometres west of Geraldton, is that I fish for my passage with local wetliner Mel McRae and his deckie Jason.

Mel doesn't think it's much of a day as far as fishing goes. With our three handlines, we only pull in about 60 kilograms of coral trout and 30 kilos of dhufish, a few groper, two red emperor and assorted other less valuable species, all headed for the tables and restaurants of Perth.

Mel is one of twenty-three Geraldton wetliners fishing the waters of the Abrolhos. He's a guy with a ready laugh, a ruddy complexion and large gobs of suntan cream slapped through his short beard. He catches the great majority of fish. If we ever catch one at the same time, he has spiked his neatly in the brain, tossed it in the ice slurry and rebaited his gang hooks before I've even got the hooks out of mine.

It takes a while, but I start pulling in my share.

'Looks like you're getting the touch,' he says. 'If this book thing doesn't work out, there's always a job here for you.'

Sounds tempting.

'Don't go writing how nice it is, though,' he warns. 'We'll have every man and his dog out here doing it.'

All day we've been fishing in sight of a group of distant islands that appear to have skyscrapers on them. As we approach the pastel cityscape, however, the buildings shrink back to become shacks. They had only looked so huge because the islands they inhabit are so flat – mere platforms of limestone about two metres above water.

These are the Houtman Abrolhos. The word 'Abrolhos' was first applied to the map here in 1619 by Dutchman Frederick de Houtman after he went close to crashing into the limestone platforms. The word is commonly thought to be Portuguese for 'keep your eyes open', but in fact comes from *abri vossos olhos* meaning 'spiked obstructions', according to Henrietta Drake-Brockman's *Voyage to Disaster*. To Spanish navigators, the word sounded like their *abre ojos*, 'open your eyes'. Abrolhos became a common expression among early navigators, meaning 'look out, low rocks, danger'.

When Houtman saw these flat shelves of limestone, he knew he had to warn others of them, and that's how the mongrel word came to be on an Australian map.

We arrive at the Abrolhos with blood on our hands and feet. Quite fitting, really, considering the islands played host to one of the most murderous rampages known to Australian history. It was here the Dutch ship *Batavia* was wrecked in 1629, and while the captain, Pelsart, was sailing a small boat off to get help, the third in command, Jeronimus Cornelisz, and his supporters killed more than 125 children, women and men.

Now the Houtman Abrolhos, some 122 islands scattered north–south over 100 kilometres, are home to almost no-one, except when the hundreds of leased shacks burst into life for the three months of the cray season. When the season is over, they fall silent and one of the only people left is a scientist, Dr Chris Surman, who spends half the year out here studying birds.

For ten years, he's been weighing chicks in their nests several times a day to record how often they are getting fed. This establishes how much food is in the nearby waters and the relationship it all has to the warm Leeuwin Current that comes down from Indonesia.

The current is the reason Mel catches so many tropical species like coral trout this far south, near the cold currents that bring sea lions onto these beaches so far north.

'How about this weather, eh?' Chris calls to Mel. He is tall and comfortable standing at the console of his boat with a Mercury 50 on the back. 'I hate working in good weather.'

Chris has offered to show me a bit of the islands, provided I give him a hand with his research and bring a few nice bottles of red. Soon, we are scudding along the twelve kilometres to Pelsart Island, Chris explaining that we have to be there for the 6 pm weigh-in.

Chris shows me the back of his hand. It has a variety of red and blue spots, peck marks from a decade of sticking his hand into bird nests. 'By the end of the season it's all swollen and red. Shearwaters are terrible. It doesn't matter if you wear gloves or anything.'

We land at Pelsart (named by Stokes in honour of the captain of the *Batavia*) and walk around the beach, thick coral crunching underfoot, two sleepy sea lions ignoring us no matter how close we get.

'When we get there, stay behind me and keep your head down. I've got to move quick or the gulls will move in and kill the chicks. And I've got to make sure the chicks don't run off the nest.'

He crouches towards the nests and calls out a nest number and the weight of the chicks, which I write down in columns. I can see from the column next to it that some chicks have gone up in weight by as much as thirteen grams in the last three hours, while others have gone down by almost as much. Every so often one of the chicks 'gurges' – regurgitates its dinner – and Chris whips out a little plastic bottle and throws what look like small squid into it. They are in fact something called beak salmon, which are the mainstay of these common noddies.

Chris grew up in Geraldton, the son of a high-school teacher, but got out as soon as he could. He did his zoology degree, spent some time on a pearl farm in Indonesia, then came back to Perth to do a PhD and post doc. He had come to the Abrolhos as a kid on his dad's yacht, so the chance to go back to study the lesser noddy was too good to miss. Virtually nothing was known about its ecology. And that grew into a larger study of lesser noddies, common noddies and shearwaters, and the relationship they all have to the Leeuwin Current.

The waters of the current can be twenty-four degrees in winter, while on the coast it's freezing. The warm waters are, however, a desert. When the current was really strong in 1996 and 1997, there were catastrophic breeding failures. Hardly any birds nested. Just a few flapping around forlornly, unsure whether to give breeding a go.

Initially, Chris had this vague paranoia that maybe he was disturbing them, but soon established a couple of control sites to observe nests from a distance, which assured him that they were all failing. When the cool currents returned and the breeding came back to life in 1998, it was a huge buzz.

Next day, I wake in Chris's shack, which is set back just a few metres from the blue reef lagoon. We speed back to Pelsart Island for some weigh-ins, then Chris takes me for a squiz at Basile Island. It's been inhabited by three generations of Sicilian fishermen – the Basiles, Scarpuzzas and others. It's a little Venice made of fibro and tin. Cathedral Avenue runs to the little fibro church, St Peters. All about is deadly quiet.

'You should see it in the season. It really rattles with generators and lights and activity,' says Chris.

St Peters is the only church on the 122 islands, but Finnish fishermen have built a sauna on one, and the Aussies, well, they've built two pubs somewhere to the north.

We spend a couple of days visiting bird nests, measuring adults heads, weighing babies and collecting gurges as birds hover and shit about us. On my final shift, Chris mentions that perhaps we should go trolling for pelagics – a scientist's way of saying fishing for open water fish – on the way home.

The wind is up around twenty-five knots, sending up thick curtains of spray as we plow through the chop. Eventually we have a tuna on board and are fanging home, soaked through and cold, and convinced that life is good. Chris's good mate and fill-in assistant, Mike, starts filleting the tuna as soon as we get off the boat. He hands me the odd piece of sashimi as he goes. It's still warm.

Over the last of the good red and the first of the chateau du cardboard that night, Chris mentions that he calls this island Buggery Island. He explains that when the Dutch ship *Zeewyk* ran aground twenty kilometres west of us on Half Moon Reef in 1727, the survivors camped on what is now Gun Island (Stokes found one of their small cannons there).

'There were two boys (from the *Zeewyk*) who were caught buggerising each other on Gun Island,' explains Chris. 'I suspect they probably weren't, but maybe didn't cooperate with some of the other gentlemen. What happened is they were sentenced to be banished on separate islands so they couldn't continue their wicked ways.'

They were left without water and never talked of again. No more was heard of them for more than 200 years, until people came through looking for guano.

'Years and years ago,' says Chris, 'a guy camped on this island and lay down his swag and had a sleep on a beach. There's only that beach there,' he points to a little patch of sand just fifteen metres out the window. 'He had a shit sleep, woke up in the morning and there was a skeleton – what they suspect was one of the buggery boys.'

The *Zeewyk*'s story is extraordinary. After the ship's failure to beware of the Abrolhos, drunken soldiers forced the captain to send the ship's small boat to Batavia (Jakarta), even though the captain thought it unseaworthy and had already started building a new ship. Still, he sent the ten best sailors out on the small boat, never to hear from them again.

When they hadn't been rescued after a few more months, the captain renewed his plan to build the new boat from wood on Pelsart Island. Never mind that they had to deal with the privations of living on a flat lump of coral, they built a 'yacht' in less than six months. It was no rough raft, either, being big enough to hold eighty-eight men, two treasure chests, food and water. The captain had his own cabin. She set sail on 26 March and was in Batavia by 27 April, four men having died on the way.

Returning to the mainland, I drove east out of Geraldton – 'Heart of the Batavia Coast' – daydreaming of a video I'd seen at the Geraldton Museum about the other wreck – the *Batavia* – and the murderous rampage that followed. The video ended with two of the bad guys, Jan Pelgrom and Wouter Looes, whose lives were spared by the rescuers. Cast ashore on the mainland, dressed all in black velvet and lacy white collars, these two men were the first Europeans known to live in Australia. Their fate is unknown.

Leaving the wheat belt, I drove through low, scrubby country to Walga Rock, 300 kilometres inland, where I am now sitting, in the afternoon shade of the truck, writing this. It's five to four and still stinking hot. I have just come from the rock art gallery.

To look at, Walga Rock is every bit the miniature Uluru. The colour and texture of the red granite are identical. Only, it is a mere fifty metres high, 1500 metres long and 500 metres wide.

Approaching the rock wall you see the swirl of shapes; some fading human figures with their hands up like they're praising the Lord; some hand stencils – one of which shows a wickedly crooked hand – some large bird tracks, all fading into a big blob of purple.

But over in the far left corner of the gallery, at eye level, is a painting that looks a little different in style and a lot different in subject matter. It's a sailing boat. It has two masts, rigging, some square port holes, perhaps for cannon. Below the boat are regular swirly lines, like someone who didn't know how to write, but having seen writing, has tried to fake it.

It has been suggested that the painting may have been made by descendants of shipwrecked Dutchmen who were saved by, and intermarried with, Aborigines. The most likely suspects being either Looes and Pelgrom from the *Batavia* or, more likely, survivors from yet another wreck, the *Zuytdorp*.

When Amy and I were at Zuytdorp Cliffs, the day before she left, I had begun reading the story of that wreck and felt compelled to come here, some 300 kilometres due east of the cliffs, to see where the story may have played out.

Walga Rock is a brilliant place to visit but, gee, it'd be tough to live here. As I move past the other paintings, a zebra finch hangs boldly to the rock face. He reluctantly flies away when I can almost touch him, but as soon as I pass, he returns. I elbow him out of the way again and look more closely. It is dark, mossy. Wet to touch. I have disturbed the little beggar's afternoon tipple. I wonder if I dug here, would I be able to eke out a few mouthfuls for myself.

For dinner, I throw a road-kill goanna (it tastes like chicken) and some potatoes in the fire and, reading on about the *Zuytdorp*, contemplate how feral I could go.

As the survivors of the *Zuytdorp* scrambled ashore from their wrecked ship, it is unlikely any of them would have felt particularly lucky – their doom merely delayed. On the first stage of the journey from Holland to Cape Town, 112 people had died from a total 286. This number was unusually high because she had an unusually slow journey. Still, of all the people who ever set sail for Asia with the Dutch East India Company, only one in three ever made it home.

In Cape Town, about fifty got off sick and another eighty to ninety passengers boarded, bringing the total to 200. The *Zuytdorp* failed to turn left before New Holland and she ended up smashed to pieces at the bottom of a vast line of nameless cliffs. It was early June in 1712.

The matter largely rested until 1954 when young geologist Phillip Playford was yarning round a campfire with a stockman, Tom Pepper, who told him about a wreck he'd found almost thirty years earlier. He showed Playford some silver coins.

Playford's investigations showed that a good few people must have got off the *Zuytdorp*, because at the top of the cliff he found such handy items as dividers and a set square for navigation. We also know the survivors dealt with their feelings of isolation by having an almighty booze-up because of all the square green gin bottles found up there. And it appears they had a bonfire and threw chests and whatever wood they could find onto it, because bits of melted brass and metal were found there.

Playford hypothesised that food and water would not have been a problem in the early months because there was plenty on the boat. Shellfish and winter rainwater would have been sufficient to supplement their diet. But by the beginning of summer the water situation would have been desperate. They would have had to move or perish.

The modern mystery of the *Zuytdorp* began in 1834 when Aborigines local to the Perth area said there was a story going round about a shipwreck about thirty days walk north. That there was 'white money plenty lying on the beach for several yards as thick as seed vessels under a red gum tree'. The story was said to have originated with the Wayl, Waylo or Weel Aborigines.

The colonists presumed it was a recent wreck and they immediately mounted a rescue expedition to the area we now call Zuytdorp Cliffs. (The surveyor Mr H.M. Ommanney was dispatched in a small schooner, the *Monkey*, to find and rescue the stranded people. He didn't find anybody or any wreck, but it is from his vessel that the town of Monkey Mia gets its name. Mia being the local Aboriginal word for humpy or home.)

Playford, not a chap given to fanciful reckonings, seems convinced that story was about the *Zuytdorp*: 'The largest and most important Aboriginal encampment and waterhole near the *Zuytdorp* wreck site was at a well known as Wale, fifty kilometres to the north.'

In 1990, Playford and some friends armed with metal detectors went to Wale Well and just twenty metres from it found a brass tobacco box lid buried ten centimetres below the surface. It was inscribed 'Leydon' and carried a picture of the Dutch town. It was identical to a lid found on the wreck of the *Zeewyk* of 1727.

But what of the survivors after they perhaps moved to Wale Well? The explorer A.C. Gregory came through the Murchison River district in 1848. Many years later he recounted having met a tribe 'whose characters differed considerably from the average Australian. Their colour was neither black nor copper, but that peculiar yellow which prevails with a mixture of European blood; their stature was good with strong limbs, and remarkably heavy and solid about the lower jaw . . . But though these and many other traces of their origin exist, it is singular that no trace of knowledge of the arts of civilised people remains; there is nothing in their weapons, erection of dwellings, or ornamentation of their person or belongings which is not common to the greater part of the Australian tribes.'

Daisy Bates, well known for her work with Aboriginal people, also noted 'traces of types distinctly Dutch' which she, like Gregory, attributed to the two men marooned from the *Batavia*. At that time, the *Zuytdorp*'s fate was still unknown.

But the most fun bit of all the evidence Playford found that pointed to Dutch heritage for local Aborigines is in the genes. There is a disease called porphyria variegata which is most common among white South Africans. Indeed, all 30,000 cases in the world can be traced back to two ancestors – Gerrit Jansz and Ariaantje Jacobs, who were married at the Cape in 1688.

The disease can be quite benign, manifesting itself in sensitivity of the skin and an allergy to certain drugs. Playford alerted the world expert on the disease of its existence in a part-Aboriginal man from Shark Bay. While there is no record of who the eighty to ninety passengers were who boarded the *Zuytdorp* at the Cape, Jansz did have an illegitimate son who would have been twenty-five in 1712.

Alternatively, his wife had a half sister. If the disease came through her side of the family, it may have been carried by her son Hendrik Bibault. He got into some drunken strife one night and threw a bag of meal at a magistrate, and part of his sentence was that he leave the Cape. He responded to the judge, 'Ik will niet loopen; ik ben een Afrikaner,' (I will not leave; I am an African), thus becoming the first white recorded to have called himself an Afrikaner. It didn't matter; he had to leave.

That was in 1707 when, curiously, the *Zuytdorp* first called at the Cape. Bibault may have joined up as crew. The first Afrikaner may well have also been one of the first white Australians.

Similarly, a condition called Ellis-van-Creveld syndrome, which causes birth defects such as extra toes, shorter limbs and heart problems was rife in Holland at the time. Interestingly, Aborigines in the area carry the second highest incidence of the disease in the world (the highest being the Dutch-descended Amish people of Pennsylvania).

Anyway, it was Playford who lobbied to have Zuytdorp Cliffs recognised as an official name, adding to that eclectic mix of Dutch, French, Aboriginal, English and bastardised Portuguese that makes the west coast so distinctive.

Walga Rock, Western Australia

MARK ▶ Sitting in the heat at Walga Rock, reading Playford's *Carpet of Silver* about the wreck of the *Zuytdorp*, I note an odd coincidence. When Don Hancock, of Ora Banda Inn fame, was investigating the 1982 Perth Mint swindle, the home of one of the suspects, Ray Mickelberg, was raided when they were looking for 653,000 dollars' worth of bullion. Hancock's detectives didn't find it, but did find forty-seven silver coins from the *Zuytdorp*, whose famous 'carpet of silver' was severely looted during the 1970s.

The Mickelberg brothers, later convicted for passing dud cheques for the bullion, had been abalone divers along that stretch of coast, but claimed to have bought the coins from a fisherman.

The other piece of interesting news on the radio this morning is that somebody returned to Ora Banda to finish their handiwork last night. In three blasts Don Hancock's house was destroyed, a rather large hole was blown out of the general store attached to the side of the pub, taking out two crescents of heavy stone from either side of the door, and Hancock's historic and functional eighty-seven-year-old gold battery was blown up. The battery was used by all the tin-pot prospectors in the district to crush their rocks in pursuit of the yellow stuff. But now, even that little industry appears doomed, and so the district dies another death. Hasta la vista Ora Banda.

Amy is due back in two weeks. We're going to meet at Esperance on the south coast. But first I have this urge to do something a little reckless and spend three days walking the route that my hero, Edward John Eyre, took to Lucky Bay, just east of Esperance. After turning back, disappointed, from Mount Hopeless in South Australia, Eyre proceeded to the south coast to walk across the Nullarbor Plain (which he named) to Albany in Western Australia, in one of the most heroic feats of exploration imaginable.

His overseer, Baxter, had been murdered by two Aboriginal guides back on the Nullarbor. They took off with food and water while Eyre and his remaining Aboriginal friend, Wylie, pushed on almost willing death in preference to the agonies of cold and hunger they were suffering.

They got lucky at Lucky Bay, being helped along by a French whaling ship.

I walk their last fifty kilometres to Lucky Bay, then turn around and walk back to Frank. So it is with a ski tan and cracked lips that I turn up at the Esperance bus station.

CHAPTER 27

ADIEU, PERHAPS *the* LAST TIME

Esperance, Western Australia

AMY Mark is standing there waiting for me when the bus finally pulls into Esperance. His scruffy beard a little longer, the car a little grubbier. As a welcome home treat he has decorated the front seat with synthetic pink gerberas. It's so good to be back.

It's been two days since I left Sydney; first the long flight to Perth and then ten hours on a bus. A bit of a hike, but we liked the sound of Esperance for our reunion. It means 'hope', named for a boat on the 1792 French expedition to locate the missing explorer La Perouse.

But it's not the French names scattered along this spectacular stretch of white beaches and blue seas we've come to see. It's Matthew Flinders, whose difficulties charting the southern shores from here to Adelaide, during his circumnavigation of Australia, are etched on the map, and whom family legend has it, is some kind of relative of mine.

We begin our Flinders journey just east of Esperance at a campsite overlooking Lucky Bay, its pretty beaches surrounded by huge granite outcrops. It was named by Flinders early on in his survey after he had trouble finding a sheltered bay. Continuing eastwards, though, the niggly obstacles of Lucky Bay would pale into insignificance. For when Flinders entered the waters around Eyre Peninsula he discovered the volatility of the Southern Ocean.

So we head back across the Nullarbor and into South Australia, the dizzying cliffs dropping down to the Great Australian Bight now on our right. Further east, when the highway leaves the coast, we hug the clifftops along a maze of sandy tracks and Saharan-style dunes towards Eyre Peninsula.

Rumbling past the turn-off to Cactus, we approach the place Flinders called Denial Bay.

When Flinders was born in Lincolnshire in 1774, he was earmarked to become a surgeon, like his father, grandfather and great-grandfather. All was going to plan until he read *Robinson Crusoe*. Try as his family might to dissuade him, Flinders had faraway shores on the brain. The ambitious lad taught himself geometry and navigation and, when he was fifteen, used family contacts to wangle a job in the navy as a lieutenant's servant.

Flinders headed to New South Wales in 1793. He hooked up with surgeon George Bass and during a six-year stint in the colony the pair made a name for themselves as explorers, especially for their circumnavigation of Van Diemen's Land (Tasmania) in 1798. On Flinders' advice the Governor named the strait between New South Wales and Van Diemen's Land Bass Strait.

Two other names Flinders penned in on those early explorations were Mount Chappelle and Chappelle Islands (now spelt Chappell), a tribute to the woman he had left behind in England. Ann Chappelle and Flinders had been writing regularly since he left, but Ann had become unsure of where she stood with him. She was approaching thirty and he had made no commitment. Her letters to him dwindled.

On his return home in 1800, Flinders wrote with some angst asking Ann why he had not heard from her. 'You must know, and your tender feelings have often anticipated for me, the rapturous pleasure I promised myself on returning from this Antipodean voyage,' he wrote. Even so, Flinders made his priorities clear: 'You see that I make everything subservient to business. Indeed my dearest friend, this time seems to be a very critical period of my life . . . I have more and greater friends than before, and this seems to be the moment that their exertions may be the most serviceable to me. I may now perhaps make a bold dash forward, or remain a poor lieutenant all my life.'

Indeed, Flinders was already in negotiations with the seriously influential Sir Joseph Banks about his bold dash forward.

Against her better judgement, Ann rekindled their long-distance affair and in time wrote asking about his plans.

In his reply, Matthew confessed that a ship was being fitted out for him to return to New South Wales. In January 1801 he wrote his goodbye: 'Adieu, perhaps the last time. This excess of misery is too great to be often recalled. It is seldom that I have written a letter in tears.'

By early April, Flinders had been promoted to commander of HMS *Investigator* and had made the ship his home. With his departure looming, he wrote to Ann on 6 April 1801, explaining that his career was shaping up well and he could now support a wife. If she could be happy living aboard the ship, would she marry him. And PS, could she keep it quiet. It may not go down too well with his bosses.

Less than two weeks later, they were married, and in a last-minute flurry Ann prepared to leave for New South Wales. But when the commissioners of the Admiralty visited the *Investigator* before she set sail, they were horrified to see the new Mrs Flinders aboard.

Flinders soon received a letter from Banks in which he expressed his displeasure, along with a veiled threat that Flinders would be replaced once he reached New South Wales if Ann were to accompany him. Subsequently, the Admiralty took every opportunity to blame mishaps aboard the *Investigator* – even though they were still in home waters – on Mrs Flinders' presence.

So on 17 July 1801, three months after they were married, the *Investigator* set sail for Terra Australis leaving Ann behind. She was far too distressed to even see her husband off.

Flinders didn't hear from her again until 1802, when he received two letters. In the second, dated 7 January 1802, she wrote that she had needed an operation to save her sight. The cause of which, it was said, was too many tears.

Meanwhile, the *Investigator* had reached the Australian coast at Cape Leeuwin on 7 December 1801 and Flinders set about writing himself into the history books. He sailed east along the south coast of Western Australia, past Lucky Bay, and into South Australia, below the desolate cliffs of the Nullarbor. He would become the first person to complete a close circum-navigation of the continent and subsequently recommend the country be called Australia. But the South Australian coast was to be his proving ground, and for some aboard the *Investigator*, catastrophic.

The screaming winds and tempestuous seas still drive grief onto its jagged shores.

Denial Bay, South Australia

AMY The sign reads 'Welcome to Denial Bay, Home of the Blue Swimmer Crab'. On our left is an oyster farm, producing the salty oysters we'd had last night for $7.70 a dozen, opened. The town is just a small, bland collection of modern, but not new, houses.

On the morning Flinders sailed into these waters in early February, 1802, he could see no land to the north-east. With grass and branches floating past, he entertained the idea that there was fresh water mixed in with the salt and that maybe a large river lay ahead on which to drive deep into the mainland. By 7 pm, however, he was pretty much closed in by land and realised 'no river of importance was to be expected'.

The next day, knee deep in scrub and battling the stinking, still heat, Flinders struggled to the top of a high island to check out his surroundings: 'That low land and the island upon which I stood, being the north-eastern most of this archipelago, must, I conceive, be the Isles of St Peter in Nuyts' chart . . . The bay to the northward, between these islands and the mainland, I named Denial Bay, as well in allusion to St Peter (who thrice denied knowing Christ before the crucifixion) as to the deceptive hope we had formed of penetrating by it some distance into the interior country.'

The actual bay of Denial Bay encompasses the waters between the town and nearby Ceduna, out to St Peter Island. St Peter is the patron saint of fishermen. Here, they need all the help they can get.

During my stay back in Sydney, I'd read in the newspapers about a couple of abalone divers missing in these waters. Several days later I was gripped watching the evening news as one of them, having just been released from Ceduna Hospital, recounted his epic tale of survival. I'd never seen anything like it, the way he sobbed through his story with a vacant stare, his wife stroking his arm.

Moved by the story, we feel compelled to find out more. So from Denial Bay, we move to a caravan park in Ceduna and phone the local police. They direct us to Port Lincoln, the fishermen's home town at the tip of Eyre Peninsula, to talk to the cops there and a tuna spotter named Kiwi White.

Driving down the west coast of Eyre Peninsula to Port Lincoln, we are only too aware that in a town where fishing is the primary industry, death at sea is a daily possibility. Halfway down the coast, Anxious Bay sweeps wide on our right. Flinders spent an uneasy night there weathering the difficult combination of squally rain and strong winds that threatened to blow him onto shore. We pass a Mount Misery and then a Mount Hope. Thirty kilometres before Port Lincoln, there's the turn-off to Point Avoid and Avoid Bay – Flinders' warning about all the low-lying isles and rocks exposed to dangerous southern winds. The road continues south to Flinders' Cape Catastrophe and Memory Cove.

Working between Ceduna and Port Lincoln, we piece together what happened to the two abalone fishermen.

When tuna spotter Kiwi White discovered his usual room at the East West Motel in Ceduna – the quiet one at the far end of the car park – had been given to ab diver Howard Rodd and his sheller Danny Thorpe, he went in there to give them a good rubbishing.

'Eh! What are you doing in my room?' he growled playfully, as he plonked himself down for a chat. Howard and Danny, lying on their beds, laughed.

'Have a look at this,' Kiwi said, handing over another newspaper story on sharks. There'd been so many of them since the two surfers were taken in the area a couple of months back, followed by a fatal attack on a suburban Perth beach. This latest article had an incredible photo of a white pointer in mid-air as it leapt from the water.

Danny looked up. 'I've got no worries, I'm in the boat. I'm safe.'

'Well, I've got my cage, so I'm safe,' Howard countered.

In truth, Danny was petrified of sharks. Nearly thirty years of fishing these waters and they still terrified him. Howard, too, lately. Years ago he didn't worry about them a lot. Sure, a white pointer would put the fear of God in him when he seen one, but he didn't see many. Always used to say that if there's no blood in the water and you're not stirred up, you're okay.

He's changed his mind now. It's like they're a different animal. Agitated and aggressive. Especially in this area round Ceduna. He was chased out of the water by a pointer up here last year. Had to get back in the next day to finish his quota and it was the scariest half day of his life. He won't go in without a cage and a shark pod – an electronic device that sends out a repellent vibe – when he's diving here, even if some of the other divers swear black and blue the sharks have become immune to the pods. The cages are okay, like driving a ride-on lawnmower underwater. You stick your hands through the front to get at the abalone. Maybe not quite as efficient, but it's peaceful because you don't have to worry about something sneaking up on you.

Abalone divers come here to Ceduna at the end of every season because they're allowed a bonus 600 kilograms of abs outside their normal quota. It usually takes five or six days to chalk that up. Some of the young guns bowl it over quicker, but Howard is semi-retired, taking it easy. Howard and Danny had taken Sunday off, so by Monday morning, their fourth day in Ceduna, they still had a bit over half their quota to fill.

Danny has been Howard's sheller for thirteen years. They are good mates. They love the life. Danny is known to his mates as Deep Sea because he has such a feeling for the ocean. His family has been in the area for generations. When the forty-seven-year-old built his Port Lincoln home it had to be on a hill so he could see the water. He put in stained-glass windows with dolphin images and began work on an anchor and treasure chest letterbox.

For Howard, the thrill is in the water. The buzz of hitting a good patch of abs, chipping 'em off, filling the bags. The free and easy lifestyle. All the islands and bays, like little paradises. Pristine, untouched, breathtaking.

Their wives back in Port Lincoln know it. They don't like all the risks, but they know their blokes never light up as much as when they talk fishing.

Howard was raised on the rhythms of the tuna seasons. Born in the New South Wales fishing town of Eden, his father was a tuna fisherman and they would move between Eden and Port Lincoln following the schools. When his father realised tuna were being overfished he got out and went into prawns in Port Lincoln. Then the prawn catch started falling, so they went up to the Gulf of Carpentaria chasing banana and tiger prawns. They kept their house in Port Lincoln, though. It was home. Each year they would steam back, unload their catch into the Adelaide market and have two months off.

When an abalone licence came up for sale in Port Lincoln years later, his father bought it. Howard worked for his dad for years then bought the licence from him. Back then it was open slather. You'd work as hard as you liked, catch as much as you liked. But you had to be fit. You couldn't afford to get the flu and have weeks out of the water. They were catching eighteen to twenty tonne of abalone meat a year. Nowadays, under the quota system, you catch eight tonne of meat, although people are starting to buy bits and pieces of quota off other divers for around 800,000 dollars a tonne. But it's been four or five years since anyone sold any, so it's hard to tell.

And it's a hard game. Howard knows it.

That Monday, the two mates headed out to Goat Island, tucked in behind St Peter Island, where they spent the morning. Howard down amongst the rocks and seaweed safe in his shark cage, Danny up on the six-metre aluminium boat, shelling abs and steering.

Sometime around lunch, they decided to knock off early. It was Howard's forty-fourth birthday and his son's fourteenth the following day. He wanted to be home for that. They'd have time for a couple of beers and still make the four to five hour drive back to Port Lincoln.

Danny was driving the boat. Howard was in his wetsuit watching Goat Island recede behind them when out of nowhere the boat spun around and was taking on water. Howard supposed they'd hit a tide line – wind and swell going in one direction, tide going the other, waves standing right up. The bow must have dug in. The deck was covered in water.

'Flatten it!' yelled Howard.

Danny accelerated, sending all the water surging to the stern and it was only then, knee deep, that Howard realised how much of it there was. The stern started to go under. One of the engines stopped. The boat rolled.

The men hauled themselves onto the upturned hull and took stock. Goat Island wasn't far off; Howard wanted to swim for it, but Danny wasn't budging. No bloody way. Sharks. So Howard duck-dived under the boat and grabbed the electronic emergency beacon. He flipped the aerial up, set it off and waited to be rescued. They sat there for hours, drifting further from the island. The afternoon wore on. No help came. Howard dived under the boat again and again, grabbing flares and safety gear and anything else they could use. A prawn boat came by, not far off. They let off flares. But the trawler kept going.

That's when Howard decided to swim. He thought their odds would be better. He tried again to convince Danny to join him, but his mate just couldn't get in the water for all the sharks. Nor would he put on the spare wetsuit.

He'd look like a fucking seal, he argued. Anyway, he'd never get found in a black suit, he said. His wet weather gear was fluorescent. He'd leave that on.

So Howard tied the emergency beacon to the boat, leaving Danny the life jackets and anything else that floated: eskies, empty fuel drums.

Howard was wearing a sleeveless wetsuit, jacket, booties and flippers. He carried an esky lid, not so much for buoyancy as for something to cling to, something to protect his belly from anything that might ram him from below.

Well I'll be having a beer in Ceduna before you, Danny said as Howard started for Goat Island.

The hours rolled on. Howard hadn't made much headway swimming into the breeze. He couldn't see where he was going. It was dark now and there was no light on Goat Island to guide him. All he could see was the glow of Ceduna. Denial Bay is so big, he knew he couldn't reach the glow, but he didn't have any choice now. It was his only landmark, so he swung more to the north and headed for the lights. Time became irrelevant, immeasurable.

His eyes stung from the salt water. The world blurred. He could hardly see a thing. He swam on, very slowly. He didn't want to thrash around and make a noise. If you thrash around, something is going to find you.

Sandy Rodd had been trying to ring her husband on his mobile all night for his birthday. She was at home in Port Lincoln with three of their four boys. Why wasn't he answering? It worried the hell out of her when Howard was working away from home.

'Oh, I know where they'll be,' she thought to herself. 'Down at the pub having a few birthday beers. So he should be.'

He swam all night. Blind and scared. It was the third time he'd been through this and he never wanted to do it again. Ever.

Howard was about twenty-two when they were steaming back from the Gulf of Carpentaria and their prawn trawler hit a shipping container in Bass Strait at 3 am. They rode right up over it, hit the propeller, flooded the engine room and down she went. They lost everything but the pyjamas on their backs.

Howard and the skeleton crew were in a life raft for three days and nights, freezing in T-shirts and jocks and living on barley sugar and water, before they washed up on a beach between Port Fairy and Portland. That accident shook him, but not enough to turn him off the sea.

Years later, Howard was diving for abalone between Coffin Bay and Avoid Bay with a fill-in sheller working up on the boat. As abs piled up waiting to be shelled, the boat over-balanced and sank. Howard, deep in the water, saw it drift down past him. He had to swim the sheller ashore, probably only a kilometre away.

That didn't bother him too much. Gave him a bit of a fright, but nothing like Bass Strait, and nowhere near what he was going through now. He was never going to put himself through this again.

An hour or two after daylight, Howard saw a tiny headland through his swollen eyes. He concentrated on that, swam to it, clinging to his esky lid. The tide picked up again and he knew he had to get to that headland. He swam harder and harder, the pain in his eyes excruciating.

Then, right in front of him, a large fin cut across his path. 'This is the end,' he thought. 'I'm dead.'

Then he heard it breathe. A dolphin. He swam on.

It was Tuesday morning, their son's birthday, and Howard still hadn't rung. By nine-thirty, Sandy was starting to worry. Maybe he and Danny had just had a big night. Maybe they were staying with that bloke Pat the Farmer. They often did that when working around Ceduna. Sandy didn't know Pat the Farmer's full name or phone number. No, this wasn't right. It was their son's birthday.

She phoned the East West Motel and they checked her husband's room.

Their beds had not been slept in.

A search by police found the men's four-wheel drive and boat trailer in a car park by a boat ramp, so it was clear they were on the water. Timing was crucial. If there'd been an accident, the police were already twenty-four hours behind. Chief Inspector Mal Schluter smelt doom. This would be one of his first jobs in his new post as the head police officer in Port Lincoln. He had traded in his job as a surveillance detective and didn't know much about sea rescue, but he drove the four hours up the coast from Port Lincoln to Ceduna to take charge.

Hours blurred one into the other as Howard swam for the headland. His chest and throat were burning, his eyes stinging. He was so bloody thirsty.

Finally, he made it to shore. He climbed rocks and, using his wetsuit top, flippers and esky lid, formed an arrow for the search planes, making sure it didn't look like they'd been washed up.

He had to get water. He checked the rockpools at the bottom of the limestone cliffs but there wasn't any water there. He was as tired as he was thirsty. He laid down.

When he got up, he crawled up the cliff to the top of the headland to look for a track. He found one through the sand dunes but he was having trouble following it. The wind had blown the sand clean and he could barely see, anyway, with his eyes so swollen. Eventually, he went back to the most distinct part of the track and used rocks to form another arrow.

He had to get help for Danny, but he realised he'd be hopeless in the bush. He just couldn't see where he was going, so he headed back to the beach, to follow it to Ceduna.

Darryl Wright from the South Australian Police Water Operations Unit had just started his afternoon shift in Adelaide when the call came through from Ceduna. A notification that a boat was overdue. He made some contingency plans, checking the rosters to see who they could bring in, and calling the air wing. Unfortunately there was a guy, believed to have already killed at least one person, running amok in the Adelaide Hills. They needed the helicopter there. If a search was called at Ceduna, they'd have to run with fixed wings.

Shortly, the Ceduna police rang back. They were going ahead with the search, starting on their own with planes from the fishing industry. Within the hour Wright was in the police aircraft, on his way to Ceduna to be the search and rescue mission co-ordinator.

It was 7.30 pm, approaching dark, when he arrived, not long after Chief Inspector Schluter had driven into town and taken charge. With the last minutes of light, Wright went up in a plane to make a quick sweep over the islands and coastline.

By that stage there were three planes in the air and boats had been directed to the Goat Island–St Peter area, which they knew from local fishermen was where Howard and Danny had been planning to go.

The winds were from the south-east and Wright learnt from the locals that the surface currents are generally the same as the wind. So they cordoned off a search area, which was small for a sea search because the wind blowing into shore confined it.

The land searchers picked up a fuel can, identified as belonging to Howard and Danny.

Their emergency beacon also turned up on the beach, its aerial broken off. It was the old type, designed to be picked up by aircraft rather than satellite. It was still operating without the aerial, but only sufficient for a low-flying plane to pick up a faint signal directly overhead.

Wright thought the gear picked up on the beach that night had drifted there quickly. That was bad, because if the guys were alive they should have drifted in too.

Howard had been walking for a long time when he came to the mouth of what he thought was a big river. He knew he should swim across it, stick to the coast, but he couldn't bring himself to get back in the water. He was so tired, so weak.

He could hear planes and thought, if he just stayed in the open they would find him. The lining of his wetsuit was bright red, so he turned it inside out. He walked and he rested, following the waterline. The planes just seemed too far away.

He swam a little creek which flowed into the river. On the other side of the creek he found a bed of razor fish. He had to keep his strength up, so he broke open some of the shells and ate. Their saltiness made him thirstier.

In the mangroves he found a mossy area, but he couldn't get any water out of the muddy sludge so he took his underpants off and soaked them in it, sucking the moisture out. It was still salty, but not as bad as sea water.

Just on dark, three search planes flew over him — two to the north and one to the south. He could see them, but he knew there wasn't enough light for them to see him. He'd be out there another night.

The mosquitoes were maddening in the mangroves, so he bundled up armfuls of seaweed and went out in the wind where they weren't so bad. He piled the seaweed over himself to keep them and the sandflies off. He tried to sleep, but just lay there.

Tuna spotter Kiwi White's cousin Peter was on the phone: 'Kiwi, there's been a problem up at Ceduna. They're missing a couple of ab divers.'

'Who?' Kiwi asked.

'Howard and Danny.'

'You've got to be joking. I was only talking to them yesterday morning.' Oh hell, Kiwi thought, I've got to do something.

It was eight o'clock on Tuesday night and fifty-six-year-old Kiwi was back home in Port Lincoln. The police planes were already up looking. 'A fat lot of good the police planes are going to do,' he thought.

He rang the police and volunteered his services. He had the plane, he had the expertise, but they didn't seem that keen.

'I don't care, I'm coming up there anyway, 'cause I want to look,' he said.

The police said they'd get back to him. Kiwi was pissed off. He'd been involved in a few searches over the years but he always found it frustrating. Tuna spotters seemed to be the last people called. He's honed his skills over twenty-one years of looking in the water hour after hour, day after day, but the police have all their protocols: this is where you go; only look in the water for twenty minutes at a time or you'll lose your concentration. That's bullshit. Spotting a seagull sitting on the water, a buoy off a cray pot, a school of bluefin, it's all second nature. If there's a body there, or an upturned boat, he's going to see it. Not patting himself on the back, that's just what he does.

He's had two engine failures in his time and has often wondered if he ever goes in the drink whether it will be the other tuna guys who find him.

Just before midnight, the phone rang and it was the Ceduna police. They asked him to be up there by 6.30 am.

Howard had at last dozed off when the tide came in and soaked his bed. He was wet and tired, it was still dark, but he wasn't going back into the mangroves, not with the mosquitoes. So he walked.

He heard an outboard coming along the coast from Denial Bay. He figured if it kept coming, it would reach him. But it didn't keep coming. He knew it wasn't far away. Yelled out to it.

He kept walking. Rain fell before dawn. It only lasted a few minutes but it was enough for him to put his jocks on his head and get some moisture from them. He got some more by rubbing the jocks over mangrove leaves.

The sun came up at last and he could see where he was going. He spotted a fence line. A track ran alongside and he followed it, but he was out of strength. Had to keep stopping.

At 6 am that Wednesday morning, Mal Schluter and Darryl Wright were holding a briefing with the searchers. They'd both been up until the early hours planning the search, defining the perimeters. Schluter drew on Wright's expertise.

There were three briefings: land, sea and air. They now had four aircraft, ten boats and about twenty land searchers – Emergency Services volunteers and abalone divers.

Wright had prepared search grids for the air and sea searchers. He laid his Perspex grids over the charts, showing the pilots how he'd divided the air into four parallel columns. One for each plane. They would fly at different altitudes to minimise the risk of collision, each pilot slowly working his way up and down his column of air space.

Up in his plane, Kiwi got more frustrated. There was no sign of Howard or Danny. His pilot came right down and they spotted a blue esky and a life jacket on the beach. The SES came and picked up the pieces.

More and more debris was found in a concentrated area of beach, so Wright knew they were searching the right place. Anybody floating, alive or dead, would go the same way. If someone was swimming they could vary the direction, but Wright knew from locals that it was extremely hard to swim against the surface currents.

Howard, however, had done just that, reaching shore several kilometres east of the zone.

Sandy was waiting for any news of Howard back in Port Lincoln. Danny's wife Debbie, a nurse at the local hospital, was there too with their three children. So were Danny's parents.

Sandy had started phoning relatives, bringing them over, expecting the worst. She called their eldest son in Queensland and told him he'd better come home.

Howard followed the fence line to a road at a Y-junction. He thought it was best to keep going north, and placed sticks on the road to indicate the fork he was taking.

He kept walking, using a stick to support himself. He followed birds to try and find water. There wasn't any. He may have slept. Were they water tanks up ahead? No, just seed storage bins. He had to keep going. God, he should never have left the coast. What should he do? He had to get help for Danny. Had to find water. Had to sit down. It was so hard to get back up. Had to keep going. Walking, resting, walking.

Then he heard some sheep. Water! He found tanks and a trough and drank so much he was sick.

He laid in the trough. Washed himself and the wetsuit and it felt good. Now he had a chance.

He continued north up the road and came to a five-way intersection. Somebody would have to pick him up here. He waited and waited. He fell asleep again. It was good to close his eyes. They felt better.

He woke up and was washing his eyes out with spit when he saw the roof of a farmhouse. He ran.

He got there and it was abandoned. He could still hear planes. He broke into the house through a window but there was no food, so he drank from the rainwater tank, then found some matches and an old pair of clothes. He wanted to light a big fire, but it was so dry he worried about starting a bushfire. He got an old drum and rolled it into a clearing, put some cardboard boxes into it and lit it up.

He heard the planes returning so he shoved some old tyres in the drum too. Black smoke spewed out, but the planes flew on. His last chance was to get back to the intersection.

Judging from where the debris was washing up, Wright guessed Howard and Danny had come to grief around Goat Island. Concentrating the search back in that direction, one of the planes spotted an orange air hose floating on the surface. Two boats were called in. On board one of them was a diving mate of Howard and Danny's, Norm Craig. Norm dived down and discovered the sunken boat.

It was forty-eight hours since the accident. No-one was holding out much hope.

The police aircraft was due for a service in Adelaide and had to leave that afternoon. The rescue helicopter was flying over to replace it, with a second search and rescue co-ordinator to replace Wright, who'd virtually worked around the clock. Having located so much debris, the land searchers were returning to Ceduna, the boats and planes coming in to refuel.

Lynton and Beryl Gurney were in the Ceduna deli that afternoon when they heard the boat belonging to the two missing fishermen had been found, sunk.

The Gurneys live out west of Ceduna, at Coorabie, but had come into town to run errands.

By the time they left Ceduna, around 2.30 pm, they could see all the search boats coming into port and the police plane flying back towards Adelaide. They presumed the search had been called off.

Rather than follow the highway home, the couple took Denial Bay Road. The dirt road is slower than the highway, but Lynton, whose job is to keep starlings out of Western Australia, was keen to look for the birds, and Beryl, a grain classifier, wanted to see the wheat crops.

They were about thirty kilometres west of town when they saw a small person shuffling north up a crossroad.

'It looks like a kid,' said Beryl. 'Wonder if there's been an accident or something.'

As they pulled up, the kid turned towards them. They saw now it was a man, maybe in his forties, and there was something wrong with him. Maybe drunk. Lynton wound his window up.

The guy was feeling his way, like he couldn't see.

In the car, Lynton suddenly realised: 'He's got a wetsuit on his shoulder!' He had wetsuit boots on, too. Lynton wound the window back down.

'Are you okay?'

'Help me. Find my mate.'

The Gurneys jumped out and gave him a drink of orange juice from the car fridge. They loaded him into their troopie, three squeezed in the front. Howard kept wiping his eyes, huge red puffy balls full of gunk. All he wanted to know was whether they'd found his mate. He was desperate to get to the police.

The couple didn't want to tell him about the boat being found; about the plane they saw going back to Adelaide; about the gear they heard had washed up.

'They're still out looking,' said Lynton. 'We'll take you to the hospital.'

They arrived in Ceduna at 3.20 pm. It had been over two days since Howard's boat had capsized. He'd swum fifteen kilometres to shore and walked twenty kilometres through sand, mangroves and farmland, but he insisted on going to the police station rather than hospital.

No-one was at the front counter when they walked in the station, so Lynton went through and stuck his head into a room full of people. He sang out, 'We've got one of the guys here from the boat.'

Wright and Schluter were debriefing a group of searchers and paid no attention. Both thought it was just one of the searchers.

Lynton tried again: 'No, there's a survivor out the front!'

The place exploded. Wright and Schluter ran to the front office where Howard was slumped on the floor. Wright was concerned about his health, but he also knew he was going to need Howard if they were to find Danny.

Howard was in a bad way. Distraught over his mate, distressed by his eyes, hypothermic.

They called an ambulance, bathed his eyes and gave him some fluids.

While the ambulance officers tended him, he started to talk, but he was confused about what day it was, confused about where he'd come ashore. Wright showed him a chart and Howard wrongly identified Point James as the point, rather than

Point Peter, four nautical miles away. But he did say he walked along the beach and across Davenport Creek.

Howard was taken to hospital, and the reinvigorated search crews went back out to find Danny. If one of them had made it to shore . . .

The land troops were sent into the Davenport Creek area, where Howard had come through the mangroves. Jet skis and dinghies roared in. The newly arrived police helicopter flew low over the swamp.

Schluter visited Howard in hospital later that afternoon. This time the fisherman correctly pinpointed Point Peter as the spot he had come ashore. A land crew was sent to get his gear.

The search continued until nightfall, resuming at six o'clock next morning, but things weren't looking good for Danny. The police knew now that he wasn't wearing a wetsuit. He would be vulnerable to cold. Wright believed it would be near impossible for anyone to have survived a second night in the water.

He concentrated on the land search. It's a harsh reality, but his job is to find people alive, and there's no point putting resources into an area where you're going to find them dead. Plus, Howard had proven that you could get ashore. But then, Howard was a fit, strong swimmer. Danny was a smoker, believed to have some kind of emphysema.

Howard identified a lunch box from the boat. It was imprinted with large teeth marks. Then they looked more closely at the life jacket found by searchers. Howard identified it as Danny's. It was shredded.

Denial Bay, South Australia

AMY We drive out along Denial Bay Road to where the Gurneys picked Howard up. Paddocks sway under shin high golden grasses. The abandoned farmhouse is less than a kilometre away. Even up close it doesn't look long abandoned. Mock Grecian pillars hold up the front verandah. The rear is fibro. It's surrounded by cactus and out the back, between the house and the car graveyard, we find a drum with a burnt tyre in it.

We measure back down the narrow dirt road. Howard walked eight and a half kilometres to get here from the mangroves. He had crossed the far busier Davenport Creek Road.

The next day we drive to the mouth of Davenport Creek and see three other vehicles pottering about in the area. There's a four-wheel-drive track out to the beach, which runs for several kilometres to the point where Howard landed. About halfway along you cross over some dunes back down to Davenport Creek. We find a family camped there with a caravan. The father is fishing with razor fish, his son is playing behind him. Says they've been there two days. The fishing's not bad.

We attempt to walk along the creek to where Howard would have crossed, but mangroves soon block our way, about 400 metres still from the mouth. By going the intuitive way towards Ceduna, Howard had walked away from a popular area into a wilderness.

On our return, the father asks: 'Did the mozzies get ya?'

'Sure did.'

'I should've warned you.'

By the time Howard was released from hospital and fronted that intimate, distressing media conference, the search for Danny was being wound down. No-one knows what happened: whether he drowned and was eaten by a shark; whether he was attacked while he was still alive; how the emergency beacon's aerial came to be broken off.

Danny's widow Debbie, their three children, Kelly, twelve, Bonney, ten and James, eight, and Danny's parents Sid and Hazel, held a memorial service on 10 December 2000. Hundreds gathered at the Marina Hotel in Port Lincoln to say their goodbyes. Debbie and the kids placed flowers in the water. Sid and Hazel thanked the searchers in an article in the *Port Lincoln Times*.

It emerged later that Sid and Hazel Thorpe were actually angry. Not with the searchers but with the organisers, the government. They should have called in the army, should have had Orions up there. And they were angry with the abalone industry, calling for more stringent safety measures and full overhauls of the ab boats.

We read in the *Port Lincoln Times* Sid Thorpe saying he had always told Danny, 'Never leave the boat.'

'I might have even put the idea in his head years ago.'

In Port Lincoln, from where we hope to visit Flinders' Cape Catastrophe, we call the Thorpes and they agree to speak with us, but when we turn up they have changed their minds, preferring to save it for the coroner.

Howard and Sandy Rodd, however, have agreed to meet us. As Sandy tells me over the phone, Howard knows this coast better than anyone.

CHAPTER 28

I CAUSED *an* INSCRIPTION *to be* ENGRAVEN

Port Lincoln, South Australia

AMY Port Lincoln is an extremely wealthy country town, too prosperous to keep most of the historic buildings it must have built in its 160-year history. The flash new marina, Lincoln Cove, could have been shipped in from the Gold Coast. Perfectly homogeneous and colour co-ordinated, the canal estate houses seem at odds with the working boats parked in the channels: tuna boats, prawn boats, cray boats, sturdy-looking things built for angry seas, all netting, rope and cable. They give the Pleasantville marina some charm.

Discreetly parked away in a semi-private canal are the huge luxury cruisers, or 'stink boats' as we've heard them called. As in stinking rich. The fishing industry is worth about 300 million dollars a year to Port Lincoln. But it comes at a high price.

Outside the Marina Hotel is a striking monument, the centrepiece of which is a rippling stone sculpture. At first glance it looks like any undecipherable piece of modern art. Up close, the ripples are revealed as the bowed heads of grieving women on one side, men being swallowed by the sea on the other.

It's called 'Fishermen Lost at Sea'. Engraved in the rocks circling the sculpture are the names of men and boats lost since 1959. There are forty-five names on it and there is room for plenty more. Several bunches of dead flowers rest at the base, presumably from Danny Thorpe's memorial service a week ago.

We have arranged to meet Howard and Sandy Rodd in the Grand Tasman Hotel, overlooking the town jetty. It is an anxious wait as the minutes of the appointed hour for our meeting tick by.

We wonder how anyone can recover from the trauma Howard has been through. Danny died only a few weeks ago, the image of Howard sobbing on television is still so vivid: 'I never should have left me mate. I should have stayed with him. You're not supposed to split up – you're supposed to stay together.'

He had said then that he would never return to sea. 'I've been fishing all my life, but I'm sick of losing friends and people.'

We recognise the couple immediately. We knew Howard was short but he is also well built. What's more striking is the gentleness about him. Even vulnerability. You can't help but wonder if he is shell-shocked. He is shy, speaks in a low voice, slow and deliberate, still with the thousand-yard stare we'd seen in the press conference. His skin looks soft, his hair feathery.

Sandy, on the other hand, looks strong and protective. She has dark hair and wears confident lipstick. She also has a maternal gentleness. She calls us 'sweetheart' and 'darling', and it's nice.

We talk about the fishing industry and the names Matthew Flinders left along this coast: Denial Bay, Anxious Bay, Cape Catastrophe and Avoid Bay. Far from avoiding it, the crayfishermen love it in there, Howard says.

They both think this is God's country with its stunning, secluded beaches. Howard loves the diving, the big blue gropers, the abalone and crayfish, the thrill of swimming with southern right whales.

These places are so calm and beautiful most of the time, Howard says, and then you'll get a day when the wind and tide just whistle through and they are suddenly treacherous.

'Boats sink and fishermen live with that. It'll keep happening – probably on an average of one a year, sometimes two a year. Ab boats get swamped and tipped over – it just happens. Very often it doesn't happen like what happened to us, when you're travelling. You're more vulnerable around the rocks and the reefs and in close. Usually when you're travelling you think you're safe as houses.'

Howard and Sandy were late because they were held up with their solicitor, doing the paperwork to lease out the abalone licence.

'So you're not going back to sea?' I ask.

'Well, I'm just sort of debating it at the moment. I'm not going back diving anymore, as far as the abalone diving's concerned it's finished. But I don't know about the fishing side of it just yet. I might do it on a part-time sort of basis, I'm not sure. Just a little bit of professional fishing, probably catching whiting and squid and a bit of snapper. Just close to Port Lincoln and that'd be about it, I think.'

'At least the abalone licence has proven to be a good asset,' Mark says.

'Yes, I think the kids'll take it over in time. Just want to see how time goes on.'

'Is your nineteen-year-old interested in fishing yet?'

'Not yet,' the two say together.

'He's away in Queensland at the moment trying to find himself a little bit,' Sandy says. 'Some kids are responsible and some aren't, well, he was not responsible . . . so he's better off learning under somebody else's wing and doing something else first. Learning to appreciate what he's really got. And I think this little episode has helped him a great deal, sad as it may be.'

Even though there was often a ball of anxiety in the pit of Sandy's stomach when Howard was out diving, she'd be happy for her children to go into it.

'I've always done what I wanted to do, and the guys love fishing, you listen to them talk about it. My God, it's their life, you know.

'Nuh, my kids can do whatever they want to as long as they're happy at what they're doing. If they never even want to go out in a boat, I couldn't give a hoot,' Sandy says.

It's hard to reconcile this love of the sea with the horrors Howard has been through. As he tells us, it just happens. Still, we notice Howard can't seem to bring himself to speak Danny's name. He hesitates each time it comes up and then calls his mate of thirteen years 'the sheller'.

 When Matthew Flinders sailed the *Investigator* round the bottom of what is now Eyre Peninsula, he nestled in behind some islands. Seeing no land to the north-east, he pondered the glorious possibilities.

'Large rivers, deep inlets, inland seas, and passages into the Gulph of Carpentaria, were terms frequently used in our conversations of this evening; and the prospect of making an interesting discovery seemed to have infused new life and vigour into every man in the ship,' Flinders wrote.

Early next morning, 21 February 1802, he stepped ashore on the largest of the islands – which he named Thistle's Island 'from the master who accompanied me' – and surveyed the mainland coast.

'In the opening between Thistle's Island and the main are several small isles; and the two southernmost so much contract the entrance of the passage that one mile and a half of its breadth, between the main land and western isle, are alone safe for ships; I gave to this the name of Thorny Passage.'

The ship's water casks were just about empty, so Flinders and Thistle searched the island for water. Unsuccessful, they returned to the ship with the intention of running over to the mainland to search there.

But back on board, Flinders discovered that the bearings he had taken were substantially different from the longitude observed by his brother, Lieutenant Samuel Flinders. The only option was to retake the measurements. It would be nearly dark by the time it was done, so he had to send Thistle to the mainland in search of water. Thistle went across in the cutter with a crew of seven.

Just on dusk, the cutter was sighted under sail returning to the *Investigator*, hopefully with the news they had found water and an anchorage for the night. Half an hour later, however, Thistle still hadn't reached the ship. The cutter had disappeared into the darkness.

The crew on board the *Investigator* shone light on the water, and Lieutenant Fowler was sent out in a boat to find the men. Two nerve-racking hours passed without sight of the little boat, nor any word back from Fowler. Finally, a gun was fired from the *Investigator*. Fowler returned, reporting that near the spot where they had last seen the cutter, he had met with such a strong rippling of tide, his own boat had nearly come to grief. It was too dark to see anything more.

Flinders knew it was bad. The tide was ebbing south. Anything floating in the water would be carried straight out to sea. What's more, only two of the eight on board could swim.

At daybreak, he set sail across Thorny Passage for the mainland, towards where the cutter had last been seen. He steered into a small sandy cove and dropped anchor.

A search boat was sent out 'and presently returned towing in the wreck, bottom upward; it was stove in every part, having to all appearance been dashed against the rocks. One of the oars was afterwards found, but nothing could be seen of our unfortunate shipmates,' wrote Flinders. 'The boat was again sent away in search; and a midshipman was stationed upon a headland, with-out side of the cove, to observe everything which might drift past with the tide. Mr Brown and a party landed to walk along the shore to the northward, whilst I proceeded to the southern extremity of the mainland, which was now named Cape Catastrophe. On landing at the head of the cove I found several footmarks of our people, made on the preceding afternoon when looking for water.'

He climbed to the top of Cape Catastrophe and searched for the missing men with his telescope, but there was no sign. Over the next few days, the crew split up to continue the search for the eight men, at the same time charting the coast. A few more pieces of debris washed up.

'The recovery of their bodies was now the furthest to which our hopes extended; but the number of sharks seen in the cove and at the last anchorage rendered even this prospect of melancholy satisfaction extremely doubtful; and our want of water becoming every day more pressing, we prepared to depart for the examination of the new opening to the northward. I caused an inscription to be engraven upon a sheet of copper, and set up on a stout post at the head of the cove, which I named Memory Cove.'

Six islands lie within Thorny Passage, and two islets just outside of it. With the largest already named for Thistle, Flinders named the remaining seven islands in memory of his lost crewmen.

They said their goodbyes and sailed into an inlet to the north, which Flinders named Port Lincoln after his birthplace.

Port Lincoln, South Australia

AMY Since we arrived in Port Lincoln, we've been trying to find someone who will take us by boat to Cape Catastrophe and Memory Cove. But we gather it's only the crayfishermen and abalone divers who go out that way. And we haven't been able to convince any of them. None of the cruise boats do it. Even the advertised trip to another Flinders-named place, Dangerous Reef – where underwater scenes for *Jaws* were filmed – no longer exists.

Ringing around some of the smaller charter companies, it emerges that, while no-one usually goes down that far, there is one guy who might take us.

'Paul at the dive shop' is, it seems, our last shot. When we track him down, Paul tells us it will depend on the weather; he will only do it if and when the conditions are absolutely right.

We'll wait. We're enjoying our tent site in the caravan park overlooking Boston Bay. The view is fantastic, the southerlies have finally dropped, it's almost Christmas and we're living on fresh prawns and tuna. In the evenings, kids gather at the wharf below us to jig for squid.

By Wednesday morning, the weather's fine and at last we're going to Cape Catastrophe. We steam out of Lincoln Cove past the high-bowed fishing boats with their towering crow's nests. Past Boston Island and the 105 tuna farms.

Our skipper, Paul Twikler, is impossibly chirpy and energetic at this early hour. Most of Paul's dive business is taken up working the tuna cages, but he also takes out diving and fishing charters. He visited here five years ago and saw the money being generated, the fortunes made. Knew there had to be something here for him.

We round Cape Donington and enter Thorny Passage. The swell is jagged. Jarring as we thwack down each wave. The tide is going out, the wind and swell coming in. A serrated sea and queasy tummies.

We're sitting in the wheelhouse of the *Snapper Trapper*, a thirty-foot aluminium Reefmaster, trying to keep our eyes on the horizon. The talk inevitably turns to sharks.

'I'd never surf here,' says Paul. 'And snorkel – I rarely snorkel; floating on the surface, you look like a seal.'

This coming from a tuna farm diver – a job something akin to being a shepherd on the Serengeti. His theory is that if you just dig in at the bottom, sharks can't get the momentum to hit you. 'They attack up, not down.'

Paul tells us he dived off Cape Catastrophe recently. He saw dolphins, sea dragons and big blue gropers. I ask about Dangerous Reef, but he says he'd never dive there. Pointer territory. It's a good fishing spot, though.

He recently took a woman there to mark the twentieth anniversary of her father's death. Her father had been on a cray boat that went down on the reef. Both men on board were lost. It's a huge reef, with only a fraction above the water. 'That's why it's called Dangerous Reef.' Anyway, he adds, it stinks of seagull shit.

The islands named for Flinders' lost crew come into view, dull and hazy grey. Their protection brings a welcome calm to our ride.

'Little got shafted,' Paul comments as we pass Little Island. 'His one's only a little island. Thistle and Taylor did okay.'

Soon we are deep within the arc of islands, in view of Cape Catastrophe, approaching the gap between it and Smith Island. Nearing the vicinity where the little cutter went down with Flinders' men. So many times in the past week we've been told how the wind and tide can just whistle through this passage. And, Paul adds as we near, when the tide is going in one direction and the wind and swell in another, it becomes a big pool of slop, jacks right up. It had looked smooth, but as we round the Cape the swell grows huge, tossing us high and smacking us back down. Mark and I are astounded.

'This is nothing,' says Paul. 'Fifteen foot swell, tide going out, eight men in a little ketch – I wouldn't be getting in it.'

We head into the sandy cove on the western side of the Cape. We can only imagine that this was where Thistle went looking for water and Flinders found footprints in the sand. The beach rises steeply into sandy cliffs, mottled green.

We drop anchor and ponder the lost men's fate over a cup of coffee. Then we try a bit of fishing. The fish are literally jumping onto our hooks; two on each line. Hauling up double headers. Cod and a big parrot fish, leather jacket and an assortment of pink and purple and orange fish. We settle on a lovely snapper from the smorgasbord, and take it home for dinner.

A few days later we leave the sea and head to the heavy green vines, rose gardens and rolling hills of the Barossa Valley for Christmas, where we snuggle up in a motel in Lyndoch for a festive and romantic couple of days. It's the first time we've stopped since I came back and everything feels right with the world.

With the Map rolled out on the bed, *Carols By Candlelight* on the tele, we focus our attention south of Adelaide, on the Fleurieu Peninsula, and a trail of dots we will whiz by on the way into Victoria before catching the ferry to Tasmania.

CHAPTER 29

HEAVENLY RIVER

Fleurieu Peninsula, South Australia

MARK▶ Driving up the side of Mount Terrible, a line of cars starts to accrue behind us. Mount Terrible was a horror spot for the old bullock drivers and still looks tough for the modern motorist. We are in a zone where the South Australian Government puts little red and black posts by the road to mark accidents, red for injuries and black for fatalities. As we go up from the coast, with Mount Terrible's peak one of the nobby, grassy hills to our left, we tally a dozen injuries and two fatalities in the kilometre or two into the town of Myponga.

When we've finished denying it was Our Ponga, we get down to finding the place we've really come to see, the River Parananacooka. This, according to *Manning's Place Names of South Australia* is: 'A corruption of the Aboriginal words "excreta and urine of the autumn stars", due to the intense brackish water at the end of the river in summer.'

There, by the river of excreta and urine of the autumn stars, we find a lovely old mill with a National Trust plaque on it and a 'For Sale' sign out the front. I'd been boring everyone (i.e. Amy) with my thoughts that all South Australian towns should be chocka with ye olde arts and crafts shoppes and other yokel industry.

They'd done it here at Second Valley, and poor old Leonards

Mill Motel and Reception Centre was clearly out of business, as was the arts and craft shop over the road. Oh well.

The river of heavenly poo and wee is dry. So we head downstream to where it meets the sea at the Second Valley caravan park.

Leaving the car in a little car park, Amy starts covering her nose.

'Can't you smell that?'

'No. Oh, maybe a little bit.'

We can't figure out whether it is the river that stinks or the yellow brick toilet block above it.

Next day sees us crossing what the South Australians insist on calling the River Murray, as opposed to the Murray River, and on to Coonalpyn – a dull, flat town dominated by a wheat silo and nothing else. A tunnel under the railway tracks is signposted as a tourist attraction because some school kids painted murals in it.

In Peg's Shoestring Kitchen and Tourist Information, I plan to trick Peg. Go in there, ask a few tourist questions and then inquire how the town got its name. It all goes to plan and she answers. 'It's Aboriginal.'

'What for?'

'Barren woman.'

Uh huh. I have her right where I want her. It is here that I was to draw on my knowledge from *Manning's Place Names of South Australia* and say: 'Oh, really. I thought it meant mouse poo.' But Peg is such a phenomenal talker I never get the chance, and end up walking out of there with a wheelbarrowful of brochures, and am particularly taken by the albino kangaroo somewhere nearby.

Defeated, we push on, east into Victoria and the New Year, along the Great Ocean Road. Holidays are not the best time to do the cardboard-cutout tourism thing in Victoria. Especially in a heat wave. Just finding a parking spot is hard enough as we move in a herd from one beauty spot to the next.

Park. Lock car. Stand behind people until they leave the front of the viewing platform. Gasp. Think about taking photo. Smelly people invade personal space. Gasp again. Leave. Unlock car, and on it goes.

Hot and bothered we learn that all the campgrounds are full and we find ourselves in Port Campbell's overflow area – next to the oval in the Port Campbell recreation reserve. It's a scorcher. A swim and an iceblock beckon. The ocean is about the same temperature as the iceblock and despite the incredible heat it's impossible to stay in for more than a few minutes. All the kids around us – who clearly knew better – have wetsuits.

We retreat to the tent. There's been something on Amy's mind for a while. She wants me to cut her hair. I think she's crazy.

Port Campbell, Victoria

AMY Having dwelt on it for at least a year, I decided on New Year's Eve that I was ready to chop off my shoulder-length hair. I'd given Mark's hair and beard a trim back at Port Lincoln and thought, why not? He assures me he has a great deal of experience, having cut his own hair often enough. He also used to give flat tops at boarding school for two dollars a pop.

Mark feels I'm putting too much trust in him. We've had so many people say to us over the past months that if we can make it through a year in a car and a tent together, we'll make it through anything. But I think he feels that making it through this haircut will be a far greater accomplishment.

He is somewhat confused by my lack of fear. I can't really explain it, either. It's as though when I made the resolution, I went into some kind of trance, immune to it. So I sit under the tent awning, wearing my bikini and hand him the scissors. His first step is to cut a wonky bob – still shorter than I've had it since I was thirteen. He makes me look in the car's side mirror and gives me an out.

No, keep going, I tell him. So he chops and chops. Great chunks of hair cover my back and stomach. Then, the wind picks up, it starts to rain and wet hair blows around, sticking to everything. The conditions aren't exactly ideal. Keep going, I say.

As it gets shorter, he becomes unsure what to do next, and tells me to look in the mirror. Big mistake.

It looks as though I've just hacked at my head with a knife. Like I've gone nuts or have lice or something. All I want to do is cry, but I'd assured Mark over and over that I wouldn't be upset if it didn't work out.

'It's okay,' I say, to reassure us both. 'We'll be in Melbourne in a couple of days. I can get it fixed up there.'

But, really, my brain is spinning.

Keep going, I tell him. Shorter.

And he does.

Shorter, shorter.

And after maybe an hour of tension, it's done. Back to the mirror. Well, it doesn't look too bad. I still feel I've made a big mistake. There are a few bits sticking out, but he has actually done a pretty good job.

I, however, am on a roller coaster.

'No worries,' I say. 'I can get it fixed. It'll grow. Sorry babe, it's not your fault. I just don't like it. I'll just have to wear a hat for the next few months.' I can see Mark is taking it personally, but do I stop?

'You just can't look at me for a couple of months, okay?'

His shoulders drop. He knew this whole thing had the potential to go horribly wrong, and now it has. He looks as though he doesn't know whether to yell at me for being so childish or run and hide in a corner. Instead he says, 'But I want to look at you.'

'Don't look at me!' I insist, covering my head.

'I am going to look at you.'

'Don't push me.'

'I'm not pushing you.'

'Don't push me!'

The tears well up in my eyes. Ah, yes, this outcome always had good odds.

'You look so pretty,' he keeps saying. He fixes a couple of the sticky-outy bits and we head back to the mirror. He's smiling. 'It really suits you.'

Suddenly, I love it. Phew.

'Let's celebrate.'

We buy a bottle of Lambrusco and some fish and chips for dinner, then follow it up with a bottle of cheap 'champagne'. It's a big splurge but I'm suddenly on a high. So free and happy and joyful with this short, short hair. Strangely, it makes us feel romantic and close.

The next morning at about nine o'clock I ring Mum and tell her Mark chopped off my hair.

'Have you two been drinking?' she asks.

CHAPTER 30

I HASTENED *from this* GOLGOTHA

Bass Strait

MARK▶ I've spent the last few days in Melbourne steering Amy away from good mirrors, fearing my handiwork won't stand up to the scrutiny. Thankfully, a hairdresser friend of ours, Harry, made all the right gushing noises. (Thanks, mate.)

Now we're heading to Tassie where hopefully hair doesn't matter so much. It certainly doesn't matter right now.

Only minutes after the *Devil Cat* leaves Port Phillip Bay, it turns from a cruise ship into a hospital ship. The captain announces winds gusting up to thirty knots from the east-north-east with a three-metre swell from the west-south-west. I now know that when people talk about lumpy seas they're not just talking about the water.

'There's spew everywhere,' reports Amy early in proceedings. 'The crew are all wearing white gloves to clean it up. If I had known this I would never have come.'

You have no idea of the venom with which this last statement was delivered.

That's the thing about Amy. She has a cast iron stomach when it comes to motion sickness. Hell, she has just polished off a chicken loaf, mayonnaise and walnut sandwich washed down with a meat pie, and it's staying down fine. Just the slightest hint of someone else being sick, however, will have her hand shooting to her mouth to contain the retch.

I'd never noticed how common chunder was in movies until I started going with Amy. I'm like a father protecting his child from crude sex scenes, but never quick enough. Strangely, her entire family suffers the same complaint.

Protecting her here is far more difficult. She only has to look up. We are in a bad spot near the toilets. A man walks out wiping his mouth. A woman doesn't quite make it in. And as the Devil Cat moves further into Bass Strait and more and more passengers succumb, crew members bring them to a spot in the middle of the boat under the stairs near us. They lay them out with blankets over their bodies and wet towels over their heads. Corpses.

And those of us still going, our faces are becoming shapeless, saggy. The barman is the least worked man on the planet.

Sitting here, trying to watch *What's Eating Gilbert Grape*, the swell is coming directly from the side. So looking out the windows, you see only ocean one moment, then the boat swings back and you see only sky.

'They should have an exclusive no vomit zone,' says Amy, desperate. 'If you even *think* you are going to vomit, you can't go in this area.'

About five hours after departure and with about two hours to go to George Town, we come into the lee of Flinders Island and the swell subsides. The barman serves a drink. Shape returns to faces. Amy looks up.

Ten years after Sydney was settled, nobody had noticed that a strait separated Van Diemen's Land from the mainland. But in December 1798, George Bass and Matthew Flinders edged into it in a chunky little yellow boat called the *Norfolk* with a modern-looking rig of jib and mainsail.

The strong easterly wind made no impression at all on the stronger westerly swell. That convinced them that 'a very wide strait did really exist betwixt Van Diemen's Land and New South Wales, and also now that we had certainly passed it'. They were at the north-western tip of the island 'terminated by steep black cliffs'. The coast looped round to the south-east for '7 or 8 miles in high dismal-looking cliffs, which appear as if they had not had a respite from the dashing of a heavy sea almost up to their summits for this thousand years . . . The night was very dark and tempestuous.'

They called it Cape Grim, and its history would get a lot grimmer yet.

Smithton, Tasmania

MARK▶ We had read about something called the Cape Grim Baseline Air Pollution Station, so we drop in at their office in Smithton to see how we can get out there. The boss of the show is Dr Neil Tindale, a Kiwi whose thirteen years in the United States remain thick in his accent. He is neat in jeans and joggers, with a mo and big, square glasses that shrink his eyes.

He explains that in the 1950s industrialised countries started to realise that air quality problems were no longer confined to the cities, but were spreading like blankets over large regions of Europe and North America.

They didn't know how dirty their air was, however, because they didn't know how clean it should be. A string of 'baseline' air quality stations were set up down the Pacific from Alaska to the Antarctic, to measure clean air. 'If you don't have that baseline you can always argue that that level of pollution is natural,' says Tindale.

'If you go upwind of us, south-west, you pass underneath South Africa. You have to go all the way to South America to hit a land mass.' That's why, when the wind is blowing in its usual direction from the south-west, Cape Grim can lay claim to the cleanest air in the world. It's official.

And when world leaders gather for their climate change summits, data coming from Cape Grim and the other Baseline stations is very much at the forefront of all the posturing that goes on. Cape Grim was one of the most important measuring stations for telling the world that the ban on chlorofluorocarbons (CFC) that was introduced to save the ozone layer through the 1980s, was actually starting to have an effect. The amount of CFCs in Cape Grim's air started to level off in the early 1990s and has just started to drop.

That's all great, but Tindale tells us we aren't allowed out to the station, which is fifty kilometres west of here. To go to Cape Grim, we need the permission of the Van Diemen's Land Company.

Of all the royal charter companies, such as the East India Company and the Hudson Bay Company, that were set up by royal command to trade and conquer new territories, the Van Diemen's Land Company is the only one left. Sourly unprofitable since it began in 1825, it's as if it has been forgotten out here on the top left corner of Tassie on this huge property called Woolnorth.

We are picked up at the gate by Stephanie Porteus–Else, the wife of the company's beef, cattle and sheep manager, Ken Else. Stephanie met Ken when she applied to be a tour guide on the property nine years ago. Now she runs the show. She is a pretty blonde with enormous energy and enthusiasm, thoroughly engaging. There's barely a question throughout the day she can't answer.

As she drives us the twenty-two kilometres from the gate to the homestead we pass a lot of modern brick houses and skinny-rumped dairy cows. They are milking a whopping 9000 of them at the moment, with ten sharefarmers running ten dairies. The country is greenish, drying at the edges, and she tells us it's been in unprecedented drought for four years, so the dairy numbers are coming down. The largest milking shed is down from 1800 to 1400.

Stephanie gives a potted history of the place as we drive. 'The Van Diemen's Land Company didn't want to come here, they wanted to go around the Mersey River, but the governor of the day, Arthur, had a rule that every new settlement had to be west of the previous one, so they found themselves out here, beyond the ramparts of civilisation,' she says.

We arrive at the Woolnorth homestead, a mix of modern buildings and white-painted convict cottages, one said to be haunted by a broken-hearted Scot named Mason.

Then Stephanie drives us on to the dramatic cliffs at Cape Grim. The wind is blowing hard, but unfortunately it's from the east, so it's not that 'cleanest air in the world'. She says they clocked a gust here recently at 176.9 kilometres an hour. 'That was only a gust, but it sat steadily at 170 kilometres an hour for an hour. We had friends ringing up and saying, "are you alright?". And we'd go, "Yeah . . . Why?". And they'd say they just heard on the radio about this gale we were having. It was a bit windy but it just went over the top of us.'

'Danger Cliff Face', declares a sign at the edge. 'Do Not approach edge of Cliff'. Which is of course the first thing we do when we get out of the car. Two great lumps of rock, the Doughboys, are just across a deep channel, and down below us to our right is a deep gorge of a bay, with black sand and strange shallow rock under the water.

'Is that Suicide Bay?'

'Yep.'

Off to our left, the cliff is called Slaughter Hill, and some-where behind us is Victory Hill. The stories of these names were recorded, but not named, by George Augustus Robinson, one of the greyest characters in Australian history. We had become interested in Robinson during our early research because he left a whole string of placenames, telling of his travails and triumphs, as he explored unknown parts of Tasmania seeking out the last remaining Aboriginal people – Friendly River, Welcome Plains, Mount Hope, Mistake River, Success River and Mount Deception.

George Robinson came to Cape Grim in 1830 on his 'Friendly Mission', attempting to bring the 300 or so remaining Tasmanian Aborigines into the protection of white civilisation.

These few remaining tribal people had fought a moderately successful campaign against encroaching white settlement and against the constant stealing of women by sealers and shepherds. They'd struck fear into the hearts of most whites, who presumed there were thousands still left out there, and who for the most part wanted them dead.

Attempts at their organised obliteration had been inefficient and costly. And that's how Robinson came onto the scene as the great conciliator. He would roam the land, win the trust of the tribal people and bring them in, out of harm's way.

There is an 1840 painting of Robinson with a group of tribal Aborigines dressed in skins and holding spears, entitled *The Conciliation*, by Benjamin Duterrau. All eyes are on Robinson, centre stage, his navy and white ensemble crowned by a navy hat – a giant soufflé rising airily from his head. A blue bow flounces just so around his neck. His round, rosy cheeks fairly reek of innocence. His female interpreters show the way for tribal Aborigines into Robinson's circle. In the front of the painting Robinson's dog and a wallaby sniff each other out.

His companions through this were a group of Bruny Islanders and, in particular, a girl called Truganini, described by a biographer as 'an intelligent, tantalising slip of a girl . . . Tiny, slim and exquisitely formed, she had long lashes over huge, dark eyes so bright and mischievous that people who gazed into their depths never forgot their sparkling beauty.'

She and her father were the only members of their family not to have been killed by Europeans.

When Robinson and Truganini got to Cape Grim they learned from a Van Diemen's Land Company shepherd of a massacre that took place there several years earlier. Shortly after hearing this, Robinson went out to the nearby islands where, in his self-righteous way, he warned the sealers off their Aboriginal women. Even so, the sealers were quite hospitable to him and gave him a kangaroo skin bed and dry clothes.

While waiting to get a boat back to Cape Grim, Robinson didn't use the skin bed, preferring to stay up and talk, 'especially as I wanted information . . . The night was remarkable fine and the sealer women made up a fire and danced and sung until it was time to depart.'

From their stories and from the shepherds, he pieced together the spiralling violence that began in late 1827 when some shepherds attempted to 'take liberties' with local women of the Pinimukiya language group. Their men resented this, spearing one of the shepherds in the thigh. An Aboriginal man was shot dead in retaliation.

In early 1828, the Aborigines hit back by driving more than 100 well-bred sheep over the cliffs of Cape Grim. The spot thus became known to the shepherds as Slaughter Hill, immediately below the modern air pollution station.

A few weeks later, a party of Aborigines, mainly women and children, was at the beach on a fine day. The sea was calm, so a group left the children with the elderly and swam to the nearby islands, the Doughboys, to catch mutton birds (shearwaters). The birds were tied with grass and brought back for a feast on the beach.

While the people sat around the cooking birds, four shepherds attacked from above. The bodies of those who could not escape were thrown into the nearby bay, which would later be known as Suicide Bay, although it appears the name doesn't relate to this incident.

Going by what a shepherd and the Aboriginal women told him, Robinson thought thirty people had been killed. However, the Van Diemen's Land Company's main man, Edward Curr, said that Robinson's principle informant, a convict named Charles Chamberlain, was a notorious troublemaker and liar who had played on the conciliator's gullibility. Curr said that his inquiries suggested the number of Aborigines killed was more likely three.

In February 1828, the Woolnorth shepherds attacked again. Curr reported that after a long fight the natives had 'left six of their number dead on the field, including their chief, beside several severely wounded . . . I have no doubt this will have the effect of intimidating them, and obliging them to keep aloof.'

The site of this battle was thus named Victory Hill, a name that descendants of the Tasmanian Aborigines reportedly find offensive.

On 24 June 1830, Robinson stared out to sea from the top of Cape Grim. 'Whilst I stood gazing on this bloody cliff me thought I heard the shrieks of the mothers, the cries of the children and the agony of the husband who saw his wife, his children torn forever from his fond embrace. I was shewed a point of rock where an old man who was endeavouring to conceal himself, was shot through the head by one of the murderers – who mentioned these circumstances as deeds of heroism. I went to the foot of the cliff where the bodies had been thrown down and saw several human bones, some of which I brought with me, and a piece of the bloody cliff. As the tide was flowing I hastened from this Golgotha . . .'

Cape Grim, Tasmania

MARK Standing there above Suicide Bay, it's easy to deduce where the events played out. The wind is whipping us towards the edge and when I knock my sunglasses off my head, they fly away and I lose sight of them. Only Stephanie sees them go and she fetches them some five metres away, well beyond the 'Danger' signs.

We retire to morning tea in the shearing shed where we meet Ken Else. Ken came here thirty-three years ago as a seventeen-year-old farmhand. Both he and Stephanie are keenly interested in the history of Woolnorth, so we ask about the shepherds' naming of Victory Hill.

'That's said to be where they ran the last Aboriginal women to ground,' says Ken.

'But the other story is that's where they killed the chief in a battle,' offers Stephanie.

What about Suicide Bay?

'Well, I heard that the Aboriginal women used to jump off there rather than be taken by the sealers,' says Stephanie. 'This was before Woolnorth was settled.'

The other story there, according to Ken, is that after the 'victory' at Victory Hill, when the women were chased by white men, they actually jumped off there, rather than let themselves be captured. 'But I've read quite a bit of the history and never seen anything to substantiate that,' says Ken. 'That's the thing with these names, you just don't know exactly where they came from.'

We had been given the story by the Tasmanian Nomenclature Board that Suicide Bay came from fishermen. That it was suicidal to fish in there, except on calm days.

Ken doesn't think so. 'Well, it's one of the calmest bays around, so I don't know about that.'

Neither Ken nor Stephanie are convinced by Robinson's claim that thirty people were killed in Suicide Bay.

Stepanie tells us they engaged their own historian to look into it. 'He noted that in those days they just had big, old single-fire shotguns, and it was very time-consuming to reload. If they were accurate, they may well have killed three or four and may have tried to grab them and club them, but they were quick and good swimmers. The reason they were in Suicide Bay was to swim out to the Doughboys.

'Robinson also said he found bones there two years after the murders, but we had two schools of whales washed up there a few years ago, and within six months everything of them was gone. The waves crash in there and just take everything away. So there's no documented evidence on either side to say exactly how many were killed.'

The other curiosity about Robinson's visit to Cape Grim was that it revealed the truth of his relationship with Truganini. The Woolnorth superintendent Joseph Fossey, one of the men who may have played upon Robinson's gullibility in exaggerating the massacre, subsequently wrote him a letter: 'Please remember me to Ligugee (Robinson's pet name for Truganini) and Pagela (her friend), and tell the former that I often think of her most singular expression respecting me, and could I meet with one as faithful as she is to you whether black or white it might wreak a great change in me: an evening companion would be exceedingly agreeable in this secluded and remote quarter . . . '

Throughout her life Truganini had many lovers but no children. It is believed she contracted a venereal disease causing sterility. She later became famous as the last surviving full-blooded Tasmanian Aborigine, although this is no longer thought to be the case.

When we ring the Tasmanian Nomenclature Board to inquire about all the placenames that had first got us interested in Robinson, we learn that they are all gone.

Of the people Robinson rounded up and took to Flinders Island, civilisation's diseases killed them quicker than guns could have. So the settlers' problem had been dealt with. To them, Robinson and his conciliation had been a raging success and the names he left behind could be forgotten as quickly as the people.

Ironically, Robinson also faithfully recorded Aboriginal customs, words and placenames. And while the names he bestowed have been wiped away, many of the original names are appearing on maps for the first time, thanks to him being the only one to bother writing them down.

A week after we leave Woolnorth, we go into the library at St Helens, the biggest town on the east coast, and ask about books on Robinson. One of the people there in the history book/visitor information centre doesn't know who he is, and as a little guy in shorts and long white socks starts to explain, a dark-skinned woman says, dismissively: 'He's the fella who gathered my ancestors and took them to Flinders Island.' And she walks out before we have a chance to talk to her.

CHAPTER 31

HOLIDAY ISLAND

Port Arthur, Tasmania

MARK Try as we might, we can't put the Port Arthur massacre out of our thoughts when we visit the convict ruins fifty kilometres south-east of Hobart. Perhaps in fifty or one hundred years it will be just another grisly tale from this strange place, but now it's too close. We keep seeing memorials to the events of 28 April 1996 but none of them actually say what happened. We wonder if foreign tourists understand that the tragedy spoken of is actually the murder of thirty-five people. The killer's name is never used, and only in one place do we see any hint of him at all – 'a lone gunman'.

I was here two and a half months before the massacre. Since then a flash new visitor centre with interpretive displays has been added. I thought the Broad Arrow Café, where this nameless man started his rampage, had been levelled, but in fact the stone walls stand, with no roof nor windows. It looks like another 150-year-old ruin, but has the feel of a shrine.

We watch two men take long video footage of the memorial plaque outside it and we pity their families back home. World's Boringest Home Videos. Port Arthur is strange and ghostly enough without all this.

The ferry to the Isle of the Dead still leaves hourly. The 'lone gunman' had apparently planned to catch it to begin his massacre there, but changed his mind.

On the ferry, we buy a copy of a little booklet, *Isle of the Dead*. The attendant takes it forward to be signed by the skipper, Peter Roche, who we presume is the author. In it, we read the story of Dennis Collins.

Dennis Collins lost a leg in battle for the Royal Navy. No longer able to sail, he was awarded a pension by the Crown, but some years later this was revoked without explanation. Collins petitioned King William IV to have it restored, but was refused.

Facing the poorhouse, the peg-legged old tar found himself at the Ascot races one day in 1832. Had he carried a gun, his name might be reviled to this day. Instead, he carried a stone and was to set in train his own anonymous doom. For as soon as King William and Queen Adelaide showed themselves at the window of the Royal box, he threw the rock. It was a good shot, hitting the King's hat 'with such violence as to cause a deep indentation'.

The King exclaimed that he had been hit, thinking it was a gun shot.

Collins was arrested, and for making the monarch look foolish was promptly found guilty of high treason and was sentenced to be hanged, drawn, beheaded and quartered.

He had already lost one quarter of his body in service to the King, so the best they could have actually done would have been to third him. In any case, the sentence was commuted to transportation for life.

Fifty-eight-year-old Collins arrived at the penal settlement of Port Arthur clad in yellow like all new prisoners. He had a 'vicious and irritable temper' according to his records. 'Conduct for the first six weeks most disorderly, insubordinate, refractory and that of a madman.'

After about six weeks, Collins calmed down and offered no more resistance, but he refused to eat the King's food. There being no other, he became weak and finally died on 1 November 1833, less than three months after arriving.

Linus Miller, convict assistant to the chaplain, describes what awaited Collins: 'When a prisoner died, his remains were dissected, put in a rough coffin in a state of perfect nudity, carried to the wharf by four men, placed in a boat, and amid the jeers and curses of the boatmen, conveyed to the landing place at the Isle of the Dead. Here it is left until the clergyman arrives, when it is borne to the grave.'

So Collins was buried in a common unmarked grave with up to six other bodies. If he was not the last in the hole, they would have covered his naked body with lime until such time as death filled the vacancies.

Collins has the distinction of being one of the first men buried on the Isle of the Dead. He who had known the noise and smell of battle, the surgeon's bloodied tools, found himself buried out there, anonymous, belittled, but unbowed.

Isle of the Dead, Tasmania

MARK Disembarking at the little green island we are met by our guide, Helen Kerrsmith. She is dressed like a flight attendant in a blue double-breasted jacket and cravat, but with a wide straw gardening hat tied down with a yellow ribbon.

In 1842, Australia's first playwright, David Burn, described the island as 'a picturesquely lovely spot – so soothing in its melancholy'. We find it so today. A large gum tree shades the boardwalk up the ramp from the boat. At various times the island has been completely overgrown or completely cleared of vegetation. Now it is a pleasant mix of manicured garden and wild bush.

Helen walks us up a small rise and begins with the convicts, all buried on the low side of the island. Even in death, perhaps especially so, the class system held. It was only after 1853, when the anti-transportation movement was gaining strength, that convicts were allowed the dignity of a headstone.

Helen has a clipped style of delivery, honed by thousands of practice runs, but she doesn't seem bored. She opens a book and shows an old picture of the island with body-length lumps rising out of the ground at regular intervals and with the grave digger's hut behind. The hut is gone now, and only two of the men to occupy it are known to history, she says.

One was John Barron, who was charged with assaulting an eight-year-old girl. 'The details of the trial,' stated the local newspaper, 'were wholly unfit for publication . . . The prisoner was sentenced to be hanged. No hope of mercy being holden out to him.'

But mercy he got.

Years later, writer Anthony Trollope visited him here on the Isle of the Dead. 'Of all the modes of life into which a man may fall,' wrote Trollope, 'surely his was the most wonderful. To the extent of the Island, he was no prisoner at all, but might wander whither he liked, might go to bed when he pleased, and get up when he pleased, might bathe and catch fish or cultivate his little flower garden – and was in very truth monarch of all he surveyed. Twice a week his rations were brought to him, and in his disposal of them no one interfered with him. But he surveyed nothing but graves. All who died at Port Arthur, whether convicts or free, are buried there, not fitfully and by hurried task-work, but with thoughtful precision – having one always made for a Roman Catholic and one for a Protestant inmate. In this regularity he was indeed acting against orders – as there was some prejudice against these ready-made graves, but he went on with his work and was too valuable in his profession to incur serious interference . . . He has been here for ten years, digging all the graves in absolute solitude without being ill for a day.'

Trollope noted that Barron was not given over to fear of ghosts, but he wouldn't grow vegetables. Wouldn't eat the fruits of this soil.

'The other known gravedigger,' continues Helen, 'was a cantankerous old coot named Mark Jeffrey. He got about with a limp because his legs were ulcerated from years in the chain gangs.'

Everybody in Port Arthur disliked him. They were glad when he requested to be the gravedigger. He would return to the settlement only on Sundays to attend both church services.

He ate well on the vegetables he grew in the tainted soil, but after about ten years in the job, he woke one night to find his whole hut aglow. 'The image of the satanic majesty was there before him.' Next morning, he lit a bonfire to signal for the military to come and get him. They found him in a state of agitation, demanding to be taken off the island. He never returned.

'He spent his last days,' says Helen, 'as an identity around Launceston, famous for beating at anyone who came close enough with his two walking canes. He had dug his own grave here, but he was buried in Launceston.'

And so Helen takes us around the rest of the headstones, all wonderfully ornate and well preserved. The decorations are those of roughly taught convict stonemasons, with flowers and flourishes like none I've ever seen. She walks us through more stones, more stories. All told on a first-name basis.

We stop in front of a headstone too clearly new.

In Memory of Henry Savery
Australia's first novelist
Businessman, forger, convict and author

Helen explains that it isn't a headstone at all, because Savery died before convicts were allowed them. It is a memorial placed here by admirers in 1992 on the 150th anniversary of his death.

'Henry came from a well-to-do family in Bristol,' she begins. 'His father was a prominent banker and Henry started out in sugar mills, and later newspapers, but was unsuccessful at each.'

Henry resorted to writing cheques in false names. He may have been unaware of the fact this was a hanging offence. However, the public execution of a notorious forger, Henry Fauntleroy, watched by 100,000 people, appears to have focused his mind. He boarded a ship to America, but thirty minutes before it was due to sail, an ex-business partner turned up with the constabulary. Savery threw himself into the sea, and was dragged out, thence expressing his 'agony of mind' by banging his head against the walls of the ship.

From this time on, Savery suffered bouts of insanity and had to be restrained to prevent suicide. He pleaded guilty to forgery and was sentenced to execution, but his pleas for clemency were answered. He got transportation for life.

Upon arrival in Hobart in 1825, being a literate gentleman, he found himself almost immediately working for the Treasury as a convict. He vigorously petitioned for his wife, Eliza, and son Henry Oliver, to be allowed to join him. When Eliza turned up in Hobart in 1828, however, she was somewhat disappointed that her husband's rank in the colony wasn't quite as high as he'd led her to believe. And when colonial tongues started wagging about Mrs Savery having a shipboard affair on her way to the colony, well . . . 'He was a volatile sort of bloke,' says Helen. 'He attempted to cut his throat.'

Mrs Savery and Henry Oliver returned to England three months after arriving.

In 1830, Savery was assigned to a Major Macintosh in the New Norfolk district and was sufficiently well treated to sit down and make the heartbreak by a 'once tenderly attached wife' the centrepiece of Australia's first novel, *Quintas Servinton*. In 1832 he won his ticket of leave.

He turned to farming but wasn't very good at it and sank deeper and deeper into debt. Once again, he started signing fictitious bills and wasn't good at that either. He was sentenced to life imprisonment and sent to Port Arthur in 1840.

During this lagging, he wrote another book, *The Hermit of Van Diemen's Land*, a series of sketches of Hobart life and characters.

One summer Sunday in 1842, he was visited at Port Arthur by dramatist David Burns. Our first playwright found our first novelist in the hospital.

'There upon a stretcher lay Henry Savary (sic) the once celebrated Bristol sugar-baker . . . The forgery and the miraculous escape from execution of this unhappy man cannot have escaped the public mind . . . I would that my ancient antagonist, His Grace of Dublin, or even his ally of the *Colonial Gazette*, could have stood, as I did, by Savary's pallet – could have witnessed the scarce healed wound of his attenuated throat – the laclustre glare of his hollow eye: I think even they would have felt inclined to doubt the syren's blandishments.

'Knowing, as I once did in Bristol, some of Savary's wealthy, dashing, gay associates, I could not contemplate the miserable felon before me without sentiments of the deepest compassion mixed with horror and awe. There he lay, a sad – a solemn warning.'

Savery's third suicide attempt later that year was successful and that's how he finished up on the Isle Des Morts, as Port Arthur's posh referred to it. The common lags called it Deadman's Island. Or just Dead Island.

Last week we visited Port Arthur's predecessor, Sarah Island in Macquarie Harbour on Tasmania's west coast. Our guide there, who was a real Laurence Olivier, had pointed with a flourish across to that settlement's cemetery – now called Hallidays Island.

'We thought it might have been a permutation of the name of the first man buried there, Ollorey, but it turns out it was referred to as "Ollorey's 'Oliday". Death being the ultimate holiday from this place.'

We had gone to the west coast to see yet another Hell's Gate, the narrow passage into Macquarie Harbour, so named because it was both a hellish nautical crossing and the gateway to hell on earth for the convict system's most recalcitrant rabble. You couldn't read *For the Term of His Natural Life* or *The Fatal Shore* and not come away with dark images of this place and its tales of freezing degradation, of cannibalism and of convicts who murdered one another just for the chance to go to Hobart, get a square meal and be hanged.

The trouble with Hell's Gate, though, when we camped out

there by the side of the narrow inlet, was that it's such a nice spot. Fishermen lined the tea-coloured water for the salmon that jumped onto their hooks. Huge modern cruise boats were heavy with tourists and it was on one of these that, the following day, we made our way to Sarah Island, where the penal settlement had been. In its first seven years, an average of 6560 lashes per year were inflicted on the backs of the 175 inmates.

As the boat approached Hell's Gate, thick brown smoke spewed from the button grass hills to our left. Then we saw a wall of orange flame with thick black plumes.

'I don't think we'll go into Hell's Gate,' announced the captain. But he pushed on anyway and just a few hundred metres short of the ocean we were lost in the blanket of smoke. Our world turned a surreal yellow. Visibility was effectively zero. The boat stopped.

'No, I'm sorry. I can't risk going any further,' he said as he turned the boat around in the narrow channel. He continued to apologise, but most of the passengers seemed delighted to have seen Hell's Gate so appropriately engulfed. The gravedigger Mark Jeffrey would have been suitably horror struck.

Leaving Port Arthur, and just before Eaglehawk Neck – where there once lived a line of hungry bulldogs put there to chew escaping convicts – we detour into Doo Town. Its nondescript weatherboards and beach shacks have one distinguishing feature: their names.

In 1939 one of the newly arrived holiday shack owners, Bill Eldridge, told his neighbours, 'This'll do us.' And so the shack 'Doo Us' was created. Soon the neighbours matched him when a handful of new names appeared overnight: Doo Me, Doo All, Doo Nix and Doo I.

We drive in. Amy's note book scorches as she notes the houses: Rum Doo, Xanadu, Wee Doo, Mal's Doog House, Doo Write, Doo Nothing, Thistle Doo Me, Doodle-Doo, Kakadoo, Gunnadoo, Make Doo, Nickle Doo, Dr Doo Little, Yabba Dabba Doo (with a picture of Fred and Wilma Flintstone), Love Me

Doo, Doo Little, Af 2 Doo, Much A Doo, Didgeri-Doo, Just Doo It, Doo F--- All, Sheil Doo, and the tiny caravan at the end of the street, Ittle Doo 4 Now.

That will doo us 4 now in Tassie too. The southern route on our Map of Misery is approaching its end. But back on the mainland we still have two things left to do. Amy has been bugging me to go horseriding, and a last-minute name has come to our attention in the Victorian high country. A name that could surely only exist in Australia.

CHAPTER 32

THE ROAD *to* MOUNT BUGGERY

Mansfield, Victoria

AMY We feel a bit conspicuous wandering around Mansfield asking, 'You don't know how Mount Buggery got its name, do you?'

So as a conversation starter we've opted for the more indirect, 'We're interested in some of the evocative names out around the Crosscut Saw: the Devil's Staircase, Hell's Window, Mount Despair, Terrible Hollow and, um, Mount Buggery.'

But I just heard Mark on the phone tell some poor woman from the historical society that he was interested in some of the more 'erotic' names in the mountains.

These names have done funny things to Mark. For some reason he feels the need to revert to his pirate's voice for them. 'Arghhh me hearties, where be the Devil's Staircase then?'

Mount Buggery never earnt a red dot on our Map. We only came across it recently in Peter Carey's *True History of the Kelly Gang*. Carey has a scene where young Ned Kelly and his bushranging mentor Harry Power survey the difficult ride ahead, across the Great Divide. Harry points out the Crosscut Saw, Mount Speculation, Mount Despair and Mount Buggery.

We bought a map of the Victorian high country and found a veritable ode to the dark side.

We spend three days sweltering in Mansfield – a town close to the Mount Buller ski resort but not close enough to benefit from the cold mountain air – harassing unsuspecting locals about impure names. Finally, we have our first breakthrough on Mount Buggery. Helen, the school librarian at Timbertop, comes across it in P.D. Gardner's *Names of the Victorian Alps*.

'Mount Buggery: one of the few coarse stockmen's names to have survived the bureaucratic censor.'

That's all.

So we search around town for old mountain cattlemen and eventually get on to Jack Lovick, whose family has been in the area for generations. Jack's cattle lease is one of the few that remains in the high country east of here, towards Mount Buggery. As a bonus, he also leads horserides up there. Jack says he's got a five-day ride coming up that will go out that way, so we drive the twenty kilometres to Jack's place to book ourselves on the trip.

Jack invites us into his farmhouse, basic and messy. He hobbles before us into the lounge room, stooped and limping with his left foot twisted inwards.

'I just got back from a ride last night. The heat almost got to me. We didn't have any water and I thought I'd had it. I flopped down off me horse. I just needed to lie down,' he says, flopping into a comfy chair.

'One of the other fellas thought he'd better take over, but I told him we'd all just stop there till it cooled down. He wanted to go back a different way but he woulda got lost. None of them know the area like I do.' His eyes twinkle.

The room, littered with clothing and papers, is that of a man in his eighties living alone. Pictures of horses line the walls. One, a painting of a man on a rearing steed, is taken from a photo of a younger Jack. The accompanying plaque declares him to be a Victorian Living Treasure.

His profile got a huge kickalong from the 1981 film *The Man From Snowy River*. Jack was the horse and location consultant and, suddenly, everyone wanted to ride like mountain men.

Jack is one of those people who cherishes the art of story-telling. You get the feeling his yarns have been enjoyed many times over the years. So we sit back and listen, two kelpie puppies scrapping at our feet.

Jack says he first went to the mountains when he was three years old.

'See, that's how you're brought up as kids in the bush – you're just taken out. And I can remember going out with an old uncle I had there, he thought the world of me as a kid. Well, he actually brought me up. Taught me to ride. He was a dear old fella.'

The uncle told him how a lot of the mountains were named, one of which is Mount Lovick, after Jack's great-grandfather William, an ex-convict who settled here in 1862. He ran the Merrijig pub just over the river.

'He was into cattle. That's how he got his name on the mountain up there.'

As for Mount Buggery, Jack's got a story, but he's saving it for later.

'There's lots of them names out there, all practical. There's a steep section of Mount Clear going down to the river. If you went down it when it was wet, the horse would just slide straight down it into the river. They were innovative, the old fellas, they called it Slither Arse.'

'What about Bastard's Neck?'

'Well, that was a bastard, too. You took horses and pack horses up it, you had to twist to go up it,' he's twisting his body to demonstrate, 'and as soon as you got up onto this little bend, you had to completely turn around to go down. They've got a road around it now, but the Bastard's Neck is still there.'

Once, he says, as a young boy, he was riding in the mountains with an old bushman named Bill Hearn, past Hell's Window.

'I can remember him telling me, "You have to file past where the devil looks down on you. Make sure he doesn't get you when you go past."

'I tell the same stories now. Old Lucifer goes from there down the Devil's Staircase and into the Terrible Hollow below. This Hell's Window, that's in the film – have you seen it? I hope you have – where Harrison told Jim Craig to go out and find the lost cattle. We took cattle straight down the face of Hell's Window. It was a spectacular scene with the old cows coming down, and straight after them came Jim Craig.

'When I was a kid, that's how I used to ride. Go for your life. You didn't give a damn what happened. That's how you learnt to ride properly. Straight down the mountainside, you didn't have a care in the world.'

Such is Jack's delight in discussing *The Man*, we don't admit that my memory of the film is a little hazy and Mark has never seen it. I'm sure Jack would never believe that. He seems to wander between scenes from the movie and reality with little distinction.

To hear him tell it, the whole film was his idea. Producer Geoff Burrowes had been out with him on several safaris in the mid-1970s, and had made a documentary for the state government called *The High Country*. It was during one of these trips Jack says the idea for a movie was first floated. 'And I said to them, "What could be more Australiana than a film on the Man from Snowy River?"

'And they said, "Yes, but you couldn't put in a two and half hour film just on that." I said, "What about all the stories we've got on tape? Give that to the scriptwriters and we'll get a script out of it." And away it went like that.'

Whether or not it unfolded that way, Jack was certainly in the thick of it. And Burrowes wouldn't argue, because he's now Jack's son-in-law.

Among Jack's jobs on the film was playing minder to Hollywood veteran Kirk Douglas.

'When he got to Melbourne the papers asked him if he was going up country to learn to ride like the man from Snowy

River. He said, "I've done all mah ridin' in mah own films and I can hold mah own with any of these mountain men."

'So right from the start we let him see that he couldn't hold his own with the mountain men. He was a scared rider, he'd just sit there barely. He complained of course: "These goddamned horses are not film trained!" '

That cracks Jack up. It's something we are yet to learn. You don't dare presume to know anything when you are out with Jack.

We arrange to meet back on Friday night, for a Saturday morning start into the mountains.

Saturday morning at Jack's is a shambles.

'You can tell this is organised by men – no offence, Mark,' says one of the other paying guests.

Our departure time drags on with no sign of Jack. Utes are packed and the horses saddled up. We discover our five-day ride is now to be a two-day local jaunt followed by a four-day quest to reach Mount Buggery.

Jack eventually hobbles through the chaos to match us with horses. He picks one for me, and Ross, one of the staff, sets to adjusting my stirrups. 'You're slipping, Ross,' Jack interrupts. And then, without any warning, Ross is cupping his hands around my bottom and giving it a good squeeze, ostensibly to decide whether I need a sheepskin on my saddle. I don't remember anything like this ever happening at pony camp.

We leave Jack's farm on horseback at a walk. Jack sits on his horse a bit like an old man might ride a motorised wheelchair, all hunched and with his limp wrists and huge, nobbly hands extending forward. But his horse, Jackson, responds intuitively to his lurches and flaps of the reins.

Ten minutes into the ride we're in a paddock and out of the blue Jack starts whooping. Jackson takes off at a canter and suddenly we're all off. Never mind that most of us are only novices. Mark has never been beyond a trot before and just manages to hang on as his horse veers off on its own. Still, good to know the Nanny State hasn't got here yet. No-one mentioned helmets.

The gratuitous bum squeeze and the unexpected cantering set the pace for the weekend. When we're not thundering through narrow bush tracks, jumping dead logs blinded by grit and slapping branches, or pounding through streams, Jack continues to encourage his all-male staff to 'cop a feel' when they can. It is exhilarating (the riding, not the harassment) but also a little disconcerting, considering this is just a prelude to our main trip.

We had thought it would be a good way to ease ourselves into the saddle. Instead, we return to Jack's place at Merrijig two very sore cowpersons. The four other women leave us and we pick up new guests for our trek to Mount Buggery and the devil's playground.

The new group consists of four men in their forties, wearing crisp jeans and polished boots. The dynamics will clearly change. Indeed, one of the blokes, Tony, is reluctant to say in front of me what constitutes a ringer's breakfast. After some prompting he lets on: 'A piss and a look around.'

We first became suspicious that there may be a problem with staff for the second stage of our trip when, over the weekend, two of the female guests who had barely ridden before were asked if they'd like to stay on and work. Which seemed odd, because when we booked onto this ride, Jack had explained that the price was due to all the staff he employs. Cook, farrier, alternative lead rider, driver . . .

By Monday morning, his list is looking rather slim. Only the unpaid cook has been persuaded not to go home. Like the two horsemen who have now returned to Melbourne, she had only come up for the weekend, but is staying on for the next four days, still without pay, as a favour to Jack. She is a very sweet, middle-aged minister's wife, with debilitating nervousness. A serial apologiser, optimism is plastered on her face so desperately you fear she will crack at any moment.

She learnt the most important lesson of all about Jack on her first night when he dropped his steak on the floor.

'Are you alright?' she asked.

'Don't ever say that to me,' he snarled, then picked the steak off the floor and ate it with his fingers as dinner continued in stony silence.

There's also an old Geordie named Alby. He's an invalid pensioner who lives at Jack's and does odd jobs around the place. He's great for rustic photo opportunities but his arthritis renders him pretty useless at anything more than getting the fire started, cussing Jack under his breath and calling out, 'Dave, there's a problem here, laddie'.

Dave Saunders is the workhorse of the trio. Going by his reckoning, the reason that there is a drop in staff now is that there are no single girls on the trip.

Dave is thirty-eight and has worked for Jack for a year. 'Before me, they had a dozen blokes through. Most of them only lasted a day or two. Shot through in the middle of the night. Stuff the pay. It wasn't worth it.'

Dave does everything from shoeing horses and mending fences to doing Jack's laundry and copping his tantrums.

He was running around feral up at the Daintree River rainforest until Joh Bjelke-Petersen put the controversial road through in the mid-1980s. He wears shirts with the sleeves ripped off at the shoulder and has a tattoo on his arm of a knife in a sheath. The sheath has a sash on it where you'd expect to see a woman's name. His is empty.

As Monday snarls along, it becomes clear Dave does everyone's job. He works his tail off trying to get us out the gate. We had anticipated driving up the mountain at about 9 am, but hours later, still at Jack's place, the prospect of jumping into the saddle anytime today looks bleak.

As lunchtime passes, it becomes clear we are getting the ringer's lunch out of The Smiling Cook. It's only later that we realise she's just too plain scared to do anything without Jack's say-so. Since he never says, 'Get lunch', we don't get it.

By 3 pm, tensions are running high. Tony, Rick, Ed and (another) Mark have been planning their trip for a year. They've come all the way from Queensland, only to be starving in the back of a four-wheel drive, still not having touched a horse.

Then The Smiling Cook turns to us from the driver's seat: 'You've got some snacks in there, haven't you? Can you please give one to Jack?' Her eyes plead. 'Please?'

We look at her blankly. Unbelieving. 'Please,' she implores, and Rick hands one over.

The horses are rounded up and finally we look to be heading into the mountains.

The Smiling Cook has never driven a four-wheel drive before, and especially not one with a trailer on the back and six customers on board. Jack's criticisms and incomprehensible directions to her only make things worse.

In the back, we're making incredulous eyes at each other. An accident feels inevitable and Rick, anticipating a huge payout, asks Jack what his liability insurance is like.

Then Rick speaks up to say that the car won't make it round the back of a hut because of the steep slope. Jack goes off.

'You are not telling me what to do in my own country. I've been here all me life. You only just got here. You know nothing.'

So The Smiling Cook tries to go where Jack tells her but doesn't get past some logs, which grate up the side of the vehicle like nails down a blackboard. Back and forward.

Jack yells at her to reverse, but now she has to do a three-point turn with the trailer and it isn't working.

Tony weighs in with some calm, concise advice. 'Hard left. Back. Stop. Now hard right. Forward.'

The situation swings around. We are just about right when Jack pipes up again, biting Tony's head off and delivering the final instructions.

We drive on in silence, like children on eggshells wishing the fighting would stop.

We are all stewing when, like a lightning bolt from the great god Murphy, the horse trailer in front of us gets a flat.

Mark and I stay in the car while the Queensland blokes get out to offer a hand.

'See, this is a good test for these fellows,' says The Smiling Cook. 'They're all tense. This'll be good for them.'

'They didn't pay 140 dollars a day to be tested,' Mark growls.

'Shut up. Shut up, shut up, shut up,' she implores, not angry, but scared, as though Jack must never hear such insolence.

'Don't you tell me to shut up,' says Mark. He stares The Smiling Cook down in the rear vision mirror. His top lip quivering.

'No, look, I know exactly how you feel. In the church I get this all the . . .'

'Don't give me your Christian bullshit. We're paying a lot of money to sit here and do fuck all.'

Jack pipes up: 'You want your money back?'

'Yes, please, and a lift off the mountain, but I'll be leading the way down.'

Jack goes quiet, and Mark gets out of the car. The Cook grabs his arm through the window on his way past.

'No, you see I get so frustrated with those bitches at my church . . .' and she's off on a tangent that Mark doesn't entirely understand, but he suddenly feels a great warmth for her and they share a moment.

The tyre on the trailer is changed. We push on. Black Dog Creek passes by off to the left as the gravel track clings to the side of the wooded valley.

I hear Jack complain about the muesli bar his customers supplied.

'It's not much is it. Just honey and nuts.'

'It's better than nothing,' says Smiley.

'That's about all it's better than.'

It's now 7.55 pm and at last we are at Lovick Hut, where we will camp the night. The Queenslanders are on their mobiles (Mount Buller resort gives great coverage) regaling their wives with the day's horrors. I sit by the fire to write it all down. Our ascent has brought us into the spectacular sub-alpine country, where the liquid limbs of grey and white snow gums are covered in pale green moss.

The rest of the journey up here was slightly more tame. The blokes finally got on horseback to ride the last hour or so up the mountain.

Still too sore from the weekend, and faint from hunger, I piked out and drove up with The Smiling Cook, following Alby in the ute. I wished I hadn't after we arrived because Alby had me out in the dam, squelching through mud to fix the pump, which his arthritis had somehow rendered him incapable of doing. He instructed me from the bank, leaning on his walking stick. His S-bend pipe sitting comfortably in the groove it's carved out of his grey beard.

There just wasn't enough water in the dam for the pump to work, so we can now add a water shortage to our list of woes. Not that Mark and I feel the need to shower. We've been living on the ripe side for a year now, but these Queenslanders look like they need one.

No-one had told us to bring bedding or a tent, but we are relieved that we did, otherwise we'd be sleeping on bare boards in the pretty little hut. Mark and I set up our hiking tent and wander into the historic shack. The blokes are outside getting into a beer. Inside, Jack is on his own in front of the fire. I only see him from the back, but he is a sad, lonely sight: shirt off revealing pale, thin skin, his head drooping forward, thin white hair sticking out in odd directions.

Apart from cooking steaks, Jack doesn't do much around the camp. He has had three hip replacements, after all. Three seems excessive, but the horrifying story Dave tells us is that he stuffed one of them up while on the job.

On the bed next to him various pills and lotions spill from a paper bag. I can't help but feel for the strapping man he must have been, the man shaped by an Australian legend, now emasculated by his frail body and isolated by his arrogance.

You get the feeling you are looking at the end of something special when you watch Jack nodding off in his chair. Dave sees it too. He admits that's why he puts up with so much shit. He wants to learn all he can from Jack.

'Then maybe I'll become living history myself. There's no-one else learning it. There's Jack's generation and then my generation, with no-one in between,' he says, farting occasionally, but always excusing himself.

Out by the fire, the guys are reminiscing about the smoked salmon they'd had for breakfast only two mornings ago at the Sheraton Towers, Melbourne. The pure, unadulterated flabbergast at what we have seen today is the only other campfire conversation until The Smiling Cook calls that the steak, mashed potato and mashed pumpkin is ready at 10.15 pm. It tastes good, but what wouldn't.

Tuesday morning

'Where's the bacon and eggs?' Jack asks, long after we've had porridge.

'I didn't put it on because I wasn't sure if you wanted it,' The Smiling Cook laughs. 'How silly of me.'

Today we were meant to ride out to Mount Buggery. However, Jack has decided that since we don't have enough water, we will camp here another night. Before we head out for a local ride, Jackson waits patiently while Jack finds a log to help haul himself into the saddle.

Jack is acting as though nothing happened yesterday. He seems like a different man. Charming almost. He tells us his dogs and horses are always happiest up in the mountains. Him too, it seems.

'People say to me, "Why don't you retire? You're not that short of a dollar that you can't retire, go and live somewhere else." I say, "You want me to die straight away, do you?" If the people, the horses and the dogs and my mountains weren't around me, I'd pine away. You can understand that, can't you?'

We make our way up the hill to the King Billy tree – an old,

old snow gum with beautiful gnarly branches twisting out in all directions. We stop here because Jack has a yarn for us, which he asks Mark and I to re-enact.

'Mark, you go over and stand by Amy.'

So Mark leads his mount, Drummer, over to me and Jack launches into his story about a customer he brought to the King Billy tree to propose to his girlfriend. The woman started crying, 'there were tears everywhere'. On the way back to camp, they again stopped at the tree, and this time the man started crying. 'Because he realised what he'd gotten himself into,' says Jack with a wry laugh.

And while Jack is telling his story with everyone huddled around, I can see Mark fumbling through his shirt pocket and I wonder if this is a set-up. Mark reaches into his pocket and my knees quiver.

'Amy, will you marry me?' he asks, slipping a ring of dried apple on my finger. Everyone laughs. We kiss dramatically and it feels perfect. Then I get a grip and realise Mark was just getting into character. I feel like a complete goose, grateful that my sunglasses had hidden the tears of joy that had sprung up. I feed the engagement ring to my horse, Ginny.

Riding on I can't help but wonder about what has just happened. It felt so real.

'Did you mean that?' I eventually ask.

'Yeah, I did actually.'

'No you didn't. Don't play with me.'

'I did. Really.'

'Really?'

'I did. I'd been meaning to do it for a while. It seemed like a good time. I was just amazed that I hadn't fed the ring to Drummer. Hey, where is your engagement ring?'

'Ginny ate it.'

And then we both start to cry.

A day's riding, exquisite views and Jack's yarns have largely dissolved yesterday's tensions. After dinner, the blokes ask him to come and sit out by the fire with us. They want him to recite Banjo Paterson's *The Man from Snowy River*.

'I used to know it off by heart and I'd sing it,' Jack says, 'but I've forgotten it now.' Instead he launches into stories of brumby mobs and mountain life.

'I've got a good story about old Charlie MacNamara,' he says, 'but I can't tell it here in front of Amy. Oh bugger it, I'll tell you anyway.'

He is interrupted by his mobile phone (a fixture that doesn't quite fit the legend) then resumes the yarn about the late Charlie MacNamara, 'a real tough old character, call a spade a spade, self-made man'.

'We were having a lot of trouble with wild dogs, dingoes,' Jack says. 'They come in and kill the sheep and make a hell of a mess with them. Killed thirty or forty sheep a night, and they had a lot of protests into the government . . .

'They asked [the then Premier of Victoria] Joan Kirner up to hear the complaints of the people in Omeo hall. They were all saying how many sheep they lost . . . It came her time to speak and she got up and she assured everybody at the meeting that the poison campaign and the trapping campaign had gone wrong, so they were providing a contraceptive bait to aerial spread around the bush to make the dingoes sterile . . .

'Old Charlie jumped up on his feet and bellows out at the top of his voice, "Minister! Minister! You've got the whole thing wrong. These dingoes are killing our sheep, not fucking them."'

Wednesday morning

Resting our horses atop Mount Magdala, Jack points to Mount Buggery's smooth summit sitting in behind the serrated form of the Crosscut Saw. Poking up behind Buggery is Mount Speculation.

From Magdala, the track narrows. The horses negotiate the rising, rocky ground while we negotiate wayward branches and knee-capping tree trunks.

We emerge from the bush. Plunging away, centimetres to our left, is a deep gully carpeted in grass and white snow daisies. A foot wrong in that direction and you'd slide down the first hundred metres, then go over the sheer cliff and freefall the next hundred.

High up to our right, a near-vertical black cliff face lurches up out of the snow daisies to Hell's Window. It is breathtaking.

We file below the gap in the rock.

'The Devil's looking down from there,' says Jack.

Rounding the bend onto an open flat, everyone starts laughing and chattering with thrilled relief. Jack prefaces the next leg of our journey.

'Mount Howitt was named after Dr Howitt, the explorer who came with Baron von Mueller. They argued on top of Mount Speculation over where to go. Howitt said, "You can go to buggery, I'm not going there. I'm going to this mountain over here."

'He went over that way and then he couldn't get off it, so he called it Mount Despair. It's pretty rough country. Von Mueller went the other way and said, "Well, this must be buggery", and called it that. It's fair enough.'

The wind is deafening when at last we reach the grassy plains atop Mount Howitt. From up here we can see Buggery and now Mount Despair, too. We have climbed above the tree line to a grassy alpine plateau, surrounded in all directions by the blue-green mountains and deep valleys.

As we make our way along Mount Howitt, Jack points to Terrible Hollow below (which takes its name from a place in Rolf Boldrewood's *Robbery Under Arms*). Around the bend is the craggy black Devil's Staircase. We descend a ridge and there, in front of us, is the Crosscut Saw: a jagged ridge with certain death falling away on both sides for over three kilometres to Mount Buggery.

'That's the most awe-inspiring landscape we've seen all year,' Mark says, having something close to a religious experience.

Jack nudges Jackson out along the cowpad-width track. Rick and Mark follow. I don't want to. Neither, apparently do the three blokes behind me. 'It's getting late. Rick, look at the time.'

Jack has stopped to weigh up the decision. The reluctance of the three guys swings him. He pushes on, Rick and Mark in tow. I follow unwillingly, my horse inching precariously along the tightrope. The three lads hang back on the spur: 'Rick, we don't want to be stuck out here.'

Vertigo turns my stomach to goo. Swirling far, far below on my right is Terrible Hollow.

'I'm shitting myself,' I whisper to Mark.

'What's so scary about this?'

Gee, thanks, tough guy.

We go on for maybe a hundred metres, creeping closer to Buggery. Jack wonders aloud where we will be able to turn around. He wonders?

Thankfully, we reach a slightly wider chunk of ridge. Jack parks himself frighteningly close to the edge as we sit and contemplate the magnificent scene. He drops his reins and starts peeling an orange, slow and deliberate.

'Your reins are on the ground, Jack,' says Rick.

'Oh my God, I'm going to go off the edge!' he mocks, stuffing a piece of orange in his mouth.

Jack's loving it out here. Says he hasn't been out along the Crosscut Saw for twenty years – not since the movie was made. 'Nobody wanted to come out here. Why did you want to come here?'

'For this. To see Mount Buggery,' says Mark, aware how dumb that might sound.

But the answer seems to make perfect sense to Jack, who is reluctant to leave the landscape so inseparable from his being. We linger. He's soaking it in like this could be his last ride along the Crosscut.

'Thanks for bringing me out here,' he says. And we head back down the mountain.

EPILOGUE

Sydney, New South Wales

MARK & **AMY** We never did find out if Jack's story about the naming of Mount Buggery was true. From our perusal of the Mitchell Library it seems that Alfred Howitt and Baron Ferdinand von Mueller never went up into the mountains together. And their published works are so refined it is hard to imagine them carving such a vulgarity onto the map.

Like so many names in Australia, the real origin is probably lost. But maybe there's enough truth in the myth.

In January 2000, coinciding with our preparations for this journey, The Australian National Placenames Project was starting up – setting out to document the what, when, who and why of all Australian placenames. Its funding had only just come through, and so it was that as we were sticking little dots on our Map of Misery, the founders of the project, Flavia Hodges and David Blair at Macquarie University, were embarking on their own gargantuan task. In Britain, a placenames project was started in 1925 and is steaming along towards completion in the first half of this new century. A similar time frame is expected here.

Our journey lasted just a year – and Australia is huge. In fifty-one weeks we travelled 53,000 kilometres, Mark ticked off

334 birds, we ate 153 dinners of packet pasta, changed nine tyres and went through half a bottle of shampoo. And the more of the country we saw, the more we realised was out there still to see.

What we did see a lot of, though, was each other. Family and friends had none too subtly said that if we survived a year in a stiff-springed four-wheel drive we could survive anything. We were taking each other on a long, intense test drive.

Of course there were a few dodgy batteries, flat tyres and blow-outs along the way, not to mention the odd bog, but by the time Jack lead us to the King Billy tree, we were sold. It felt strangely as though Jack knew what magic he was creating when he launched into that engagement yarn.

We've returned to Sydney with a swag of new dreams, all sounding dangerously like some corny country and western song. We've fantasised about moving into a caravan on the edge of town, about buying a few acres somewhere, about staying on the road, forever. Right now, they're just dreams, and we're about to move back into the closed spaces of a Surry Hills flat. But we won't be there for long.

3 September, 2001: Just as we were going to press, news came from Perth that the owner of the Ora Banda Inn, Don Hancock, had been killed by a remote-controlled bomb. Hancock, 64, and his friend, former bookmaker Lawrence Lewis, 63, were reportedly returning from the races in Lewis's car, just pulling into Hancock's suburban driveway, when the dynamite bomb detonated, killing both men.

ACKNOWLEDGEMENTS

We owe huge thank yous to so many people who went out of their way to help us during our travels and the subsequent writing of this book.

Firstly, we want to thank everyone who appears in *The Road to Mount Buggery* – whether you were pulling us out of a bog, making us a cup of tea, showing us around or telling us stories, without you we may never have made it home, and we certainly wouldn't have this book.

There were many more who are not in the book but whose generosity was greatly appreciated. To Rob Green, for the fine advice that helped us choose Frank; Graham from four-wheel drive school for giving us the handle from his jack; Trans Media for the loan of equipment and hospitality in Darwin; David Barlow for pulling us out of our first bog; Julietta Jameson for putting us up in Tibooburra and for ongoing support; Melissa Brown and Telstra for giving us work along the way so we could pay for petrol; Kendall Hill for giving us the book he was reading; Anthony and Briony Schofield, for Scho's computer genius and Brin's patience; and Paul and Fred from Wodonga for the twelve-volt light.

Thank you also to Christian Coulthard from the Gammon Ranges, Syd Coulthard from Ukaka, Mark Manando and Grant Streeter from Broome, Jenny Green, Gavan Breen and Robert

Hoogenraad from the Institute for Aboriginal Development, Heatherbell Lambert from the Gulf Savannah, and Megan Lewis from *The Australian*, all of whom pointed us in the right direction. And we are enormously appreciative to so many from historical societies, local libraries and placenames boards, always on hand to answer our questions. Your communities are lucky to have you.

To wonderful friends and family who put us up and cooked us meals as we travelled through – Anna and Murray, Harry and Sadi, Glenn and Andy, Maree and James, Michael and Gordana, and Mick (who also helped out with computers and other stuff along the way) – we owe you big time.

This book, of course, began life as a magazine article, and for that we have Candida Baker, then editor of *The Australian Magazine*, to thank. Also, Mark wishes to thank Campbell Reid, then editor of *The Australian*, for allowing him the time off to track our Map of Misery.

And a heartfelt thank you to Amanda Hemmings, former publisher at Pan Macmillan, and to Tom Gilliatt, who subsequently took us on with gusto. Tom, together with our editor Cathy Perkins, could see what we wanted and helped us to get there. We are extremely grateful.

Very special thanks to Maree Whittaker, for help with laborious research while we were on the road; Pat Whitely, for your enthusiasm, opinions and the beautiful song you wrote for us; and to Claudia Zines, John van Tiggelen and Tristram Miall for taking the time to go over our manuscript and for your feedback.

We would each like to let our siblings know how much we value all the help with the boring fiddly bits. And, finally, we owe the greatest debt to our parents. To Alice and Bill Whittaker – thanks for the cakes, vitamins and encouragement. Sorry about the title. To Carol Willesee – thank you for the coffee, superb dinners and for loving every word we wrote; and to Mike Willesee – for your faith in us and some wise advice, right when we needed it.

BIBLIOGRAPHY

Absalom, Jack
Safe Outback Travel
The Five Mile Press, 1992

Andersen, John
Bagmen Millionaires: Life and People in Outback Queensland
1983

Andrews, Alan E.J. (ed.)
Hume and Hovell, 1824
Blubber Head Press, Hobart, 1981

Bach, John (ed.)
The Bligh Notebook: Rough Account of Lieutenant William Bligh's Voyage in the Bounty's Launch from the Ship, Tofua and thence to Timor
Allen and Unwin, 1986

Barker, Sue; McCaskill, Murray; Ward, Brian
Explore the Flinders Ranges
The Royal Geographical Society of Australasia

Barrass, Tony
'Outback Hit'

The West Australian
7 April, 2001, pp. 1, 8–9

Barrie, Douglas R.
The Heart of Rum Jungle – The History of Rum Jungle and Batchelor in the Northern Territory of Australia
S. & D. Barrie Northern Territory, 1982

Beaglehole, J.C. (ed.)
The Journals of Captain James Cook on His Voyages of Discovery
Cambridge, Hakluyt Society, Great Britain, 1955

Blake, Les
Place Names of Victoria
Rigby, 1977

Bowman, Robert (ed.)
An Account of the Mutiny on the HMS Bounty
Alan Sutton & Humanities Press, 1981

Brunton, Paul (ed.)
The Endeavour Journal of Joseph Banks – The Australian Journey
Angus & Robertson

Cannon, Michael
The Exploration of Australia: From First Sea Voyages to Satellite Discoveries
Reader's Digest, Sydney, 1987

Carey, Peter
True History of the Kelly Gang
University of Queensland Press, 2000

Clarke, Marcus
For the Term of His Natural Life
The Tasmanian Book Company, 1995

Cockburn, Rodney
What's In A Name? Nomenclature of South Australia
Ferguson Publications, 1984

Corke, David
Partners in Disaster: The Story of Burke and Wills
Thomas Nelson Australia, 1985

Cribbin, John
The Killing Times: the Coniston Massacre 1928
Fontana Books, Sydney, 1984

David, Andrew
The Voyage of HMS Herald to Australia and the South-west Pacific 1852–1861 under the command of Captain Henry Mangles Denham
The Miegunyah Press, 1995

Drake-Brockman, Henrietta
Voyage to Disaster
Angus & Robertson, Sydney, 1963

Durack, Mary
Kings in Grass Castles
Constable & Co Ltd, Great Britain, 1959

Dutton, Geoffrey
Australia's Last Explorer: Ernest Giles
Faber and Faber, London, 1970

Dutton, Geoffrey
Edward John Eyre: The Hero as Murderer
Penguin, 1977

Edwards, Hugh
Crocodile Attack in Australia
J.B. Books Australia, 1998

Edwards, Hugh
Islands of Angry Ghosts: Murder, Mayhem and Mutiny, the Story of the Batavia
Hodder & Stoughton Ltd, London, 1966

Edwards, Hugh
Shark Bay: Through Four Centuries 1616 to 2000
Edwards, Perth, 1999

Eyre, Edward John
Journals of Expeditions of Discovery into Central Australia, and Overland from Adelaide to King George's Sound, in the Years 1840–1
T. & W. Boone, London, 1845

Feeken, Erwin H.J.; Feeken, Gerda E.E.; Spate, O.H.K.
The Discovery and Exploration of Australia
Nelson, 1970

Flannery, Tim (ed.)
The Explorers
Text Publishing, Melbourne, Australia, 1998

Flinders, Matthew
A Voyage to Terra Australis Undertaken for the Purpose of Completing the Discovery of the Vast Country
G. & W. Nicol, London, 1814

Frost, Alan
The Voyage of the Endeavour: Captain Cook and the Discovery of the Pacific
Allen & Unwin, 1998

Gaunt, C.E.
'The Birth of Borroloola'
The Northern Standard, 13/10/31

Giles, Ernest
Australia Twice Traversed: The Romance of Exploration, Being a Narrative Compiled from the Journals of Five Exploring Expeditions Into and Through Central South Australia, and Western Australia, From 1872 to 1876 (Vols 1 and 2)
Sampson Low, Marston, Searle & Rivington Ltd, London, 1889

Haynes, Roslynn D.
Seeking the Centre: The Australian Desert in Literature, Art and Film
Cambridge University Press, 1998

Henderson, James
Sent Forth A Dove: Discovery of the Duyfken
University of Western Australia Press, 1999

Holthouse, Hector
River of Gold – The Wild Days of the Palmer River Gold Rush
Angus & Robertson, 1967

Hordern, Marsden
King of the Australian Coast: The Work of Phillip Parker King in the Mermaid and Bathurst 1817–1822
The Miegunyah Press at Melbourne University Press, 1997

Hordern, Marsden C.
Mariners are Warned!: John Lort Stokes and H.M.S. Beagle in Australia 1837-1843
Melbourne University Press, 1989

Horner, Frank
The French Reconnaissance – Baudin in Australia 1801–1803
Melbourne University Press, 1987

Horner, Frank
Looking for La Perouse – D'Entrecasteaux in Australia and the South Pacific 1792–1793
The Miegunyah Press, 1995

Hughes, Robert
The Fatal Shore
Collins Harvill, 1987

Hughes, Thea Stanley
Matthew Flinders
Movement Publications, 1984

Jensen, Jo & Barrett, Peta
John Oxley
Future Horizons Publishing, 1996

Kennedy, Brian & Barbara
Australian Place Names
Hodder & Stoughton, Sydney, 1989

Kimber, R.G.
The End Of the Bad Old Days: European Settlement in Central Australia, 1871–1894
State Library of the Northern Territory, 1991

Kynaston, Edward
A Man on the Edge – a Life of Baron Sir Ferdinand von Mueller
Allen Lane, 1981

Loney, Jack
Wreck of the Ly-Ee-Moon
A Marine History Publication, Geelong

Loney, Jack
Wrecks on the Queensland Coast 1791–1992
Lonestone Press, 1993

Mack, David
The Village Settlements on the River Murray in South Australia 1894–1909 – A Chronicle of Communal Life and Hardship
Self-published, 1993

McKinlay, John
McKinlay's Journal of Exploration in the Interior of Australia (Burke Relief Expedition)
F.F. Bailliere, Melbourne, 1862

Manning, Geoffrey H.
Manning's Place Names of South Australia
Self-published, Adelaide, 1990

Mort, S.W.
Points North – Points of General Interest Between Cairns and Torres Strait
Torres Strait Pilots

Munn, Jean M.
The History of Waikerie – Gateway to the Riverland
Waikerie Historical Society, November 1994

Oakley, Vivienne
'Tears For Lost Mate'
The Advertiser
25 November 2000, p. 1

Oxley, John
Journals of Two Expeditions into the Interior of New South Wales, Undertaken By Order of the British Government in the Years 1817–18
John Murray, London, 1820

Pearl, Cyril
Five Men Vanished – The Bermagui Mystery
Hutchinson of Australia, 1978

Pedersen, Howard & Woorunmurra, Banjo
Jandamarra and the Bunuba Resistance
Magabala Books, Broome, 1995

Pierce, Peter (ed.)
The Oxford Literary Guide to Australia
Melbourne Oxford University Press, 1987

Playford, Phillip
Carpet of Silver: The Wreck of the Zuytdorp
University of Western Australia Press, 1996

Plomley, N.J.B. (ed.)
Friendly Mission – The Tasmanian Journals and Papers of George Augustus Robinson 1829–1834
Tasmanian Historical Research Association, 1966

Quammen, David
The Song of the Dodo – Island Biogeography in an Age of Extinctions
Hutchinson, London, 1996

Radok, Rainer
Capes and Captains – A Comprehensive Study of the Australian Coast
Surrey Beatty & Sons, NSW, 1990

Rae-Ellis, Vivienne
Black Robinson – Protector of Aborigines
Melbourne University Press, 1988

Retter, Catharine & Sinclair, Shirley
Letters to Ann – The Love Story of Matthew Flinders and Ann Chappelle
Angus & Robertson, 1999

Robson, Frank
'The Fatal Shores'
The Good Weekend, Sydney Morning Herald
3 February 2001, p. 18

Roche, John
The Isle of the Dead: Port Arthur's Unique Island Cemetery
Port Arthur & Isle of the Dead Scenic Cruises

Rodd, Howard
'A story of survival'
The Advertiser
25 November 2000, p. 8

Scott, Ernest (ed.)
Australian Discovery By Sea
London and Toronto: J.M. Dent and Sons Ltd.
E.P. Dutton & Co. Inc., New York, 1929

Sharp, Andrew
The Discovery of Australia
Oxford, 1963

Singe, John
Among Islands
Torres News (publications), Thursday Island, 1993

Spencer, Matthew & Plane, Terry
'Signs Pointed to Shark Horror'
The Weekend Australian
30 September – 1 October 2000, p. 1

Stephen, Leslie (ed.)
Dictionary of National Biography
Smith, Elder & Co., London, 1889

Stokes, John Lort
Discoveries in Australia
T & W Boone, London, 1846

Sturt, Charles
Narrative of an Expedition into Central Australia
T & W Boone, London, 1849

Tolcher, H.M.
Drought or Deluge: Man in the Cooper's Creek Region
Melbourne University Press, 1986

Trollope, Anthony
Australia and New Zealand
1874

Walker, Mary Howitt
'A.W. Howitt 1830–1908'
The Gap Magazine
1966

Whitehead, Anne
Paradise Mislaid: In Search of the Australian Tribe of Paraguay
University of Queensland Press, 1997

Whitelock, Phil
Greencape Lighthouse – Eden, NSW
1992

Whittaker, Mark
'Map of Misery'
The Australian Magazine
16 January 1999

Yarrow, Stephen & Batchelor, Lesley
Every Name Tells a Story – The Origins of Major Town Names of Western Australia
Self-published, 1979

H. Ling Roth
The Aborigines of Tasmania
First published 1890
This edition a facsimile from the 1899 edition
Published in England by Halifax
F. King & Sons, Printers and Publishers
Facsimile: Fullers Bookshop Pty Ltd
Cat and Fiddle Arcade, Hobart, Tasmania

'"Deep Sea" – a character in the fishing industry'
Port Lincoln Times
30 November 2000

'What's Behind the Name?' (Northern Territory)
Northern Territory Department of Education
October 1978